Yale French Studies

NUMBER

Literature and the Ethical Question

Yale French Studies

Claire Nouvet, *Special editor for this issue*
Liliane Greene, *Managing editor*
Editorial board: Ora Avni (Chair), Sahar Amer, Peter Brooks,
   Shoshana Felman, Denis Hollier, Didier Maleuvre,
   Christopher Miller, Kevin Newmark, Eliza Nichols,
   Charles Porter, Allan Stoekl
Staff: Kathryn Oliver
Editorial office: 82–90 Wall Street, Room 308.
Mailing address: 2504A-Yale Station, New Haven,
   Connecticut 06520.
Sales and subscription office:
   Yale University Press, 92A Yale Station
   New Haven, Connecticut 06520
   Published twice annually by Yale University Press

Designed by James J. Johnson and set in Trump Medieval
Roman by The Composing Room of Michigan, Inc.
Printed in the United States of America by the Vail-
Ballou Press, Binghamton, N.Y.

ISSN 044–0078
ISBN for this issue 0–300–05000–3

CLAIRE NOUVET

Foreword

Let me introduce this issue by commenting briefly on its cover. The imposition of a drawing on the cover of an issue devoted to the ethical question should not be taken for granted. In view of the fact that the relation of the ethical to the aesthetic is, to say the least, problematic, it might even seem highly inappropriate. If a drawing by Antonin Artaud was nonetheless chosen, it is as a testimony to the extent to which his graphic works both challenge the aesthetic categories that we might want to impose on them and resist the aesthetic gratification that we might want to derive from them. Commenting on them, Artaud himself insists that they are not to be judged from an "artistic point of view" which would allow the beholder to dismiss them simply as either technically deficient or overly academic:

> My drawings are not drawings but documents, you have to look at
> them and understand what is *inside* . . .
> I mean that there is in my drawings a sort of moral music that I made
> by living my strokes not with the hand only, but with the scraping of the
> breath of my trachea, and with the teeth of my mastication.[1]

The drawing on the cover functions therefore as a reminder; it reminds us of that which remains unaccounted for by a purely aesthetical approach, a remainder which, irreducible, insistently returns to prod us: the ethical question.

It is this question and its urgency that are addressed in this issue. I say this question, for what is at stake here is not simply the relation of literature

---

1. Antonin Artaud, *Œuvres complètes* (Paris: Gallimard), vol. 21, 266–67. [All translations P. Weidmann.]

YFS 79, *Literature and the Ethical Question*, ed. Claire Nouvet, © 1991 by Yale University.

to ethics, but the relation of literature to ethics as a *question*, and moreover as a twofold question. In the "ethical question," the word "ethics" is indeed to be read as both that which questions and that which is called into question. This volume enacts this ambiguous status by addressing the "question of ethics" in two overlapping ways. Firstly, how does ethics come to question literature and literary analysis? Specifically, how, when, and why does ethics intervene in a literary analysis and become an unavoidable question? Secondly, how do literature and literary analysis come, in turn, to question ethics? And again, specifically, how do literature and literary analysis re-think notions which either ground an ethical discourse or traditionally belong to the field of ethics? What role does the notion of "ethics" play in the writing process? How can we situate and reassess the return of "ethics" in contemporary theories?

This double questioning leads to a critical reassessment of some major and interrelated issues such as the status of the subject and of the other; the economy of violence, be it under the guise of agressivity, murder, sacrifice, or genocide; the notions of responsibility and liberty; and the very possibility of history. Finally, a question recurs throughout this issue which the drawing placed on its cover already addressed to us: the question of our humanity. As Artaud reminds us, "the human face (*visage*) has not yet found its face (*face*), and it is up to the painter to give it one."[2] Creating the portrait of a human face should not, however, be confused with a simple humanistic gesture. Responding to a demand as imperative as it is enigmatic, it requires a certain "cruelty" which remains to be interrogated:

> My portraits are those that I wanted to represent, they themselves wanted to be, it is their destiny that I wanted to represent without concerning myself with anything other than a certain barbarity, yes, with a certain CRUELTY outside of any school, but who would know to find this in the middle of the species?[3]

2. In: catalogue of the *Portraits et dessins* by Antonin Artaud exhibit, Galerie Pierre, 4–20 July 1947.

3. Manuscript excerpt in: catalogue of the *Antonin Artaud: Dessins* exhibit, Centre Georges Pompidou, 30 June–11 October 1987.

I.

MAURICE BLANCHOT

Enigme

Chère Madame,

Pardonnez-moi de vous répondre par une lettre. Lisant la vôtre où vous me demandez un texte qui s'insèrerait dans le numéro d'une revue universitaire américaine (Yale) avec pour sujet "La littérature et la question éthique," j'ai été effrayé et quasiment désespéré. "A nouveau, à nouveau," me disais-je. Non pas que j'aie la prétention d'avoir épuisé un sujet inépuisable, mais au contraire avec la certitude qu'un tel sujet me revient, parce qu'il est intraitable. Même le mot "littérature" m'est soudain étranger.

Qu'en est-il de la littérature? Et ce "et" entre litterature "et" éthique? Si je ne me trompe pas, Adorno, dans un de ses livres sur Alban Berg dont il fut l'élève et l'ami, rapporte qu'un jour Schumann parla de son horreur de la musique.[1] De même Alban Berg (se rappeler la symphonie, si simple qu'elle soit, de Haydn, intitulée "la symphonie des adieux") a cherché à donner forme par la musique à la disparition de la musique. Et je me souviens d'un texte sur la littérature où il est dit que celle-ci a un clair destin qui est de tendre à la disparition. Pourquoi alors parler encore de la littérature? Et si on la met en rapport avec la question de l'éthique, est-ce pour nous rappeler que l'exigence d'écrire (son éthique) ne serait rien d'autre que le mouvement infini par lequel elle en appelle vainement à la disparition?

Déjà Hölderlin:

> *Pourquoi être si bref?*
> *N'aimerais-tu donc plus*

---

1. Je doute de cette citation. Schumann a certes souffert d'un excès de musique et a ainsi pu dire dans des moments de dépression ou d'exaltation: "Trop de musique."

YFS 79, *Literature and the Ethical Question*, ed. Claire Nouvet, © 1991 by Yale University.

5

> *Comme autrefois le chant! Toi qui, plus jeune,*
> *Aux jours de l'espérance quand tu chantais*
> *Ne savais plus finir!*

* * *

Et encore une fois Mallarmé.

Dans un texte ancien (une lettre écrite dans la spontanéité de l'abandon), il fait sienne l'opinion de Poe:[2] *nul vestige d'une philosophie, l'éthique ou la métaphysique, ne transparaitra; j'ajoute qu'il la faut incluse et latente* (mais ici Mallarmé ne restaure-t-il pas l'éthique? Cachée, elle garde son droit). *Eviter quelque réalité d'échafaudage, demeuré autour de cette architecture spontanée et magique n'y implique pas le manque de puissants calculs et subtils, mais on les ignore, eux-mêmes se font mystérieux exprès.* C'est l'essence en littérature de n'être libre que par les règles ou les structures qui se dérobent intentionnellement; elles n'agissent plus, si elles se montrent.

Mais Mallarmé nous propose alors une affirmation dont nous percevons la beauté, mais qui semble récuser ce qu'il vient de dire. Paroles toujours hors d'atteinte: "*Le chant jaillit de source innée, antérieure à un concept, si purement que refléter au dehors mille rythmes d'images.*"

Obsession de l'antériorité. On la trouve sous maintes formes: "*Au ciel antérieur où fleurit la Beauté*" et ailleurs (Hérodiade): "*Par le diamant pur de quelque étoile, mais / Antérieure, qui ne scintilla jamais.*"

N'est-il pas "clair" alors que ce qui est premier, ce n'est pas l'éthique (exigence morale)? On serait tenté de le dire, s'il ne fallait dire aussi que, pour Mallarmé, "premier" ne suffit pas, ne convient pas: *Antérieur* à ce qui serait premier et nous voilà entraînés par un mouvement sans fin. Aussi, après avoir affirmé: "Le chant jaillit de source innée, antérieur à un concept," Mallarmé en revient à se donner des limites: "*l'armature intellectuelle du poème*" qui est moins dans l'arrangement des mots (les rimes ou les rythmes) que dans l'espace qui les isole. "*Signicatif silence qu'il n'est pas moins beau de composer, que les vers.*"

On comprend, j'espère, que si je parle de contradictions, c'est pour mieux en éprouver la nécessité. Le pur jaillissement de source. Et cependant les calculs qui n'agissent qu'en se dérobant. Ou l'armature intellectuelle qui se compose (espace, blanc, silence), donc travail et maîtrise. Et cependant *quelle foudre d'instinct renfermer, simplement la vie, vierge, en sa synthèse et illuminant tout.* Innée et se donnant des règles; antérieure à tout principe et simplement la vie, vierge. Contradictions sans conciliation: il ne s'agit pas de dialectique.

---

2. Citations empruntées aux "Ecrits sur le livre" (Éditions de l'éclat).

Et j'ajouterai pour balbutier une réponse à votre question sur l'écriture et l'éthique: libre mais servante, face à *autrui*.

Enigme que tout cela? Oui, énigme comme l'évoque la parole de Hölderlin:

> *Enigme est le pur jaillissement de ce qui jaillit.*
> *Profondeur qui tout ébranle, la venue du jour.*

Et pardon encore pour cette lettre terminée si abruptement, comme s'il n'y avait plus rien à dire que s'excuser, sans se mettre hors de cause.

Maurice Blanchot

MAURICE BLANCHOT

Enigma

Dear Madam,

Please forgive me for answering you with a letter. Reading yours, in which you ask me for a text to be placed in the issue of an American university journal (Yale) on the topic: "Literature and the ethical question," I was frightened and nearly in despair. "Once again, once again," I said to myself. Not that I pretend to have exhausted an inexhaustible subject, but on the contrary with the certainty that such a subject returns to me* because it cannot be dealt with. Even the word "literature" is suddenly foreign to me.

What of literature? And of this "and" between literature "and" ethics? If I am not mistaken, Adorno, in one of his books on Alban Berg, whose student and friend he was, tells us that one day Schumann spoke of his horror of music.[1] In the same way Alban Berg (remember Haydn's symphony, simple though it may be, entitled "The Farewell Symphony") sought to give shape through music to the disappearance of music. And I remember a text on literature where it is said that it has a clear destiny which is to tend towards disappearance. Why then still speak of literature? And if one puts it in relation with the question of ethics, is it to remind us that the necessity to write (its ethic) would be nothing other than the infinite movement by which it vainly calls for disappearance?

Hölderlin already:

> *Why be so brief?*
> *Do you no longer love?*

---

*Can also be read "is my due." [Translator's note]

1. I question this citation. Schumann certainly suffered from an excess of music and may thus have said, in moments of depression or exaltation: "Too much music."

YFS 79, *Literature and the Ethical Question*, ed. Claire Nouvet, © 1991 by Yale University.

Song as once before! You who, younger,
In the days of hope when you sang,
Knew not how to finish!

* * *

And once again Mallarmé.

In an old text (a letter written in the spontaneity of abandon), he makes Poe's opinion his own:[2] *"No remnants of a philosophy, the ethical or the metaphysical, will show through; I add that it must be included and latent."* (But isn't Mallarmé here restoring ethics? Hidden, it reserves its rights.) *"To avoid some building reality, remaining around this spontaneous and magical architecture does not imply a lack of powerful calculations and subtle ones, but one does not know about them, they themselves make themselves mysterious on purpose."* It is the essence in literature to be free only in the rules or the structures which intentionally slip away; they no longer act, if they show themselves.

But Mallarmé then offers us an affirmation whose beauty we perceive, but which seems to challenge what he has just said. Words always out of reach: *"Song surges from innate source, anterior to a concept, so purely as to reflect outside a thousand rhythms of images."*

An obsession with anteriority. We find it under many forms: *"To the anterior sky where Beauty blooms"* and elsewhere (Hérodiade): *"By the pure diamond of some star, but/Anterior,* which never shone."

Isn't it "clear", then, that what is first, is not ethics (moral requirement)? We would be tempted to say so, if we did not also have to say that, for Mallarmé, "first" is not sufficient, is not suitable: *"Anterior* to what would be first and here we are caught in an endless movement. Thus, after having stated: "Song surges from innate source, anterior to a concept," Mallarmé comes back to setting himself limits: "The intellectual armature of the poem" which is less in the organization of the words (the rhymes or the rhythms) than in the space which isolates them. *"Significant silence no less beautiful to compose, than verses."*

One will understand, I hope, that if I speak of contradictions, it is to better experience their necessity. The pure surging from the source. And nevertheless the calculations which only act by slipping away. Or the intellectual armature which composes itself (space, blank, silence), thus work and mastery. And nevertheless *to contain what lightning of instinct, simply life, virgin, in its synthesis and illuminating everything.* Innate and setting rules for itself; anterior to all principles and simply life, virgin. Contradictions without conciliation: it is not a question of dialectics.

And I will add, to stammer an answer to your question on writing and ethics: free but a servant, in front of *the other.*

2. Citations borrowed from "Writings on the book" (Éditions de l'éclat).

An enigma, all this? Yes, enigma such as evoked by Hölderlin's words:

> *Enigma is the pure surging of that which surges.*
> *Depth that shakes everything, the coming of the day.*

And again forgive me for this letter so abruptly ended, as if there were nothing left to say but to apologize, without exonerating oneself.

Maurice Blanchot

Translated by Paul Weidmann

GEORGES BATAILLE

The Reasons for Writing a Book . . .*

The reasons for writing a book can be traced back to a desire to modify the relations that exist between a man and his fellow-creatures. The extant relations are judged unacceptable and are perceived as an agonizing affliction.

Yet as I wrote this book I discovered that it was powerless to remedy this affliction. At a certain point, the desire for *human* interactions that are perfectly clean and that escape general convention becomes a desire for annihilation. Not that interactions of this order are impossible, but that they are conditioned by the death of the one who proposes them. Thus I found myself before a dilemma more piteous than tragic and still more shameful than miserable; that which I desired to *be for others* excluded by *being for me,* and it was only natural that the use to which I wanted to be put by others—and without which my presence was tantamount to an absence—require that I cease to be, that is, in words more immediately intelligible, *that I die. To not be* had become an imperative exigency of *being,* and I was condemned to live not as a real being but as a fœtus that had been tainted before term and as an unreality.

I do not believe that my affliction will ever become acceptable, but although I remain bound to my profound niggardliness, I will no longer seek to escape from it by paltry subterfuge.

When at some time or other my attitude will have become intelligible which, it seems to me, cannot fail to happen, it will be sufficiently clear that my attitude is tied to a hatred for authority that does not accept the possibility of defeat.

Translated by Elizabeth Rottenberg

*This text is drawn from *Oeuvres complètes* of Georges Bataille, *Ecrits posthumes 1922–1940* (Paris: Gallimard, 1988), vol. 2, 143. [translator's note]. With the permission of Gallimard.

YFS 79, *Literature and the Ethical Question,* ed. Claire Nouvet, © 1991 by Yale University.

II.

GEORGES BATAILLE

Reflections on the Executioner and the Victim*

David Rousset, *Les Jours de notre mort (The Days of Our Death)*, novel,*
Edition du Pavois, 1947, in-8°, 787 pages, "Le Chemin de la vie" (series
directed by Maurice Nadeau).

"In the four weeks that we were away from Helmstedt, we'd been to the
extreme limit of ruin. The structure of the camps had ripped apart and the
men had broken all the dams. Me, us, everyone. Of what we learned in
abjection, it will never be spoken. As we are now, miserable and frightening,
we carry with us, despite it all, with us and beyond us, a triumph for the
entire community of mankind. We never gave up the fight, we never repudiated a thing. We never blasphemed against life . . ." (760).

*"This book is structured like a novel." Discovering no doubt in novelistic
techniques a richer means of expression and a subordination of language to
life that were not at the disposal of a historian, the author specifies, however:
"Fabrication has no part in this work. The facts, the events, the persons are
all real. It would have been silly to invent when the truth so exceeded the
imaginary." We know that David Rousset published *L'Univers concentra-
tionnaire* (*The Universe of the Concentration Camp* which we acknowledged previously: *Critique*, n°5, October 1946, 441) as an introduction to
this big book, in which he sets forth the central themes which he would later
expound in the tangled, dense narrations of *Les Jours de notre mort*. The

*This text is drawn from *Oeuvres complètes* of Georges Bataille, *Ecrits posthumes
1922–1940* (Paris: Gallimard, 1988), vol. 2, 143 [translator's note]. With the permission of
Gallimard.

YFS 79, *Literature and the Ethical Question*, ed. Claire Nouvet, © 1991 by Yale
University.

criticism, misreading perhaps the ambiguity in the subtitle "novel," dwells on the overwriting and the repetition in the narrations: in principle the criticism represents the "normal world" that requires respect for the convention that founds it, even as another voice reaches it from "another world," the other voice founded upon the very rupture of that convention. Let us say that the overwriting and the repetition help us to hear this other voice, exactly as it may be, voice to which David Rousset has given strength and severity. This book is already a discovery for us of the ground (and needless to say, of the muck) from which humanity rises.

If an extreme possibility has been given to life, not in the furtive time of normal death, but in the endless repetition that the addition of hundreds upon thousands of prolonged agonies offers to it, it is surely for this possibility that David Rousset became a memorialist. He describes the singularity of his experience: forced to observe, he nonetheless remained a guinea pig. And at the end one observes that the guinea pig triumphantly claims victory over life put to the test, by looking death and calamity in the eye.

*

But the insolent conclusion of Rousset's book does not remove from his experience its value as a negating contention: "Never," are we told, "will normal people be able to understand. They live at the surface. And not only of social conventions. But of other conventions even more profound. And unsuspected. The conventions upon which the most intimate life tolerates itself. To say to them: the truth is that both the victim and the executioner were ignoble; that the lesson of the camps is fraternity in abjection; that if *you* did not conduct yourself with the same degree of ignominy, it was only because time was lacking and the conditions were not altogether ripe; that there only exists, in the decomposition of beings, a difference of rhythm; that the slowness of the rhythm is the attribute of great men; and that the mould, there beneath it all, rises and rises and rises, is absolutely, hideously the same thing. Who would believe it? Especially when the survivors will no longer know it. They too will invent rose-tinted images" (587–88).

*

In truth it is not the author who speaks but a prisoner whose meditation he relates: " . . . A great farce. His own, definitive way of reducing it to nothingness;" such is according to Rousset the conclusion of the wretched man who in the final moment prefers poison to torture. But nothing is clear. And it seems to me that searching the depths of reflection for a thought possible in the mind of Pröll, who is about to die, the author comes against a fundamental difficulty: never can we *establish* a limit once a man advances far into suffering; he cannot *be assured* that a barrier which resisted in the past will not be broken. And what precisely can be admired in the event of a trial survived and in the victory of life is that life, discovering itself to be in the hands of horror and knowing itself to be at the mercy of physical affliction, nonetheless *insures* its successful outcome by the excess of its steadfastness in the face of filth. Yet in a universe of suffering, of baseness and of stench, every one, at his *leisure*, could measure the abyss, the absence of limit to the abyss, and the truth that obsesses and fascinates.

*

One of David Rousset's most surprising reactions is exaltation, almost euphoria at the idea of participating in an insane experiment. Nothing more virile, nothing more *healthy*. The depths of horror—on the one hand the suffering and the degradation that it entails, and on the other hand the vile cruelty of the executioner and its unleashing of a beyond of infinite possibility—the depths of horror presents itself to human beings as the truth to discover. In other words, it is necessary for man to learn, beyond his normal state, the faraway limit of the possible. But he must pay the price . . .

*

But he who retreats and does not want to see is hardly a man: he has chosen as a foundation not to know what he is. In a sense he does know: he turns away! But he *does not want* to know it. This negation of humanity is barely less degrading than is that of the executioner. The executioner demeans himself, demeans his victim; especially as he strikes in a cowardly manner, in ignorance (no one, if he is not *inhuman*, can effectively reduce himself to a state of blind nature; a torturer is *ignorant* of the fact that he strikes himself: he adds to the suffering of his victim the annihilation of the idea of humanity). But a *kind soul* is even more cowardly and doubtless more dangerous; his failing extends that laughable region where humanity undoes itself, is naught but error and vanity, and asserts parrotlike inanities.

*

Horror obviously is not the truth; it is but an infinite possibility, the limit of which is death (the scope of death—it sets a term to pain—give pain a final and inordinate sense; death remains impossible in us until the end; it suppresses all possibles other than pain and, insofar as death limits pain, it evades consciousness). But man is made up of possible abjection, his joy, of potential pain; and if the abjection and the pain were ever to reveal themselves fully to him by any means, it would be a ragdoll disguised as a man, a Pharisee, a clown or an old maid, any false and chattering affect benumbing the remorse of a failing.

*

Nausea is not what reveals things to us, but the world is only given to us in a restrained nausea.

*

If one were to remove from us this particular domain—the possibility of pain—the world would consist of *Charlottes* and *Gustaves* of whom one would no longer laugh. But pain is always there for us, and our disgust for it defines us. And the knowledge of possible pain *humanizes:* it is pain that makes one so tender and so hard, so gay and so heavy with silence.

(Thus David Rousset marks exactly the point at which humanity fulfills itself, surviving the test without hatred and without complaints, with as much humor as lucidity.)

*

The worst aspect of the sufferings of the inmates is not the pain endured but the pain furiously desired by others. Pain resulting from sickness or accidents does not seem as horrible; the depths of horror is in the will of those who command it. A world in which many individuals suffer great pain but in which the common goal was to fight pain would be soothing. Degradation, ignominy, cowardliness multiplied—destroying little by little the fortress that reason is at the root of the civilized world—disturb us more violently than does raw suffering.

The difference, however, concerns the suffering of the victim less than our own suffering. We are far more threatened when the barriers that opposed reason and order to cruelty give way.

*

But that is not all.

We cannot be *human* until we have perceived in ourselves the possibility for abjection in addition to the possibility for suffering. We are not only possible victims of the executioners, the executioners are our fellow-creatures. We must ask ourselves: is there anything in our nature that renders such horror impossible? And we would be correct in answering: no, nothing. A thousand obstacles in us rise against it. . . . Yet it is not impossible. Our possibility is thus not simply pain, it extends to the rage of the torturer. The Toni Brunckens, the Heinzes, the Popenhauers, so many killers in combat boots with bludgeons, all cowardly and unrelenting, are there to tell us with their irrefutable rage that often cowardliness alone is the limit to violence and that there is no limit to cowardliness.

And how could we not see, in the most unpleasant silence, that such a potential simply remains the farthest away, the most inconceivable also, but *ours* without a doubt? Nothing in us can be isolated, can be safely put aside in order to say firmly that it would have been impossible, no matter what. No matter what? What we are, depended on circumstances that might have been different, that might have been, for example, those of which Toni Bruncken was the end result.

*

It is clear that life cannot be reduced to the absurd, although man's potential oversteps the limits of reason in all directions. A chain of reasonable acts is one potential sequence among others and the man whom reason enlightens always perceives in himself, at once, the reasonable and beyond, but always in himself, which puts the reasonable in question.

It is the essence of reason to be contestable, but of the essence of contention to be an effect of reason. At the limit, reason becomes an insoluble question for itself and it might then seem as if it gives in to the absurd of its own accord. But such is not the case if one wishes to see more lucidly (perhaps also painfully). The absurd cannot destroy the reasonable because reason brings about in and of itself that which the irrational does from the outside: its own endless questioning. This is precisely where man prevails over negation: he does not prevail in a decisive victory, after which rest and sleep would be granted him; he prevails by way of the doubt that *awakening* is.

Only what would this awakening be if it only illuminated a world of abstract possibilities? If it did not awake first to the possibility of Auschwitz, to the potential for stench and unalleviated fury?

*

There exists in a certain form of moral condemnation an escapist denial. One says, basically, this abjection would not have been, had there not been monsters. In judging so violently, one subtracts the monsters from the possible. One implicitly accuses them of exceeding the limit of the possible instead of seeing that their excess, precisely, defines this limit. And it is possible, insofar as this language appeals to the masses, that this infantile negation may seem effective; but in the end it changes nothing. It would be as vain to deny the incessant danger of cruelty as it would be to deny the danger of physical pain. One hardly obviates its effects flatly attributing it to parties or to races which one imagines to be inhuman.

*

And, needless to say, an awakening that requires a relentless consciousness of the possible horror is more than a means of avoiding it (or at the final moment of facing it). The *awakening* begins with humor, with poetry also. (And not the least meaning of Rousset's book is that it affirm humor too and that the nostalgia which emanates from it, never one of sated happiness, be that of movements drunk with poetry.)[1]

Translated by Elizabeth Rottenberg

---

1. Under no circumstances do I pretend, having proposed to start from the extremes of reflection, to have exhausted a work which is, in reality, a universe. Rousset's forthcoming book *Lazare ressuscité (Lazarus Risen)* will discuss the return from this other world to the normal world. How could the somber and unparalleled experience of the camps not have challenged all notions? It is in every way and incessantly that one should return to it.

JEAN-LUC NANCY

The Unsacrificeable*

Contemporary reflection on sacrifice cannot *not* be haunted by the thought of Bataille. Of this thought itself, I will be speaking later on; for the moment, I will merely remark upon three distinctive traits that give it an exemplary character:

1) Bataille's thought certainly does not arise by chance or by individual whim. It links up emphatically with a whole context—sociological, ethnological, and anthropological on the one hand, philosophical, theological, and psychoanalytic on the other—that determined it in the first half of this century. (Among many other possible confirmations one could refer, for instance, to the work of Georges Gusdorf, *L'Expérience humaine du sacrifice*, published in 1948 after having been "undertaken in captivity."[1] While Gusdorf's perspective is entirely different from Bataille's (whom Gusdorf nevertheless knew personally and cites in his text), the network of references, the importance attributed to the object, and its reaching for the idea of a necessary "overcoming" of sacrifice testify to a large community of concern at the time, above and beyond the symptomatic value of the two authors (Gusdorf, 267).

2) Bataille's thought is well-known to be not only marked by a particular interest in sacrifice, but obsessed and fascinated by sacrifice. "The allure of sacrifice" is said to respond to nothing less than the following: "what we await, from our childhood on, is this upsetting of the order we are suffocat-

*Thanks to Allan Stoekl. [Translator's note]

1. George Gusdorf, *L'Expérience humaine du sacrifice* (Paris: PUF, 1948), viii. Henceforth cited in the text.

YFS 79, *Literature and the Ethical Question,* ed. Claire Nouvet, © 1991 by Yale University.

ing in . . . the negation of this limit of death, fascinating as light."[2] Equally well known is that Bataille sought not only to think sacrifice, but to think according to sacrifice. He willed sacrifice itself, in the act; at least, he never ceased presenting his thought to himself as a necessary sacrifice of thought.

3) No less well known, however, is the slow displacement, the long drifting, that led Bataille to denounce the *theatre* of sacrifice and consequently to renounce its successful accomplishment.

Without limiting myself to Bataille alone, the questions that I want to pose here proceed from what his experience of thought exemplifies for us. What is there in the fascination of sacrifice? Where does it come from? What does it engage, what does it engage in? What, in fact, is our relation to sacrifice made of? Isn't all of the West, in some sense, determined by it? And consequently, doesn't this relation keep us riveted to the closure of the West? Isn't it time, finally, to take action: both the end of real sacrifice and the closure of its fantasm?

I

What is the nature of the West's initial relation to sacrifice? More precisely: according to what relation to the rest of humanity's sacrifices (or to the representation of those sacrifices) does the West elaborate, so to speak, its own "sacrifice"?

Socrates and Christ signify that this relation is decisive and foundational. In each case a relation at once distanced and repetitive is involved. Both of these figures—the double figure of ontotheology—deviate decidedly, and quite deliberately, from sacrifice; in doing so, they propose a metamorphosis or a transfiguration of sacrifice. What is involved, therefore, is above all a *mimesis:* the ancient sacrifice is reproduced—up to a certain point—in its form or its scheme; but it is reproduced so as to reveal an entirely new content, a truth hitherto hidden or misunderstood, if not perverted. By this fact alone, the old sacrifice is represented as having constituted no more than a preliminary imitation, a crude image of what has since come to effect a transfigured sacrifice. On the other hand, the new sacrifice does not result from its rustic precursors by way of simple transmission or natural generation: to inaugurate itself it requires precisely the gesture of this "mimetic rupture."

The mimetic rupture of the West's sacrifice (of Western-style sacrifice, if you will) proposes a new sacrifice, distinguished by a certain number of characteristics. This does not mean that these characteristics were always

2. Georges Bataille, *Oeuvres complètes* (Paris: Gallimard, 1988), vol. 11, 484. Henceforth cited in the text.

purely and simply absent from the older sacrifices—insofar, that is, as it might still be possible to retrace the truth of these "older" sacrifices (this is, in one sense, the whole problem, and we will return to it). But four characteristics are clearly required and presented by the ontotheology of sacrifice.

1) It is self-sacrifice. Socrates and Christ are both condemned, both of them by an iniquitous condemnation which, as such, neither the victims nor the executioners represent as a sacrifice. But the carrying-out of this condemnation is, in turn, represented as a desired sacrifice, willed and sought after by the entire being, by the life and the thought or message of the victims. It is, in the fullest sense of the words, and in both senses of the genitive, the sacrifice of *the subject*.

The *Phaedo* proposes nothing but an appropriative reversal of the situation by the subject Socrates: he is in prison, he is going to die, and so he designates all of earthly life as a prison, from which it is fitting to liberate oneself through death. *Philosophy* thus appears, not only as the knowledge of this liberation, but as its actual enactment: "And those who have purified themselves sufficiently by philosophy live thereafter altogether without bodies etc."[3] And so, shortly after having pronounced these words, the philosopher himself will not hesitate to drink and drain the cup of hemlock, praying to the gods that his "removal from this world to the other may be prosperous" (*Phaedo*, 117c).

As for Christ, the Pauline doctrine of *kenosis* is well known, the gesture by which Christ "being in the form of God . . . humbled himself"[4] becoming man even unto death. God, lord over the death of his creatures, inflicts this death on himself; his own life and his own love, distributed throughout creation, are thus returned to himself and to his own glory.

For both Socrates and Christ, the event of sacrifice properly speaking (if we can still put it in these terms), the putting-to-death, comes only to punctuate and to unfold the process and the truth of a life that is itself wholly a sacrifice. For the West, the issue no longer involves a life that would understand sacrifice; nor even, according to a good Christian phrase, a "life of sacrifice" alone. What is involved is a life that would be in and of itself, wholly a sacrifice.

2) This sacrifice is unique, and it is accomplished for all. Or, still more precisely, in it all are assembled, offered, and consecrated. Let us cite Saint Paul: "And every priest standeth daily ministering and offering oftentimes the same sacrifices, which can never take away sins. But this man, after he had offered one sacrifice for sins for ever . . . by one offering he hath perfected for ever them that are sanctified."[5] And Saint Augustine will say:

3. Plato, *Phaedo*, 114c. Henceforth cited in the text.
4. Philippians 2:6–8.
5. Hebrews 10:11–14.

"The whole city of the redeemed, all the assembly of saints, is offered to God, in one unique and universal sacrifice by the supreme pontiff. He himself has offered himself for us in his passion in the form of the slave, so that we may become the body of such an august head.[6]

The uniqueness of the sacrifice is thus displaced or made dialectical, from a uniqueness that is exemplary and counts as such (where Socrates ranks first and foremost; and we could add: in general, isn't the sacrifice the most exemplary of examples?) to a uniqueness of the life and the substance in which or to which all singularity is sacrificed. At the end of this process, there is, of course, Hegel: "the substance of the State [is] the power by which the particular independence of individuals and their absorption in the external existence of possession and in natural life is convicted of its own *nothingness*, and the power which mediates the conservation of the universal substance through the *sacrifice*—operating through the internal disposition it implies—of this natural and particular being."[7]

3) This sacrifice is inseparable from its being the unveiled truth of all sacrifices, or of sacrifice in general. It is thus not only unique; its uniqueness lies in its elevation into the principal or the essence of sacrifice itself.

It is remarkable that the *Phaedo* should be framed by two references to what I have termed the "older" sacrifice. At the beginning, we learn that, following the judgment, Socrates' death had to be postponed because executions were forbidden during the annual voyage to Delos that celebrated Theseus's victory over the Minotaur: the end, that is, of the sacrifice to which the Minotaur had compelled the Athenians (58b). At the end, by contrast, as is well known, Socrates, at the point of death, already half-paralyzed by the poison, utters these last words: "Crito, we ought to offer a cock to Asclepius. See to it and don't forget" (118). Interpretation here is doomed—by the text itself—to a significant ambiguity: either Socrates, recovering the health of the soul by sacrificing his body, is thanking the god of healing; or else he is leaving behind him, with distance and perhaps with irony, a sacrifice itself vain in the eyes of one who, at that very moment, is in himself accomplishing a philosophical purification. But either way, the truth of sacrifice is brought to light in its *mimesis:* the "old" sacrifice is an

6. Saint Augustine, *City of God*, cited in E. Mersch, *Le Corps mystique du Christ* (Declée, 1951), vol. 2, 114.

7. Hegel, *Encyclopédie*, trans. B. Bourgeois (Paris: Vrin, 1988), vol. 3, 325 (§ 546). A. V. Miller, in *Hegel's Philosophy of Mind*, translates this passage as follows: "Country and fatherland then appear as the power by which the particular independence of individuals and their absorption in the external existence of possession and in natural life is convicted of its own nullity—as the power which procures the maintenance of the general substance by the patriotic sacrifice on the part of the individuals of this natural and particular existence—so making nugatory the nugatoriness that confronts it" (276). [Translation from Miller modified]

exterior figure—vain in itself—of that truth in which the subject sacrifices itself, in spirit, to spirit [esprit]. And in this spirit, it is to the truth itself that the true sacrifice is offered; it is in truth and as truth that it is accomplished. In the middle of the dialogue, consecrated to the truth of the immortality of the soul, Socrates will have declared: "As for you, if you will take my advice, you will think very little of Socrates, and much more of the truth" (91 b–c).

In the wake of Saint Paul, Augustine, and the entire tradition, Pascal will write: "Circumcision of the heart, true fast, true sacrifice, true temple: the prophets have indicated that all of this is spiritual. Not the flesh that perishes, but the one that does not perish."[8]

4) So the truth of the sacrifice sublates, along with "the flesh that perishes," the sacrificial moment of sacrifice itself. And that is the reason why the final characteristic of Western sacrifice is to be itself the transcendence of sacrifice, its infinite and dialectical transcendence. Western sacrifice is already infinite in being self-sacrifice, in being universal, and in revealing the spiritual truth of all sacrifice. But it is—and must be—infinite also insofar as it reabsorbs the finite moment of sacrifice itself and thus insofar as it must, logically, sacrifice itself as sacrifice in order to accede to its truth.

This is the meaning of the Catholic Eucharist which, consumed through the finitude of sensible tokens, passes into the interior worship of the reformed spirit. And this is its speculative truth:

> The negativity of the finite can also only come about in finite fashion. Here we have come to what is generally called sacrifice. The immediate content of sacrifice is the surrender of an immediate finitude, in the sense of my testifying that this finitude ought not to be my own possession and that I do not want to keep it for myself. . . . Because the depths of mind and heart are not yet present, negativity cannot here reveal itself in an inner process . . . the subject . . . is only to surrender an immediate possession and a natural existence. In this sense sacrifice is no longer to be found in a spiritual religion, and what is there called sacrifice can only be so in a figurative sense.[9]

II

Mimesis, then: spiritual sacrifice will be sacrifice only in a figurative sense. Truly, it is "the reconciliation of absolute essence with itself."[10] Mimesis, *but* repetition: the reconciliation of essence nevertheless requires passage

---

8. Blaise Pascal, *Pensées* (Paris: Gallimard, 1954), 569; Brunschvig, 683.

9. Hegel, *Philosophie de la religion*, trans. Gibelin (Paris: Vrin, 1971), vol. 1, 223–24; *Lectures on the Philosophy of Religion*, ed. Peter Hodgson (Berkeley: University of California Press, 1984), 384 n.

through absolute negativity and death. "Sacrifice" means appropriation of the Self in its own negativity. And if the sacrificial gesture has been abandoned to a finite world, it is only so that the infinite sacrificial structure of this appropriation of the Subject may emerge more clearly. The appropriation, by means of the transgression of the finite, of the infinite truth of the finite, might be termed "trans-appropriation." In a sense there is no longer sacrifice: there is a process. In another sense, this process only matters through its negative moment, in which the finite must be annihilated; and this moment remains nonetheless a transgression of the law, the law of self-presence. This transgression occurs in suffering, even in horror. For Hegel, for instance, it is the somber, bloody, yet ineluctable face of history itself.

Such is the result of the mimetic rupture: sacrifice is sublated in its finite functions and its exteriority. Yet a fascinated gaze remains fixed on the moment of sacrificial cruelty as such. "Flesh that does not perish" remains flesh cut out of an adorable body, and the secret of this horror continues to cast an obscure light from the center of the sublation, from the heart of the dialectic. Truly, Hegel notwithstanding, it is this secret that makes this heart beat. Or else, even more seriously, it is the dialectical gesture itself that instituted this secret. Western spiritualization/dialectization invented the secret of the infinite efficacity of transgression and its cruelty. After Hegel and Nietzsche comes an eye fixed on this secret, with a clear conscience, necessary and unbearable: for instance, the eye of Bataille.

But what, exactly, does this eye see? It sees its own sacrifice. It sees that it cannot see except on the condition of an unbearable, intolerable vision—a vision of sacrificial cruelty. Or else, it sees that it sees nothing.

If it is always, indeed, a question of the old sacrifice at the heart of modern sacrifice, it must be acknowledged that the mimetic rupture has made us lose the older truth of sacrifice. Just as the specialists of our own day tell us that "sacrifice" is an artificial notion, so the spiritualizing consciousness of sacrifice may not have always had a clear awareness of its own assumption of the, after all, heterogeneous functions of sacrifice. It would be useful to follow the complicated—and doubtless poorly unified—destiny of the remission of sins, the preservation of grace, and the acquisition of glory (to mention only the three functions of sacrifice that Saint Thomas Aquinas acknowledged) through the theological literature; the three modes of sacrifice—martyrdom, austerity, works of justice and worship—no doubt follow a parallel course.[11] In reality, only one thing is clear: the interiorisation, the spiritualization, and the dialecticization of sacrifice.

10. Hegel, Phénoménologie de l'esprit, trans. Jean Hippolyte (Paris: Aubier, 1951) vol. 2, 280: the reference is to Christ.

11. Thomas Aquinas, Summa Theologica IIa qu.,22, 2C; IIaIIae, qu. 85 3 ad.2.

But this clarity is itself obscure. Indeed, what appears, in the light of spiritualization, as the "old" sacrifice is a pure economy of barter between man and the divine powers. Everything is reduced to the formula of the brahmanic ritual (or at least, to the only way we have of understanding this formula): "Here is the butter? Where are the gifts?" (Cited in Gusdorf; 45). Condemnation of this sacrificial "economism" runs through Plato and Christianity, Hegel and Bataille. Spiritualization has no doubt left us, from the outset, incapable of grasping the proper significance of the old sacrifice in its own context. When someone says to his gods: "Here is the butter. Where are the gifts?" it may be that we do not know what he is saying, since we know nothing of the community in which he lives with his gods. Similarly, to answer the other charge that is leveled at the old sacrifice—that it is nothing but a simulacrum, as long as it has not attained the level of self-sacrifice—we do not know what *mimesis* is in this context. At most we could follow Lévy-Bruhl in guessing that it may be *methexis*, participation: but we do not know what such "participation" means, if not, for us, a confusion of identity. (Similarly, Freud did not know what "identification" meant; and likewise, we could ask whether Girard knows what the contagion of mimetic violence means. Either way, we do not know what "being-in-common" means, if not the "being-one" of sacrifice—with its cruelty.[12])

Denunciations of economism and simulation run throughout the dialectical understanding of sacrifice, up to and including Bataille. Indeed—and here Bataille's contribution cannot be contested—a fascination with sacri-

12. Cf., *Les Carnets de Lucien Lévy-Bruhl* (Paris: PUF, 1949). In general, the relations between *mimesis* and sacrifice require an examination which I cannot undertake here but will pursue elsewhere. If *mimesis* is the appropriation of the other through the alternation or the suppression of the proper, is its structure not homologous to that of sacrifice? (Cf., for example, "being no one—or everyone," in Philippe Lacoue-Labarthe's analysis of Diderot's Paradox, in *L'Imitation des Modernes* (Paris: Galilee, 1986), 35. As for the relation between sacrifice and mimesis, cf., as well Jacques Derrida, "La Pharmacie de Platon" in *La Dissémination* (Paris: Seuil, 1972), for example, 152–53). So should sacrifice be founded on *mimesis*, understood now in Girardian terms, at the price of a rather problematic anthropology? (Lacoue-Labarthe has discussed these problems in *Mimesis: désarticulations* (Paris: Flammarion, 1975), as has Y. J. Harder in his "Le Sacrifice du Christ," Séminaire philosophie/psychanalyse, GRTST, Strasbourg, 1989). Or should *mimesis* not rather be thought on the basis of sacrificial *methexis*, that is, on the basis of the general question of contagion and communication (cf., e.g., Bataille OC 7 369–71)? This would require thinking both the construction of the Western sacrificial model as "communion" and the deconstruction of this model in the thought of finitude, which I will get to at the end of this piece, a thought, that is, of a *non*-communal communication. Shouldn't we ask ourselves, finally, whether, when Western thought insists on denouncing the simulacrum of the "old" sacrifice, and on presenting the new sacrifice as the "true" *mimesis* (or sublation) of the other, it does not betray *an incapacity, or a refusal, to touch on methexis:* that is, perhaps, simultaneously on a danger of contagion and, paradoxically, an "incommunion" of communication or of participation, to which ontotheology objects on principle (in its principle of appropriation by a Subject)?

fice does not prevent one from remarking on a generalized "economism" and "mimeticism" in its dialectic. Sacrifice as self-sacrifice, universal sacrifice, truth, and sublation of sacrifice, is itself the institution of the absolute economy of absolute subjectivity, which can only mimic (in the pejorative sense) a passage through negativity, from which, symmetrically, it cannot but reappropriate or trans-appropriate itself infinitely.

Everything finally occurs as if the spiritualization/dialectization of sacrifice could not operate without a formidable disavowal of itself. It disavows itself beneath the figure of an "old" sacrifice, which it pretends to know and which in reality it fabricates for its own purposes. And it approves of itself in the form of an infinite process of negativity, which it covers with the "sacred" name of "sacrifice." This double operation brings to the center, simultaneously and in a painful ambiguity, the infinite efficacity of dialectical negativity *and* the bloody heart of sacrifice.

To cast doubt upon this disavowal—this manipulation, rather—is to question this simultaneity, and to be forced to ask whether dialectical negativity expunges blood or whether, on the contrary, blood must ineluctably continue to spurt. In his desire to put an end to dialectical process as comedy, Bataille wanted blood to spurt. He wanted to weigh in the balance the horribly lacerated body and the look—distraught or ecstatic?—of a young Chinese being tortured, a famous photograph. But in so doing, Bataille was really working out the deep logic of the sublation of sacrifice, which would rescue it from its repetitive and mimetic character: *because sublation is ultimately incapable of knowing what is truly involved in repetition and mimesis, and so in sacrifice.* In return, this same logic, which claims to be both rupture with and *mimetic repetition* of sacrifice, wants, by this same movement, to be both the sublation and the truth of sacrifice. So we have to think that the victim of torture sublates into ecstasy the horror that renders him distraught. But how to think so in truth, if the eye that sees—and not the one that is here looked at—does not know what it is seeing, or even if it is seeing? How to think it, without the subject of this gaze having already appropriated, in himself, the dialectic of the distraught and the ecstatic? How to think it, that is, without having fascination constitute itself as mastery and dialectical knowledge of sacrifice?

Bataille wound up declaring: "As for nostalgia for the *sacred*, it is time to admit that it necessarily comes to nothing, that it misleads: what today's world lacks is the proposing of temptations. Or the proposing of such hateful ones that they matter only on the condition that they deceive those whom they tempt," (Bataille, *OC* 11: 55). Undoubtedly, ambiguity does not disappear entirely from these phrases; their syntax is constructed so as to sustain it. On the one hand, today's world "lacks" truly sacred "temptations," ones that are given immediately and without recourse to nostalgia; on the other hand, the world "lacks"—in the sense, now, of being lacking—because its temptations are illusory. So sacrifice—or something about sacrifice—still cannot help be lacking.

III

Even there, Bataille must have thought—only up to a certain point—to palliate this lack through literature, or art in general. (At the same time, Heidegger, speaking of art and the putting-to-work [mise-en-oeuvre] of truth, named "the essential sacrifice as one of the modes of this putting-to-work that is concentrated in art; elsewhere in the same text, he had already thought it necessary to count "gifts and sacrifice" at the heart of the existent which is open to the clearing of being.[13] I cannot comment further on this reference here.)

One link between sacrifice and art, especially literature, incontestably runs through, or doubles, the Western process of the spiritualization of sacrifice. Book V of Saint Augustine's *Confessions*, for example, begins: "Accept the sacrifice of my confessions, presented by the hand of my tongue, which you have formed and exhorted to confess your name"—and thus opens the way for everything that will spring from "confession" in our literatures. But is there, finally, a veritable limit between "confession" and literature and art? Or at least, isn't one dominant representation of art that of the transgressive exposition of a subject, who thereby appropriates himself and lets himself be appropriated? The Kantian sublime is produced in a "sacrifice" of the imagination, which "plunges into the abyss of itself and is thus plunged into a moving satisfaction."[14] The whole program of poetry is given in Novalis's note to *Heinrich von Ofterdingen*: "Dissolution of the poet in his song—he will be sacrificed among savage peoples."[15] and, moving quickly, we return to Bataille, who writes: "poetry . . . is . . . sacrifice where the words are victims. . . . We cannot . . . dispense with the efficacious relations that words introduce between men and things. But we wrest them deliriously from these relations" (Bataille, *OC* 5: 156).

More precisely, art comes to supplement, to relay or to sublate, the impasse of sacrifice. This impasse is linked to the following: "If the subject is not truly destroyed, everything is still equivocal. And if it is destroyed, the equivocal is resolved, but in the void where everything is obliterated" (Bataille, *OC* 12: 485). So the choice is between the simulacrum and noth-

---

13. Heidegger, "L'Origine de l'oeuvre d'art," in *Chemins qui ne mènent nulle part*, (Paris: NRF, 1962), 48 and 40.

14. Kant, *Critique de la faculté de juger*, "Remarque générale sur l'exposition des jugements esthétiques réfléchissants," and § 26.

15. Novalis, Heinrich von Ofterdingen, trans. R. Rovni (Paris: 10/18. 1967), 269.

ingness; that is also to say, between the representation of the "old" sacrifice and the postulation of self-sacrifice. "But"—Bataille continues—"out of this double impasse arises a sense of the moment of art, which, putting us on the track of utter extinction—leaving us suspended there for a time—proposes to man a ravishing without repose." "Ravishing without repose" is still a dialectical formula. There is ravishing inasmuch as art preserves us "suspended" on the edge of extinction, which is one way of recognizing a new form of the simulacrum here. But it is "without repose," because it brings along the intense agitation of an emotion that accedes to extinction. This emotion does not properly belong to art: it can only exist in access to the bloody heart of extinction. Farther on, Bataille writes: "the infinite festivity of works of art is there to tell us that a triumph . . . is promised to anyone who leaps into the irresolution of the instant. This is why one cannot be too interested by the manifold intoxication that traverses the world's opacity with lightning bolts of apparent cruelty, where seduction is linked to massacre, to torture, to horror." Art itself thus displaces the gaze once again: "apparent" cruelty is a singularly ambiguous effect. It is limited to the simulacral, and at the same time it matters only through the cruelty, the horror that it brings out, and which (so to speak) means something—in any case, only has force—if it is *not* simulated. Bataille's article is entitled: "Art, exercise in cruelty": it involves, whatever the detours, acceding—even if only a little—to the effective exercise of an effective cruelty, at least in its emotion. Art thus matters only if it still sends us back to the sacrifice it supplants. It cannot sacrifice sacrifice except by still sacrificing to sacrifice.

Bataille sees the difficulty—and promptly turns away: "This is not an apology for horrible facts [he is speaking of the facts of sacrifice evoked earlier in the text]. This is not a call for their return." Yet he cannot help shifting once again, to slip into his refusal (I will not say, at this point, that it is a disavowal) a certain restriction: "But . . . these moments . . . have, in the moment of ravishing, all the truth of the emotion in themselves." And further on: "the movement [of art] places him without difficulty at the height of the worst and, reciprocally, the painting of the horror reveals the opening towards the entirety of the possible." In this reciprocity—how *not* to see this?—something of the *mimesis* is annulled; or rather, *mimesis* reveals (and Bataille speaks of revelation) effective *methexis:* art lets us commune, by means of a transgression that is still effective, with horror. That is to say, with the enjoyment of an instantaneous appropriation of death.

By setting aside the horror—troublesome and reputedly ineffective—of blood spilled, and by proposing a horror ravishing but "at the height of the worst," one shows that, on the one hand, one no longer has access to real sacrifice, but also, on the other hand, that thought continues to be measured by the logic and the desire of an infinite "trans-appropriation." Yet it is still, for Bataille (and perhaps—even doubtless—obscurely, for the whole Western tradition) only a question of access without access to a moment of disappropriation. But sacrificial thought does not leave off reappropriating, trans-appropriating this access. Even the chasm of horror, its "opening to the entirety of the possible," is appropriated as soon as it is placed under the sign of sacrifice. Which it is, because the sign of sacrifice is the sign of the repetitive and mimetic possibility of access to that obscure place that both repetition and mimesis are supposed to come from. But what if that place were nothing at all, and if, consequently, there were nothing that could be sacrificed to reach it?

To put it another way, one might say: it is by appropriating death that sacrifice escapes the truth of the moment of dis-appropriation. And for Bataille himself, in the final reckoning, what is at stake in sacrifice is not death: "The awakening of sensibility, the passage from the sphere of intelligible—and usable—objects to an excessive intensity, this is the destruction of the object as such. Of course, it is not what is ordinarily called death . . . it is, in one sense, quite the contrary. In the eyes of a butcher a horse is already dead (meat, an object)" (Bataille, *OC* 4: 103). By this reckoning the substitution of art for sacrifice is more readily grasped. But it should be at the price of a true suppression of sacrifice. And it is in this same passage that Bataille inserts one of his strongest—make no mistake—condemnations of sacrifice: "it is not what is ordinarily called death (and *sacrifice, after all, is definitely a shocker* [un pavé de l'ours]). To the extent that art maintains the sacrificial moment, by its emotion "at the height of the worst," the "shocker" is not missing either. Or rather, sacrifice should not be involved in any way, and the horror of death—on a real altar or a painted one—gives access only to itself and not to any "supreme moment." One more time: if "sovereignty is NOTHING," (Bataille, *OC* 8: 300) as Bataille wore himself out thinking, is there nothing—that is, some thing—that could be sacrificed for it?

IV

Before putting this question to the test more precisely, we have to take one more step with Bataille. We have to follow him in his reflection on the Nazi camps. I will follow the movement of his most developed text on the subject (about which he wrote very little): "Reflections on the Executioner and the Victim," about David Rousset's book, *Les Jours de notre mort*.[16]

16. Bataille, *OC* 11, 262ff. For lack of space I will omit discussion of the article "Sartre," on the Jews and the camps (Ibid, 266 ff). The conclusions would converge: with-

Not once does this text pronounce the word "sacrifice." Nor do other, parallel texts of Bataille's. Nevertheless, it lays out the elements of a sacrificial logic. First of all, the camps give exposure to what is at stake by way of sacrifice: "in a world of suffering, stench, and degradation, each one had the *leisure* to measure the abyss and the absence of limits of the abyss and this obsessive and fascinating truth." But to know these "depths of horror," "the price has to be paid." This price—if I understand Bataille—is double: it consists, first, in the given conditions for a "senseless experience"—that is, the very existence of the camp—and then, of a will that does not refuse to face this horror as a human possibility. This will must be the victim's (and Bataille finds it in the "exaltation" and the "humor" he finds in Rousset). To refuse it would be "a negation of humanity scarcely less degrading than that of the torturer." An appeal is made, if not to self-sacrifice, then to the position, after all, of a subject. To be sure, Bataille specifies: "the horror is evidently not the truth: it is only an infinite possibility, having no limit but death." Access to the "fascinating" truth, however, requires that, "by some means" "abjection and pain reveal themselves in full to man." These means were found in the camps. In particular, they made it clear that "the depth of horror is in the resolution of those who demand it." It is the resolution of the executioners which would "ruin the redoubt that is the founding reason of civilized order" (Elsewhere Bataille wrote that the Jews at Auschwitz "incarnated reason."). Civilized reason, however, is precisely no more than a "redoubt," fragile and limited. What is pitted against it, namely "the rage to torture," does not come from any place other than humanity, not even from a special part of humanity ("parties or races which, we imagine, have nothing human about them"). This possibility is *"ours."* Knowing this possibility as such makes reason capable of its own "putting-into question without reservations," which assures no definitive victory but the highest human possibility that is "the awakening." "Only, what would awakening be if it illuminated only a world of abstract possibilities? if it did not awaken first of all to the possibility of Auschwitz, to the possibility of stench and irreparable fury?" There is a necessity, therefore, in the realization of this possibility.

For Bataille, this necessity evidently stems from the existence of the

---

out saying so directly, Bataille tends to consider the Jews as victims of a sacrificial immolation of "reason." Another text: 7:376–79. On the character—sacrificial or not? of the camps, cf., Lacan, who affirms it (*Séminaire 11* [Paris: Seuil, 1977], 247); Lacoue-Labarthe, who denies it but discusses an objection (*La Fiction du politique* [Paris: Bourgeois, 1987] 80–81); Derrida, who seems to suggest the affirmative (cf., *Schibboleth* [Paris: Galilée, 1986], 82–83, and "Il faut bien manger" in *Confrontations*, n. 20, "Après le sujet qui vient," 113, in the midst of a development on sacrifice as orality and on philosophies that "do not sacrifice sacrifice."

camps and from the will to face, without facile moralism, what they revealed. It is not posed as a necessity a priori. Not for an instant would I want
to suggest the slightest idea of complicity, even unconscious, on Bataille's
part. I believe only that the following should be considered: the logic followed here is quite exactly the somber reverse of a clear logic of sacrifice (at
least if it is possible to isolate such a "clarity"). This logic declares: only
extreme horror keeps reason awake. The logic of sacrifice would say: the
only awakening is an awakening to horror, where the moment of truth
transpires. The two utterances are far from being confounded. But the second can always harbor the truth of the first. If Bataille does not draw this
conclusion, and if the camps remain outside of sacrifice for him, is it not, in
fact, because the horror of sacrifice is silently toppling down here? Even
though Bataille cannot bring himself to say so, thus preserving perhaps, in
spite of all, a possibility that, at the end of the text, indicates "poetry" as a
form of "awakening" (but now we know what return of sacrifice "poetry" is
dedicated to).

Sacrifice would topple here, in silence, into a contrary that is also its
accomplishment: a revelation of horror with no access, no appropriation,
only with the revelation itself, infinite, or rather, indefinite.

A sacrificial interpretation of the camps is thus no doubt possible, even
necessary, but only on the paradoxical condition of reversing itself into its
contrary (from Holocaust to Shoah): this sacrifice leads nowhere, it gives no
access. Still, in one sense, it could be said to be a model of self-sacrifice, since
the reason that is the victim of the camps is likewise on the side of the
executioner, as the analysis of the state and technical mechanisms of extermination has constantly underlined. Bataille said, elsewhere: "the unleashing of passions that seethed at Buchenwald and at Auschwitz was an unleashing governed by reason."[17] It would not be at all surprising if a certain
rationality culminated in self-sacrifice, if self-sacrifice—whose equivalence
to all of Western sacrifice we can now understand—renders the account of a
certain process of Reason. It appropriates to itself the abyss of its own subjec-
titude (to speak like Heidegger).

But at the same time—and without contradiction—the camps represent
the absence of sacrifice, because they put into play an unheard-of tension
between sacrifice itself and the absence of sacrifice. It is not irrelevant that
the description of the privileges of the Aryan race in *Mein Kampf* culminates in the possession of the absolute meaning of sacrifice: "The Aryan

17. Bataille, OC 7: Note that a similar discussion has taken place on the subject of the
sacrificial character of the revolutionary regicide: cf., Myriam Revault d'Allones, *D'une
mort à l'autre* (Paris: Seuil, 1989), 59. There are, obviously, considerable differences. I want
only to suggest that, under the reign of Western sacrifice, sacrifice has long since begun to
discompose itself.

does not attain his full grandeur by his spiritual properties in themselves; he attains it by the measure of his readiness to put all of his capacities to the service of the community. The instinct of preservation has attained in him its noblest form, for he voluntarily subordinates his own self to the collectivity and, when the hour demands it, he will go so far as to sacrifice it."[18] Or again: "posterity forgets men who have only served their own interests, and celebrates heroes who have renounced their own happiness" (*Mein Kampf*, 329). So the Aryan is essentially the one who sacrifices himself to the community, to the race; that is, the one who gives his blood for Aryan Blood. He is thus not only "the one who sacrifices himself," he is, in essence, sacrifice, *the* sacrifice.

As is only fair, what follows immediately is the description of the race in which the instinct of self-preservation is dominant. "Among the Jewish people, the will to sacrifice does not go beyond the pure and simple instinct of the preservation of the individual" (*Mein Kampf*, 330). There is thus a double reason that the Jew not be and should not be sacrificed: on the one hand, nothing of him should be appropriated; on the contrary, one should rid oneself of his vermin as a defensive and hygenic measure. On the other hand, sacrifice is entirely present, invested and accomplished in the Aryan community as such. "We have the moral right, we have a duty towards our people to annihilate this people who would annihilate us . . . we can say that we have carried out the most difficult of duties for the love of our people. . . . You should know what a hundred—or five hundred or a thousand—corpses laid next to one another are. To have held out, and at the same time . . . to have remained honest men, this is what has hardened us. It is a glorious page of our history that has never been written and which will never be written."[19] Thus Himmler in 1943 presented to his *Gruppenführer* the sacrifice of duty that defies human strength, and which goes so far as to sacrifice the memorial of this glorious sacrifice. Thus he declares, simultaneously, that the side of the victims is intolerable and that on the side of the executioners, there is the most silent, most interior form of sacrifice.

Himmler does not use the word "sacrifice": it would, in effect, be too honorific toward the victims, and he would claim, for the executioners, too much of the glorious narrative, which must be withheld from them. It would be possible, it seems to me, to say that at this point sacrifice disappears in itself. It is the SS or the Aryan, then, who withdraws, who absorbs into himself all the power and the fruit of sacrifice, including its secret: he is already himself, in his own being, the sacrificial secret. Before him he leaves

18. Adolph Hitler, *Mein Kampf* 183/184e, Munich, 1936, 326. Henceforth cited in the text.

19. Himmler's speech of 4 October 1943, in Raul Hillberg, *La Destruction des Juifs d'Europe*, trans. M. F. de Palomera and A. Charpentier (Paris: Fayard, 1985), 870–71.

only naked horror, a parody of immolation and smoke mounting to the heavens, a parody that no longer even has the right to the name of "parody." What disappears along with sacrifice is the very possibility of considering, in whatever sense, the simulacrum. The Aryan exposes devastation, night and fog: "night and fog," however, also form the disastrous secret of his own appropriation, the regeneration of his Blood. No longer Western sacrifice, it is the "westerning" of sacrifice. A second rupture takes place, and this time it is the rupture of sacrifice itself. Or rather, its brutal interruption: in the very site of immolation itself, there is no more immolation.

V

" . . . immolation, murder . . . ": they can no longer be distinguished. Immolation itself is put to death. "Not divine," "illusory," sacrifice has lost all rights and all its dignity. Transgression trans-appropriates nothing. Or rather, it appropriates nothing but this: the victim as corpse, the charnel-house heap, and the other (for whom the name of executioner is scarcely fitting) as pure instrument of the production of the charnel-house heap. Thus, the decomposition of sacrifice not only avows itself as possible thanks to the technical means, but it delivers itself as an exemplary figure—hideously exemplary—of technique itself.[20]

This does not imply a condemnation of the said "technique." On the contrary. For what is *hideously* exemplary, that is, so to speak, exemplarily hideous, is that "technique" should be presented as the operation of a sort of sacrifice, as the last secret of sacrifice, even while it works to decompose sacrifice. The question that arises is rather the following: should not the age of technique be understood as the age of the end of sacrifice? That is to say, as the age of the end of trans-appropriation; or in other words, as the age of another mode of appropriation entirely: no longer of sacrificial trans-appropriation, but of what Heidegger tried to name with the word *Ereignis*. To force this interpretation, without being able to analyze or to justify it here, I would say: "technique" *is Ereignis*, that is, the event appropriating finite existence as such. In this sense, rather than appealing to an "essence" of technique, it may be more fitting to consider technique itself, in that, turning every possible mode of appropriation back on itself and its own "one-dimensionality," if you will, it exposes at one stroke both the question of *finite* existence as such and the question of its equally finite appropriation. The technique of the camps is doubtless one possibility of technique, but it is also its sacrificial possibility.

20. On technique, techné, art, and the work in Nazism and/or Heidegger's thought, see Lacoue-Labarthe, *La Fiction du politique*, passim.

Sacrificial trans-appropriation is the appropriation of the Subject who penetrates negativity, that sustains itself there, that survives its own destruction, and that returns to itself as sovereign. (And this negativity could well play the same role, in a subtle fashion, when it is what Bataille calls "negativity without use.") Fascination for the sacrifice formulates the desire of this transfiguration. Perhaps it is also what Lacan meant by saying (a propos of the camps) that "sacrifice signifies that, in the object of our desires, we try to discover evidence of the presence of the desire of that Other whom I will here call "the obscure God."[21] Let another's desire, obscure, consecrate as *his* my own desire, and I am constituted in absolute Self-possession, in unlimited self-presence. What is thus required is sacrifice, the production of the object as reject, even if this object were its own subject, which here, precisely, trans-appropriates itself.

But if sovereignty is nothing, if the "obscure God" is only the obscurity of desire ecstatic in the face of itself, if existence arranges itself only towards its own finitude, then we must think apart from sacrifice.

On the one hand, what is at stake since the beginning of the Western sublation of sacrifice should definitively be acknowledged: strictly speaking we know nothing decisive about the old sacrifice. We need to admit that what we consider as a mercenary exchange ("Here is the butter . . . ") sustained and gave meaning to billions of individual and collective existences, and we do not know how to think about what founds this gesture. (We can only guess, confusedly, that this barter in itself goes beyond barter.) On the contrary, we know that, for us, it is absolutely impossible to declare: "here are the lives, where are the others?" (all the others: our other lives, the life of a great Other, the other of life and the other life in general).

Consequently, on the other hand, it should be definitively acknowledged that the Western economy of sacrifice has come to a close, and that it is closed by the decomposition of the sacrificial apparatus itself, that bloody transgression by which the "moment of the finite" would be transcended and appropriated infinitely.

But finitude is not a "moment" in a process or an economy. A finite existence does not have to let its meaning spring forth through a destructive explosion of its finitude. Not only does it not have to do so; in a sense it cannot even do so: thought rigorously, thought according to its *Ereignis*, "finitude" signifies that existence cannot be sacrificed.

It cannot be sacrificed because, in itself, it is already, not sacrificed, but offered to the world. There is a resemblance, and the two can be mistaken for one another; and yet, there is nothing more dissimilar.

---

21. Lacan, *Seminaire 11* (Paris: Seuil, 1973), 247. Here Lacan expressly derives this definition from the existence of the camps.

One could say: existence is in essence sacrificed. To say this would be to reproduce, in one of its forms, the fundamental utterance of Western sacrifice. And we would have to add this major form, which necessarily follows: that existence is, in its essence, sacrifice.

To say that existence is offered is no doubt to use a word from the sacrificial vocabulary (and if we were in the German language, it would be the same word: *Opfer, Aufopferung*). But it is an attempt to mark that, if we have to say that existence is sacrificed, it is not in any case sacrificed by anyone, nor is it sacrificed to anything. "Existence is offered" means the finitude of existence. Finitude is not negativity cut out of being and granting access, through this cutting, to the restored integrity of being or to sovereignty. Finitude utters what Bataille utters in saying that sovereignty is nothing. Finitude simply corresponds to the generative formula of the thought of existence, which is the thought of the finitude of being, or the thought of the meaning of being as the finitude of meaning. This formula states: "the "essence" of *Dasein* lies in its existence.[22] If its essence (in quotation marks) is in its existence, it is that the existent has no essence. It cannot be returned to the trans-appropriation of an essence. But it is offered, that is to say, it is presented to the existence that it is.

The existence exposes being in its essence disappropriated of all essence, and thus of all "being:" the being that *is* not. Such negativity, however, does not come dialectically to say that it shall be, that it shall finally be a trans-appropriated Self. On the contrary, this negation affirms the inappropriate as its most appropriate form of appropriation, and in truth as the unique mode of all appropriation. Also, the negative mode of this utterance: "being is not" does not imply a negation but an ontological affirmation. This is what is meant by *Ereignis*.

The existent arrives, takes place, and this is nothing but a being-thrown into the world. In this being-thrown, it is offered. But it is offered by no one, to no one. Nor is it self-sacrificed, if nothing—no being, no subject—precedes its being-thrown. In truth, *it is not even offered or sacrificed to a Nothing, to a Nothingness or an Other in whose abyss it would come to enjoy its own impossibility of being impossibly.* It is exactly at this point that both Bataille and Heidegger must be relentlessly corrected. Corrected, that is: withdrawn from the slightest tendency towards sacrifice. For this tendency towards sacrifice, or through sacrifice, is always linked to a fascination with an ecstasy turned towards an Other or towards an absolute Outside, into which the subject is diverted/spilled the better to be restored.

22. Heidegger, *Being and Time*, Trans. John Macquarrie & Edward Robinson (New York: Harper, 1962), § 9.

Western sacrifice is haunted by an Outside of finitude, as obscure and bottomless as this "outside" may be.

But there is no "outside." The event of existence, the "there is," means that there is *nothing else.* There is no "obscure God." There is no obscurity that would be God. In this sense, and since there is no longer any clear divine epiphany, I might say that what technique presents us with could simply be: clarity without God. The clarity, however, of an open space in which an open eye can no longer be fascinated. Fascination is already proof that something has been accorded to obscurity and its bloody heart. But there is nothing to accord, nothing but "nothing." "Nothing" is not an abyss open to the outside. "Nothing" affirms finitude, and this "nothing" at once returns existence to itself and to nothing else. It de-subjectivizes it, removing all possibility of trans-appropriating itself through anything but its own event, advent. Existence, in this sense, its proper sense, is unsacrificeable.

Thus there is room to give meaning to the infinite absence of appropriable meaning. Once again, "technique" could well constitute such an horizon. That is once more to say, there must be no retreat: the closure of an immanence. But this immanence would not have lost or be lacking transcendence. In other words, it would not be sacrifice in any sense of the word. What we used to call "transcendence" would signify rather that appropriation *is immanent,* but that "immanence" is not some indistinct coagulation: it is made only from its horizon. The horizon holds existence at a distance from itself, in the gap or the "between" that constitutes it: *between* birth and death, *between* one and the others. One does not enter the *between,* which is also the space of the play of *mimesis* and of *methexis.* Not because it would be an abyss, an altar, or an impenetrable heart, but because it would be nothing other than the limit of finitude; and lest we confuse it with, say, Hegelian "finiteness," this limit is a limit that does not soar above nothingness. Existence alone breaks away from even itself.

Does this mean rejoicing in a mediocre and limited life? Surely such a suspicion could itself come only from a mediocre and limited life. And it is this same life that could suddenly be exalted, fascinated, by sacrifice. Neither pain nor death are to be denied. Still less, if possible, are these to be sought after in view of some trans-appropriation. At issue, rather, is a pain that no longer sacrifices, and which one no longer sacrifices. True pain, doubtless, and perhaps even the truest of all. It does not efface joy (nor enjoyment), and yet, it is not the latter's dialectical or sublimating threshhold either. There is no threshhold, no sublime and bloody gesture, that will cross it.

After all, Western sacrifice has almost always known, and almost always been ready to say, that it sacrificed to nothing. That is why it has always tended to say that true sacrifice was no longer sacrifice. Yet henceforth it is incumbent upon us to say—after Bataille, with him and beyond him—that there is no "true" sacrifice, that veritable existence is unsacrificeable, and that finally the truth of existence *is* that it cannot be sacrificed.

Translated by Richard Livingston

SHOSHANA FELMAN

In an Era of Testimony:
Claude Lanzmann's *Shoah*[1]

I

History and Witness, or the Story of an Oath

"If someone else could have written my stories," writes Elie Wiesel, "I would not have written them. I have written them in order to testify. My role is the role of the witness . . . . Not to tell, or to tell another story, is . . . to commit perjury."[2]

To bear witness is to take responsibility for truth: to speak, implicitly, from within the legal pledge and the juridicial imperative of the witness's oath.[3] To testify—before a court of Law or before the court of history and of the future; to testify, likewise, before an audience of readers or spectators—, is more than simply to report a fact or an event or to relate what has been lived, recorded and remembered. Memory is conjured here essentially in order to *address* another, to impress upon a listener, to *appeal* to a community. To testify is always, metaphorically, to take the witness's stand, or to take the position of the witness insofar as the narrative account of the witness is at once engaged in an appeal and bound by an oath. To testify is thus not merely to narrate but to commit oneself, and to commit the nar-

1. The present essay is part of a more extensive study, constituting the chapter on *Shoah* in my forthcoming book: *In an Era of Testimony: Crises of Witnessing in Literature, Psychoanalysis and History* (London: Routledge, 1991; volume coauthored with Dori Laub, M.D.)

2. "The Loneliness of God," published in the journal *Dvar Hashavu'a* (magazine of the newspaper *Davar*): Tel-Aviv, (1984). My translation from the Hebrew.

3. "To tell the truth, the whole truth, and nothing but the truth;" an oath, however, which is always, by its nature, susceptible to perjury.

YFS 79, *Literature and the Ethical Question,* ed. Claire Nouvet, © 1991 by Shoshana Felman.

rative, to others: to *take responsibility*—in speech—for history or for the truth of an occurrence, for something which, by definition, goes beyond the personal, in having general (nonpersonal) validity and consequences.

But if the essence of the testimony is impersonal (to enable a decision by a judge or jury—metaphorical or literal—about the true nature of the facts of an occurrence; to enable an objective reconstruction of what history was like, irrespective of the witness), why is it that the witness's speech is so uniquely, literally irreplaceable? "If someone else could have written my stories, I would not have written them." What does it mean that the testimony cannot be simply reported, or narrated by another in its role as testimony? What does it mean that a story—or a history—cannot be told by someone else?

It is this question, I would suggest, that guides the ground-breaking work of Claude Lanzmann in his film *Shoah* (1985), and constitutes at once the profound subject and the shocking power of originality of the film.

A Vision of Reality

Shoah is a film made exclusively of testimonies: first-hand testimonies of participants in the historical experience of the Holocaust, interviewed and filmed by Lanzmann during the eleven years which preceded the production of the film (1974–1985). In effect, *Shoah* revives the Holocaust with such a power (a power that no previous film on the subject could attain) that it radically displaces and shakes up not only any common notion we might have entertained about it, but our very vision of reality as such, our very sense of what the world, culture, history, and our life within it, are all about.

But the film is not simply, nor is it primarily, a historical document on the Holocaust. That is why, in contrast to its cinematic predecessors on the subject, it refuses systematically to use any historical, archival footage. It conducts its interviews, and takes its pictures, in the present. Rather than a simple view about the past, the film offers a disorienting vision of the present, a compellingly profound and surprising insight into the complexity of the *relation between history and witnessing*.

It is a film about witnessing: about the witnessing of a catastrophe. What is testified to is limit-experiences whose overwhelming impact constantly puts to the test the limits of the witnesses and of the witnessing, at the same time that it constantly unsettles and puts into question the very limits of reality.

Art as Witness

Secondly, *Shoah* is a film about the *relation between art and witnessing*, about film as a medium which *expands* the capacity for witnessing. To understand *Shoah*, we must explore the question: what are *we* as spectators made to witness? This expansion of what we in turn can witness is, however, due not simply to the reproduction of events, but to the power of the film as a work of art, to the subtlety of its philosophical and artistic structure and to the complexity of the creative process it engages. "The truth kills the possibility of fiction," said Lanzmann in a journalistic interview.[4] But the truth does not kill the possibility of art—on the contrary, it requires it for its transmission, for its realization in our consciousness as witnesses.

Finally, *Shoah* embodies the capacity of art not simply to witness, but to *take the witness's stand:* the film takes responsibility for its times by enacting the significance of our era as an *age of testimony*, an age in which witnessing itself has undergone a major trauma. *Shoah* gives us to witness a *historical crisis of witnessing*, and shows us how, out of this crisis, witnessing becomes, in all the senses of the word, a *critical* activity.

On all these different levels, Claude Lanzmann persistently asks the same relentless question: what does it mean to be a witness? What does it mean to be a witness to the Holocaust? What does it mean to be a witness to the process of the film? What does testimony mean, if it is not simply (as we commonly perceive it) the observing, the recording, the remembering of an event, but an utterly unique and irreplaceable topographical *position* with respect to an occurrence? What does testimony mean, if it is the uniqueness of the *performance of a story* which is constituted by the fact that, like the oath, it cannot be carried out by anybody else?

The Western Law of Evidence

The uniqueness of the narrative performance of the testimony in effect proceeds from the witness's irreplaceable performance of the act of seeing—from the uniqueness of the witness's "seeing with his/her own eyes." "Mr. Vitold," says the Jewish Bund leader to the Polish Courrier Jan Karski, who reports it in his cinematic testimony thirty-five years later, in narrating how the Jewish leader urged him—and persuaded him—to become a crucial visual witness: "I know the Western world. You will be speaking to the English. . . . It will strengthen your report if you will be able to say: '*I saw it myself*' (171)".[5]

In the legal, philosophical and epistemological tradition of the Western world, witnessing is based on, and is formally defined by, first-hand seeing. "Eyewitness testimony" is what constitutes the most decisive law of evi-

4. An interview with Deborah Jerome ("Resurrecting Horror: The Man behind *Shoah*"), *The Record*, 25 October 1985.
5. *Shoah*, the complete text of the film by Claude Lanzmann (New York: Pantheon Books, 1985). Quotations from the text of the film will refer to this edition, and will be indicated henceforth only by page number (in the parentheses following the citation).

dence in courtrooms. "Lawyers have innumerable rules involving hearsay, the character of the defendant or of the witness, opinions given by the witness, and the like, which are in one way or another meant to improve the fact-finding process. But more crucial than any one of these—and possibly more crucial than all put together—is the evidence of eyewitness testimony."[6]

Film, on the other hand, is the art par excellence which, like the courtroom (although for different purposes), calls upon a *witnessing* by *seeing*. How does the film use its visual medium to reflect upon eyewitness testimony, both as the law of evidence of its own art and as the law of evidence of history?

Victims, Perpetrators and Bystanders: About Seeing

Because the testimony is unique and irreplaceable, the film is an exploration of the *differences* between heterogeneous points of view, between testimonial stances which can neither be assimilated into, nor subsumed by, one another. There is, first of all, the difference of perspective between three groups of witnesses, or three series of interviewees; the real characters of history who, in response to Lanzmann's inquiry, play their own role as the singularly real actors of the movie, fall into three basic categories:[7] those who witnessed the disaster as its *victims* (the surviving Jews); those who witnessed the disaster as its *perpetrators* (the ex-Nazis); those who witnessed the disaster as *bystanders* (the Poles). What is at stake in this division is not simply a diversity of points of view or of degrees of implication and emotional involvement, but the *incommensurability* of different topographical and cognitive positions, between which the discrepancy cannot be breached. More concretely, what the categories in the film give to see is *three different performances of the act of seeing.*

In effect, the victims, the bystanders, and the perpetrators are here differentiated not so much by what they actually see (what they all see, although discontinuous, does in fact follow a logic of corroboration), as by what and how they *do not see*, by what and how they *fail to witness*. The Jews see, but they do not understand the purpose and the destination of what they see; overwhelmed by loss and by deception, they are blind to the significance of what they witness. Richard Glazar strikingly narrates a moment of perception coupled with incomprehension, an exemplary moment in which the

6. John Kaplan, "Foreword" to Elizabeth R. Loftus: *Eyewitness Testimony* (Cambridge, Mass. and London, England: Harvard University Press: 1979), vii.

7. Categories which Lanzmann borrows from Hilberg's historical analysis, but which the film strikingly *embodies* and rethinks. Cf., Raul Hilberg, *The Destruction of the European Jews* (New York: Holmse and Meier, 1985).

Jews fail to read, or to decipher, the visual signs and the visible significance they nonetheless see with their own eyes:

> Then very slowly, the train turned off of the main track and rolled . . . through a wood. While he looked out—we'd been able to open a window—the old man in our compartment saw a boy . . . and he asked the boy in signs, "Where are we?" And the kid made a funny gesture. This: (draws a finger across his throat) . . .
>
> *And one of you questioned him?*
>
> Not in words, but in signs, we asked: "what's going on here? And he made that gesture. Like this. We didn't really pay much attention to him. We couldn't figure out what he meant. [34]

The Poles, unlike the Jews, *do* see but, as bystanders, they do not quite *look*, they avoid looking directly, and thus they *overlook* at once their responsibility and their complicity as witnesses:

> You couldn't look there. You couldn't talk to a Jew. Even going by on the road, you couldn't look there.
>
> *—Did they look anyway?*
>
> Yes, vans came and the Jews were moved farther off. You could see them, but on the sly. In sidelong glances. [97–98]

The Nazis, on the other hand, see to it that both the Jews and the extermination will remain unseen, invisible; the death camps are surrounded, for that purpose, with a screen of trees. Franz Suchomel, an ex-guard of Treblinka, testifies:

> Woven into the barbed wire were branches of pine trees. . . . It was known as "camouflage". . . . So everything was screened. People couldn't see anything to the left or right. Nothing. You couldn't see through it. Impossible. [110]

It is not a coincidence that as this testimony is unfolding it is hard for us as viewers of the film to see the witness, who is filmed secretly: as is the case for most of the ex-Nazis, Franz Suchomel agreed to answer Lanzmann's questions, but not to be filmed; he agreed, in other words, to give a testimony, but on the condition that, as witness, *he* should not be seen:

> *Mr. Suchomel, we're not discussing you, only Treblinka. You are a very important eyewitness, and you can explain what Treblinka was.*
>
> But don't use my name.
>
> *No, I promised . . .* [54]

In the blurry images of faces taken by a secret camera that has to shoot through a variety of walls and screens, the film makes us see concretely, by the compromise it unavoidably inflicts upon *our* act of seeing (which, of necessity, becomes materially an act of *seeing through*), how the Holocaust was a historical assault on seeing and how, even today, the perpetrators are still by and large invisible: "everything was screened. You couldn't see anything to the left or right. You couldn't see through it."

Figuren

The essence of the Nazi scheme is to make itself—and to make the Jews—essentially invisible. To make the Jews invisible not merely by killing them, not merely by confining them to "camouflaged," invisible death camps, but by reducing even the materiality of the dead bodies to smoke and ashes, and by reducing, furthermore, the radical opacity of the *sight* of the dead bodies, as well as the linguistic referentiality and literality of the *word* "corpse," to the transparency of a pure form and to the pure rhetorical metaphoricity of a mere *figure:* a disembodied verbal substitute which signifies abstractly the linguistic law of infinite exchangeability and substitutability. The dead bodies are thus verbally rendered invisible, and voided both of substance and of specificity, by being treated, in the Nazi jargon, as *Figuren:* that which, all at once, *cannot be seen* and can be *seen through*.

> The Germans even forbade us to use the words "corpse" or "victim." The dead were blocks of wood, shit. The Germans made us refer to the bodies as *Figuren*, that is, as puppets, as dolls, or as *Schmattes*, which means "rags." [13]

But it is not only the dead bodies of the Jews which the Nazis, paradoxically, do not "see." It is also, in some striking cases, the living Jews transported to their death that remain invisible to the chief architects of their final transportation. Walter Stier, head of Reich Railways Department 33 of the Nazi party, chief traffic planner of the death-trains ("special trains," in Nazi euphemism), testifies:

> *But you knew that the trains to Treblinka or Auschwitz were—*
>
> Of course we knew. I was the last district. Without me the trains couldn't reach their destination . . .
>
> *Did you know that Treblinka meant extermination?*
>
> Of course not . . . . How could we know? I never went to Treblinka. [135]
> . . . .
> *You never saw a train?*
>
> No, never. . . . I never left my desk. We worked day and night. [132]

In the same way, Mrs. Michelshon, wife of a Nazi schoolteacher in Chelmno, answers Lanzmann's questions:

> *Did you see the gas vans?*

> No. . . . Yes, from the outside. They shuttled back and forth. I never looked inside; I didn't see Jews in them. I only saw things from outside. [82]

The Occurrence as Unwitnessed

Thus, the diversity of the testimonial stances of the victims, the bystanders and the perpetrators have in common, paradoxically, the incommensurability of their different and particular positions of not seeing, the radical divergence of their topographical, emotional and epistemological positions not simply as witnesses, but as witnesses who *do not witness*, who let the Holocaust occur as an event essentially unwitnessed. Through the testimonies of its visual witnesses the film makes us *see* concretely—makes us *witness*—, how the Holocaust occurs as the unprecedented, inconceivable historical advent of *an event without a witness*, an event which historically consists in the scheme of the literal *erasure of its witnesses* but which, moreover, philosophically consists in an accidenting of perception, in a *splitting of eyewitnessing* as such; an event, thus, not empirically, but cognitively and perceptually without a witness both because it precludes seeing and because it precludes the possibility of a *community of seeing;* an event which radically annihilates the recourse (the appeal) to visual corroboration (to the commensurability between two different seeings) and thus dissolves the possibility of any *community of witnessing.*

Shoah enables us to see—and gives us insight into—the occurrence of the Holocaust as an absolute historical event whose literally *overwhelming evidence* makes it, paradoxically, into an *utterly proofless event;* the age of testimony is the age of prooflessness, the age of an event whose magnitude of reference is at once below and beyond proof.

The Multiplicity of Languages

The incommensurability between different testimonial stances, and the heterogeneous multiplicity of specific cognitive positions of seeing and not seeing, is amplified and duplicated in the film by the multiplicity of languages in which the testimonies are delivered (French, German, Sicilian, English, Hebrew, Yiddish, Polish), a multiplicity which necessarily encompasses some foreign tongues and which necessitates the presence of a professional translator as an intermediary between the witnesses and Lanzmann as their interviewer. The technique of dubbing is not used, and the character of the translator is deliberately not edited out of the film—on the contrary, she is quite often present on the screen, at the side of Lanzmann, as another one of the real actors of the film, because the process of translation is itself an integral part of the process of the film, partaking both of its scenario and of its own performance of *its* cinematic testimony. Through the multiplicity of foreign tongues and the prolonged *delay* incurred by the translation, the splitting of eyewitnessing which the historical event seems to consist of, the incapacity of seeing to translate itself spontaneously and simultaneously into a meaning, is recapitulated on the level of the viewers of the film. The film places us in the position of the witness who *sees* and *hears*, but *cannot understand* the significance of what is going on until the later intervention, the delayed processing and rendering of the significance of the visual/acoustic information by the translator, who also in some ways distorts and screens it, because (as is testified to by those viewers who are natives of the foreign tongues which the translator is translating, and as the film itself points out by some of Lanzmann's interventions and corrections), the translation is not always absolutely accurate.

The palpable foreignness of the film's tongues is emblematic of the radical foreignness of the experience of the Holocaust, not merely to us, but even to its own participants. Asked whether he had invited the participants to see the film, Lanzmann answered in the negative: "in what language would the participants have seen the film?" The original was a French print: "They don't speak French."[8] French, the native language of the filmmaker, the common denominator into which the testimonies (and the original subtitles) are translated and in which the film is thought out and gives, in turn, its own testimony happens (not by chance, I would suggest) not to be the language of any of the witnesses. It is a metaphor of the film that its language is a language of translation, and, as such, is doubly foreign: that the occurrence, on the one hand, happens in a language foreign to the language of the film, but also, that the significance of the occurrence can only be articulated in a language foreign to the language(s) of the occurrence.

The title of the film is, however, not in French and embodies thus, once more, a linguistic strangeness, an estrangement, whose significance is enigmatic and whose meaning cannot be immediately accessible even to the native audience of the original French print: *Shoah*, the Hebrew word which, with the definite article (here missing), designates "The Holocaust"

8. Interview given by Lanzmann on the occasion of his visit to Yale University, and filmed at the Video Archive for Holocaust Testimonies at Yale (Interviewers: Dr. Dori Laub and Laurel Vloch), on 5 May 1986. Transcript, 24–25. Hereafter, citations from this videotape will be referred to by the abbreviation "interview," followed by an indication of the page number by its (unpublished) transcript.

but which, without the article, enigmatically and indefinitely means "catastrophe," here names the very foreignness of languages, the very namelessness of a catastrophe which cannot be possessed by any native tongue and which, within the language of translation, can only be named as the *untranslatable:* that which language cannot witness; that which cannot be articulated in *one* language; that which language, in its turn, cannot witness without *splitting.*

The Historian as a Witness

The task of the deciphering of signs and of the processing of intelligibility—what might be called *the task of the translator*[9]—is, however, carried out within the film not merely by the character of the professional interpreter, but also by two other real actors—the historian (Raul Hilberg) and the filmmaker (Claude Lanzmann)—who, like the witnesses, in turn *play themselves* and who, unlike the witnesses and like the translator, constitute *second-degree witnesses* (witnesses of witnesses, witnesses of the testimonies). Like the professional interpreter, although in very different ways, the filmmaker in the film and the historian on the screen are in turn catalysts—or agents—of the process of *reception,* agents whose reflective witnessing and whose testimonial stances aid our own reception and assist us both in the effort toward comprehension and in the unending struggle with the foreignness of signs, in processing not merely (as does the professional interpreter) the literal meaning of the testimonies, but also, some perspectives on their philosophical and historical significance.

The historian is, thus, in the film, neither the last word of knowledge nor the ultimate authority on history, but rather, one more topographical and cognitive position of *yet another witness.* The statement of the filmmaker—and the testimony of the film—are by no means *subsumed* by the statement (or the testimony) of the historian. Though the filmmaker does embrace the historical insights of Hilberg, which he obviously holds in utter respect and from which he gets both inspiration and instruction, the film also places in perspective—and puts in context—the discipline of history as such, in stumbling on (and giving us to see) the very limits of historiography. "*Shoah,*" said Claude Lanzmann at Yale, "is certainly not a historical film. . . . The purpose of *Shoah* is not to transmit knowledge, in spite of the fact that there is knowledge in the film . . . . Hilberg's book, *The Destruction of the European Jews,* was really my Bible for many years. . . . But in spite of this, *Shoah* is not a historical film, it is something else. . . . To

---

9. Cf., Walter Benjamin, "The Task of the Translator," in *Illuminations*, trans. Harry Zohn, ed. Hannah Arendt (New York: Schocken Books: 1969), 69–82.

condense in one word what the film is for me, I would say that the film is an *incarnation*, a *resurrection*, and that the whole process of the film is a philosophical one."[10] Hilberg is the spokesman for a unique and impressive knowledge on the Holocaust. Knowledge is shown by the film to be absolutely necessary in the ongoing struggle to resist the blinding impact of the event, to counteract the splitting of eyewitnessing. But knowledge is not, in and of itself, a sufficiently active and sufficiently effective act of seeing. The newness of the film's vision, on the other hand, consists precisely in the surprising insight it conveys into the radical ignorance in which we are unknowingly all plunged with respect to the actual historical occurrence. This ignorance is not simply dispelled by history—on the contrary, it *encompasses* history as such. The film shows how history is used for the purpose of a historical (ongoing) *process of forgetting* which, ironically enough, *includes* the gestures of historiography. Historiography is as much the product of the passion of forgetting as it is the product of the passion of remembering.

Walter Stier, former head of Reich railways and chief planner of the transports of the Jews to death camps, can thus testify:

What was Treblinka for you? . . . A destination?

Yes, that's all.

But not death.

No, no . . .

Extermination came to you as a big surprise?

Completely . . .

You had no idea.

Not the slightest. Like that camp—what was its name? It was in the Oppeln district . . . . I've got it: Auschwitz.

Yes, Auschwitz was in the Oppeln district. . . . Auschwitz to Krakow is forty miles.

That's not very far. And we knew nothing. Not a clue.

But you knew that the Nazis—that Hitler didn't like the Jews?

That we did. It was well known. . . . But as to their extermination, that was news to us. I mean, even today people deny it. They say there couldn't have been so many Jews. Is it true? I don't know. That's what they say. [136–38]

---

10. "An Evening with Claude Lanzmann," 4 May 1986, first part of Lanzmann's visit to Yale, videotaped and copyrighted by Yale University. Transcript of the first videotape (hereafter referred to as "Evening"), 2.

To substantiate his own amnesia (of the name of Auschwitz) and his own claim of essentially *not knowing,* Stier implicitly refers here to the *claim of knowledge*—the historical authority—of "revisionist historiographies," recent works published in a variety of countries by historians who prefer to argue that the *number* of the dead cannot be *proven* and that, since there is no scientific, scholarly hard evidence of the *exact extent* of the mass murder, the genocide is merely an invention, an exaggeration of the Jews and the Holocaust, in fact, never existed.[11] "But as to their extermination, that was news to us. I mean, even today, people deny it. They say there could not have been so many Jews. Is it true? I don't know. That's what they say." 'I am not the one who knows, but there are those who know who say that what I did not know did not exist.' "Is it true? I don't know."

Dr. Franz Grassler, on the other hand (formerly Nazi commissioner of the Warsaw Ghetto), comes himself to mimic, in front of the camera, the very gesture of historiography as an alibi to *his* forgetting.

You don't remember those days?

Not much. . . . It's a fact: we tend to forget, thank God, the bad times . . .

I'll help you to remember. In Warsaw you were Dr. Auerswald's deputy.

Yes . . .

Dr. Grassler, this is Czerniakow's diary. You're mentioned in it.

It's been printed. It exists?

He kept a diary that was recently published. He wrote on 7 July 1941 . . .

7 July 1941? That's the first time I've relearned a date. May I take notes? After all, it interests me too. So in July I was already there! [175–76]

In line with the denial of responsibility and memory, the very gesture of historiography comes to embody nothing other than the blankness of the page on which the "notes" are taken.

The next section of the film focuses on the historian Hilberg holding, and discussing, Czerniakow's diary. The cinematic editing that follows shifts back and forth, in a sort of shuttle movement, between the face of Grassler (who continues to articulate his own view of the ghetto) and the face of

11. Cf., for instance, Robert Raurisson: "I have analyzed thousands of documents. I have tirelessly pursued specialists and historians with my questions. I have in vain tried to find a single former deportee capable of proving to me that he had really seen, with his own eyes, a gas chamber." (*Le Monde,* 16 January 1979.) We have "a selective view of history," comments Bill Moyers. "We live within a mythology of benign and benevolent experience. . . . It is hard to believe that there exists about a hundred books all devoted to teaching the idea that the Holocaust was a fiction, that it did not happen, that it has been made up by Jews for a lot of diverse reasons . . . " Interview with Margot Strom, in *Facing History and Ourselves* (Fall 1986), 6 and 7.

Hilberg (who continues to articulate the content of the diary and the perspective that the author of the diary—Czerniakow—gives of the ghetto). The Nazi commissioner of the ghetto is thus confronted structurally, not so much with the counterstatement of the historian, but with the firsthand witness of the (now dead) author of the diary, the Jewish leader of the ghetto whom the ineluctability of the ghetto's destiny led to end his leadership—and sign his diary—with suicide.

The main role of the historian is, thus, less to narrate history than to *reverse the suicide*, to take part in a cinematic vision which Lanzmann has defined as crucially an "incarnation" and a "resurrection." "I have taken a historian," Lanzmann enigmatically remarked, "so that he will incarnate a dead man, even though I had someone alive who had been a director of the ghetto."[12] The historian is there to embody, to give flesh and blood to, the dead author of the diary. Unlike the Christian resurrection, though, the vision of the film is to make Czerniakow *come alive precisely as a dead man*. His "resurrection" does not cancel out his death. The vision of the film is at once to make the dead writer come alive as a historian, and to make, in turn, history and the historian come alive in the uniqueness of the living voice of a dead man, and in the silence of his suicide.

The Filmmaker as a Witness

At the side of the historian, *Shoah* finally includes among its list of characters (its list of witnesses) the very figure of the filmmaker in the process of the making—or of the creation—of the film. Travelling between the living and the dead and moving to and fro between the different places and the different voices in the film, the filmmaker is continuously—though discreetly—present in the margin of the screen, perhaps as the most silently articulate and as the most articulately silent, witness. The creator of the film speaks and testifies, however, in his own voice, in his triple role as the *narrator* of the film (and the signatory—the first person—of the script), as the *interviewer* of the witnesses (the solicitor and the receiver of the testimonies), and as the *inquirer* (the artist as the subject of a quest concerning what the testimonies testify to; the figure of the witness as a questioner, and of the asker not merely as the factual investigator but as the bearer of the film's philosophical address and inquiry).

The three roles of the filmmaker intermix and in effect exist only in their relation to each other. Since the narrator is, as such, strictly a witness, his

---

12. Statement made in a private conversation that took place in Paris, on 18 January 1987: "*J'ai pris un historien pour qu'il incarne un mort, alors que j'avais un vivant qui était directeur du ghetto.*"

story is restricted to the story of the interviewing: the narrative consists of what the interviewer hears. Lanzmann's rigor as narrator is precisely to speak strictly as an interviewer (and as an inquirer), to abstain, that is, from narrating anything directly in his own voice, except for the beginning—the only moment which refers the film explicitly to the first person of the filmmaker as narrator:

> The story begins in the present at Chelmno . . . . Chelmno was the place in Poland where Jews were first exterminated by gas. . . . Of the four hundred thousand men, women, and children who went there, only two came out alive. . . . Srebnik, survivor of the last period, was a boy of thirteen when he was sent to Chelmno. . . . I found him in Israel and persuaded that one-time boy singer to return with me to Chelmno. [3–4]

The opening, narrated in the filmmaker's own voice, at once situates the story in the present and sums up a past which is presented not yet as the story but rather as a pre-history, or a pre-story: the story proper is contemporaneous with the film's speech, which begins, in fact, subsequent to the narrator's written preface, by the actual song of Srebnik re-sung (reenacted) in the present. The narrator is the "I" who "found" Srebnik and "persuaded" him to "return with me to Chelmno." The narrator, therefore, is the one who *opens,* or re-opens, the story of the past in the present of the telling. But the "I" of the narrator, of the signatory of the film, has no voice; the opening is projected on the screen as the silent text of a mute script, as the narrative voice-over of a *writing* with no voice.

On the one hand, then, the narrator has no voice. On the other hand, the continuity of the narrative is ensured by nothing other than Lanzmann's voice, which runs through the film and whose sound constitutes the continuous, connective thread between the different voices and the different testimonial episodes. But Lanzmann's voice—the active voice in which we hear the filmmaker speak—is strictly, once again, the voice of the inquirer and of the interviewer, not of the narrator. As narrator, Lanzmann does not speak but rather, vocally recites the words of others, *lends his voice* (on two occasions) to read aloud two written documents whose authors cannot speak in their own voice: the letter of the Rabbi of Grabow, warning the Jews of Lodz of the extermination taking place at Chelmno, a letter whose signatory was himself consequently gassed at Chelmno with his whole community ("Do not think"—Lanzmann recites—"that this is written by a madman. Alas, it is the horrible, tragic truth," [83–84]), and the Nazi document entitled "Secret Reich Business" and concerning technical improvements of the gas vans ("Changes to special vehicles . . . shown by use and experience to be necessary," [103–05]), an extraordinary document which might be said to formalize Nazism as such (the way in which the most perverse and most concrete extermination is abstracted into a pure question of technique and function). We witness Lanzmann's voice modulating evenly—with no emotion and no comment—the perverse diction of this document punctuated by the unintentional, coincidental irony embodied by the signatory's name: "signed: Just."

Besides this recitation of the written documents, and besides his own mute reference to his own voice in the written cinematic preface of the silent opening, Lanzmann speaks as interviewer and as inquirer, but as narrator, he keeps silent. The narrator lets the narrative be carried on by others—by the live voices of the various witnesses he interviews, whose stories must be able to *speak for themselves*, if they are to testify, that is, to perform their unique and irreplaceable firsthand witness. It is only in this way, by this abstinence of the narrator, that the film can in fact be a narrative of testimony, a narrative of that, precisely, which can neither be reported, nor narrated, by another. The narrative is thus essentially a narrative of silence, the story of the filmmaker's *listening*; the narrator is the teller of the film only insofar as he is the bearer of the film's silence.

In his other roles, however, that of interviewer and of inquirer, the filmmaker, on the contrary, is by definition a transgressor, and a breaker, of the silence. Of his own transgression of the silence, the interviewer says to the interviewee whose voice cannot be given up and whose silence must be broken: "I know it's very hard. I know and I apologize" (117).

As an interviewer, Lanzmann asks not for great explanations of the Holocaust, but for concrete descriptions of minute particular details and of apparently trivial specifics. "Was the weather very cold?" (11). "From the station to the unloading ramp in the camp is how many miles? . . . How long did the trip last?" (33). "Exactly where did the camp begin?" (34). "It was the silence that tipped them off? . . . Can he describe that silence?" (67). "What were the [gas] vans like? . . . What color?" (80). It is not the big generalizations but the concrete particulars which translate into a vision and thus help both to dispel the blinding impact of the event and to transgress the silence to which the splitting of eyewitnessing reduced the witness. It is only through the trivia, by small steps—and not by huge strides or big leaps—that the barrier of silence can be in effect displaced, and somewhat lifted. The pointed and specific questioning resists, above all, any possible canonization of the experience of the Holocaust. Insofar as the interviewer challenges at once the sacredness (the unspeakability) of death and the sacredness of the deadness (of the silence) of the witness, Lanzmann's questions are essentially desacralizing.

> *How did it happen when the women came into the gas chamber? . . .*
> *What did you feel the first time you saw all these naked women? . . .*
> . . . .

But I asked and you didn't answer: What was your impression the first time you saw these naked women arriving with children? How did you feel?

I tell you something. To have a feeling about that . . . it was very hard to feel anything, because working there day and night between dead people, between bodies, your feeling disappeared, you were dead. You had no feeling at all. [114–16]

Shoah is the story of the liberation of the testimony through its desacralization; the story of the decanonization of the Holocaust for the sake of its previously impossible historicization. What the interviewer above all avoids is an alliance with the silence of the witness, the kind of empathic and benevolent alliance through which interviewer and interviewee often implicitly concur, and work together, for the mutual comfort of an avoidance of the truth.

It is the silence of the witness's death which Lanzmann must historically challenge here, in order to revive the Holocaust and to rewrite the *event-without-a-witness* into witnessing, and into history. It is the silence of the witness's death, and of the witness's deadness which precisely must be broken, and transgressed.

We have to do it. You know it.

I won't be able to do it.

You have to do it. I know it's very hard. I know and I apologize.

Don't make me go on please.

Please. We must go on. [117]

What does *going on* mean? The predicament of having to continue to bear witness at all costs parallels, for Abraham Bomba, the predicament faced in the past of having to continue to *live on*, to survive in spite of the gas chambers, in the face of the surrounding death. But to have to *go on* now, to have to keep on bearing witness, is more than simply to be faced with the imperative to replicate the past and thus to replicate his own *survival*. Lanzmann paradoxically now urges Bomba to break out of the very deadness that enabled the survival. The narrator calls the witness to come back from the mere mode of surviving into that of living—and of living pain. If the interviewer's role is thus to break the silence, the narrator's role is to ensure that the story (be it that of silence) will go on.

But it is the inquirer whose philosophical interrogation and interpellation constantly reopen what might otherwise be seen as the story's closure.

Mrs. Pietrya, you live in Auschwitz?

Yes, I was born there . . .

Were there Jews in Auschwitz before the war?

They made up eighty percent of the population. They even had a synagogue here . . .

Was there a Jewish cemetery in Auschwitz?

It still exists. It's closed now.

Closed? What does that mean?

They don't bury there now. [17–18]

The inquirer thus inquires into the very meaning of *closure* and of narrative, political, and philosophical *enclosure*. Of Dr. Grassler, the ex-assistant to the Nazi "commissar" of the Jewish ghetto, Lanzmann asks:

> *My question is philosophical. What does a ghetto mean, in your opinion?*
> [182]

Differences

Grassler of course evades the question. "History is full of ghettos," he replies, once more using erudition, "knowledge," and the very discipline of history, to avoid the cutting edge of the interpellation: "Persecution of the Jews wasn't a German invention, and didn't start with World War II" (182). Everybody knows, in other words, what a ghetto is, and the meaning of the ghetto does not warrant a specifically *philosophical* attention: "history is full of ghettos." Because "history" knows only too well what a ghetto is, this knowledge might as well be left to history, and does not need in turn to be probed by us. "History" is thus used both to deny the *philosophical* thrust of the question and to forget the specificity—the *difference*—of the Nazi past. Insofar as the reply denies precisely the inquirer's refusal to *take for granted* the conception—let alone the preconception—of the ghetto, the stereotypical, preconceived answer in effect *forgets* the asking power of the question. Grassler essentially forgets the difference, forgets the *meaning* of the ghetto as the first step in the Nazi overall design precisely of the framing—and of the enclosure—of a difference, a difference that will consequently be assigned to the ultimate enclosure of the death camp and to the "final solution" of eradication. Grassler's answer *does not meet* the question, and attempts, moreover, to *reduce* the question's difference. But the question of the ghetto—that of the attempt at the containment (the reduction) of a difference—perseveres both in the speech and in the silence of the inquirer-narrator. The narrator is precisely there to insure that the question, in its turn, will *go on* (will continue in the viewer). The inquirer, in other words, is not merely the agency which asks the questions, but the force which takes apart all previous answers. Throughout the interviewing process the inquirer-narrator, at the side of Grassler as of others, is at once the witness of the question and the witness of the gap—or of the difference—between the question and the answer.

Often, the inquirer bears witness to the question (and the narrator silently bears witness to the story) by merely recapitulating word by word a fragment of the answer, by literally repeating—like an echo—the last sentence, the last words just uttered by the interlocutor. But the function of the echo—in the very resonance of its amplification—is itself inquisitive, and not simply repetitive. "The gas vans came in here," Srebnik narrates: "there were two huge ovens, and afterwards the bodies were thrown into these ovens, and the flames reached to the sky" (6). "To the sky [zum Himmel]," mutters silently the interviewer, opening at once a philosophical abyss in the simple words of the narrative description and a black hole in the very blueness of the image of the sky. When later on, the Poles around the church narrate how they listened to the gassed Jews' screams, Lanzmann's repetitious echoes register the unintended irony of the narration:

> They heard the screams at night?
>
> The Jews moaned. . . . They were hungry. They were shut in and starved.
>
> What kinds of cries and moans were heard at night?
>
> They called on Jesus and Mary and God, sometimes in German . . .
>
> The Jews called on Jesus, Mary, and God! [97-98]

Lanzmann's function as an echo is another means by which the voicelessness of the narrator and the voice of the inquirer produce a *question* in the very answer, and enact a *difference* through the very verbal repetition. In the narrator as the bearer of the film's silence, the *question* of the screams persists. And so does the *difference* of what the screams in fact call out to. Here as elsewhere in the film, the narrator is, as such, both the guardian of the question and the guardian of the difference.

The inquirer's investigation is precisely into (both the philosophical and the concrete) particularity of difference. "*What's the difference* between a special and a regular train?," the inquirer asks of the Nazi traffic planner Walter Stier (133). And to the Nazi teacher's wife, who in a Freudian slip confuses Jews and Poles (both "the others" or "the foreigners" in relation to the Germans), Lanzmann addresses the following meticulous query:

> Since World War I the castle had been in ruins. . . . That's where the Jews were taken. This ruined castle was used for housing and delousing the Poles, and so on.
>
> *The Jews!*
>
> Yes, the Jews.

Why do you call them Poles and not Jews?

Sometimes I get them mixed up.

There's a difference between Poles and Jews?

Oh yes!

What difference?

The Poles weren't exterminated, and the Jews were. That's the difference. An external difference.

And the inner difference?

I can't assess that. I don't know enough about psychology and anthropology. The difference between the Poles and the Jews? Anyway, they couldn't stand each other. [82–83]

As a philosophical inquiry into the ungraspability of difference and as a narrative of the specific differences between the various witnesses, *Shoah* implies a fragmentation of the testimonies—a fragmentation both of tongues and of perspectives—that cannot ultimately be surpassed. It is because the film goes from singular to singular, because there is no possible *representation* of one witness by another, that Lanzmann needs us to sit through ten hours of the film to begin to witness—to begin to have a concrete sense—both of our own ignorance and of the incommensurability of the occurrence. The occurrence is conveyed precisely by this fragmentation of the testimonies, which enacts the fragmentation of the witnessing. The film is a gathering of the fragments of the witnessing. But the collection of the fragments does not yield, even after ten hours of the movie, any possible totality or any possible totalization; the gathering of testimonial incommensurates does not amount either to a generalizable theoretical statement or to a narrative monologic sum. Asked what was his concept of the Holocaust, Lanzmann answered: "I had no concept; I had obsessions, which is different. . . . The obsession of the cold. . . . The obsession of the first time. The first shock. The first hour of the Jews in the camp, in Treblinka, the first minutes. I will always ask the question of the first time. . . . The obsession of the last moments, the waiting, the fear. *Shoah* is a film full of fear, and of energy too. You cannot do such a film theoretically. Every theoretical attempt I tried was a failure, but these failures were necessary. . . . You build such a film in your head, in your heart, in your belly, in your guts, everywhere" (*Interview*, 22–23). This "everywhere" which, paradoxically, cannot be totalized and which resists theory as such, this corporeal fragmentation and enumeration which describes the "building"—or the process of the generation—of the film while it resists any attempt at conceptualization, is itself an emblem of the specificity—of the uniqueness—of the mode of testimony of the film. The film testifies not merely by collecting and by gathering fragments of witnessing, but by actively exploding any possible enclosure—any conceptual frame—that might claim to *contain* the fragments and to fit them into one coherent whole. *Shoah* bears witness to the fragmentation of the testimonies as the radical invalidation of all definitions, of all parameters of reference, of all known answers, in the very midst of its relentless affirmation—of its materially creative validation—of the absolute necessity of speaking. The film puts in motion its surprising testimony by performing the historical and contradictory double task of the breaking of the silence and of the simultaneous shattering of any given discourse, of the breaking—or the bursting open—of all frames.

II

A Point of Arrival

The film opens in the filmmaker's own mute voice, which addresses the spectator from within the very writing on the screen that constitutes the film's silent opening.

> Of the four hundred thousand men, women, and children who went there, only two came out alive: Mordechaï Podchlebnik and Simon Srebnik. Srebnik, survivor of the last period, was a boy of thirteen when he went to Chelmno . . .
> I found him in Israel and persuaded that one-time boy singer to return with me to Chelmno. [3–4]

Something is found, here, in Israel, which embodies in effect a point of arrival in Lanzmann's journey, as well as the beginning—or the starting point—of the journey of the film. *"I found him in Israel"* (My emphasis). I would suggest that the artistic power of the film proceeds, precisely, from this *finding*: the *event* of *Shoah* is an event of finding.

What is it exactly that Lanzmann, at the outset of the film, *finds?* The inaugural event of finding is itself already constituted by a number of implied—and incommensurable—discoveries, which the film sets out to explore on different levels.

1) The *finding*, first and foremost, is the finding of Simon Srebnik, the astonishing winning survivor, "that one-time boy singer" who was literally executed (shot in the head) and yet miraculously, more than once, fooled death and survived:

> With his ankles in chains, like all his companions, the boy shuffled through the village of Chelmno each day. That he was kept alive longer than the others he owed to his extreme agility, which made him the winner of jumping contests and speed races that the SS organized for their chained prisoners. And also to his melodious voice; several times a

week . . . young Srebnik rowed up the Narew, under guard, in a flat-bot-
tomed boat. . . . He sang Polish folk tunes, and in return the guard taught
him Prussian military songs . . .

During the night of 18 January 1945, two days before Soviet troops
arrived, the Nazis killed all the remaining Jews in the "work details" with
a bullet in the head. Simon Srebnik was among those executed. But the
bullet missed his vital brain centers. When he came to, he crawled into a
pigsty. A Polish farmer found him there. The boy was treated and healed
by a Soviet Army doctor. A few months later Simon left for Tel-Aviv along
with other survivors of the death camps.

I found him in Israel and persuaded that one-time boy singer to return
with me to Chelmno. [3–4]

2) The *finding* is thus also, at the same time, the finding of a *site* of
entering: the discovery of Israel is the finding of a place which enables
Lanzmann, for the first time, to *inhabit* his own implication in the story of
the Other (Srebnik's story).

3) The finding is the *finding of the testimony*—of its singular significance and functioning as the story of an *irreplaceable historical performance*, a narrative performance which no statement (no report and no description) can replace and whose unique enactment by the living witness is
itself part of a *process of realization* of historic truth. Insofar as this realization is, by definition, what cannot simply be reported, or narrated, by another, Lanzmann finds in Israel, precisely, that which cannot be reported;
both the general significance and the material, singular concretizations of
the testimony (Srebnik's testimony, as well as others').

4) Finally, the finding is *the finding of the film* itself: *Shoah* rethinks, as
well, the meaning and the implications of the advent (of the event) of its own
finding. To find the film is to find a new possibility of sight, a possibility not
just of vision—but of re-vision. Lanzmann finds precisely in the film the
material possibility and the particular potential of *seeing again* someone
like Srebnik whom, after his shooting, no one was likely or supposed to see
ever again. Even more astonishingly, the finding of the film provides in
general, in history, the possibility of *seeing again* what in fact was never seen
the first time, what remained *originally unseen* due to the inherent blinding
nature of the occurrence.

The Return

The film does not stop, however, at the site of its own finding(s), does not
settle at its initial point of arrival, but rather, uses the arrival as a point of
departure for another *kind* of journey, a *return trip* which, going back to the
originally unperceived historical scene, takes place as a journey to another

frame of reference, entering into what Freud calls *eine andere Lokalität*—
into another scale of space and time: "I found him in Israel and persuaded
that one-time boy singer to *return with me to Chelmno.*"

Why is it necessary to return to Chelmno? What is the return about?
Who, or what, returns?

> We are, I am, you are
> by cowardice or courage
> the ones who find our way
> back to this scene[13]
> carrying a knife, a camera
> a book of myths
> in which our names do not appear.[14]

The return in *Shoah* from Israel to Europe (Poland, *Chelmno*), from the place
of the regeneration and the locus of the gathering of Holocaust survivors
back to the prehistory of their oppression and suppression, back to the primal scene of their annihilation, is at once a spatial and a temporal return, a
movement back in space and time which, in attempting to revisit and to
repossess the past is also, simultaneously, a movement forward toward the
future.

The return to Chelmno by the boy singer for whom the Chelmno period
ended with a bullet in the head concretizes at the same time, allegorically, a
historical return of the dead. In a way, the returning forty-seven-year-old
Srebnik ("He was then forty-seven years old," [4]), reappearing on the screen
at the site of the annihilation, the improbable survivor who returns from
Israel to the European scene of the crime against him, is himself rather a
ghost of his own youthful performance, a returning, reappearing ghost of the
one-time winner of chained races and of the boy singer who moved the Poles
and charmed the SS, and who, like Scheherazade, succeeded in postponing
his own death indefinitely by telling (singing) songs. Thus, if Srebnik on the
screen at forty-seven, in the scene of Chelmno of today, embodies a return of
the dead, his improbable survival and his even more improbable return (his
ghostly reappearance) concretizes allegorically, in history, a return of the
(missing, dead) witness on the scene of the event-without-a-witness.

Srebnik had, during the Holocaust, witnessed in effect himself, in

13. "The film," Lanzmann says, "is at moments a crime film . . . , [on the mode of] a
criminal investigation. . . . But it is a Western too. When I returned to the small village of
Grabow, or even in Chelmno. . . . Okay. I arrive here with a camera, with a crew, but forty
years after. . . . This creates an incredible . . . event, you know? Well . . . I am the first
man to come back to the scene of the crime, where the crime has been committed . . . "
(*Panel Discussion*), 53.

14. Adrienne Rich, *Diving into the Wreck* (New York and London, W. W. Norton,
1973), 22.

Chelmno, a return of the dead—a return to life of the half-asphyxiated bodies tumbling out of the gas vans. But he witnessed this revival, this return of the dead, only so as to become a witness to their second murder, to an even more infernal killing (or re-killing) of the living dead, by a burning of their bodies while those are still alive and conscious of their burning, conscious of their own encounter with the flames by which they are engulfed, devoured:

> When [the gas vans] arrived, the SS said: "Open the doors!" . . . . The bodies tumbled right out. . . . We worked until the whole shipment was burned.
>
> I remember that once they were still alive. The ovens were full, and the people lay on the ground. They were all moving, they were coming back to life, and when they were thrown into the ovens, they were all conscious. Alive. They could feel the fire burn them. [101–02]

Srebnik's witness dramatizes both a burning consciousness of death, and a crossing (and recrossing) of the boundary line which separates the living from the dead, and death from life. But when Srebnik saw all that, he was not really a (living) witness since, like Bomba,[15] like Podchlebnik,[16] he too was already *deadened*.

> When I saw all this, it didn't affect me. . . . I was only thirteen, and all I'd ever seen until then were dead bodies. Maybe I didn't understand, maybe if I'd been older, but the fact is, I didn't. I'd never seen anything else. In the ghetto in Lodz I saw that as soon as anyone took a step, he fell dead. I thought that's the way things had to be, that it was normal. I'd walk the streets of Lodz, maybe one hundred yards, and there'd be two hundred bodies. They went into the street and they fell, they fell . . .
>
> So when I came . . . to Chelmno, I was already . . . I didn't care about anything. [102–03]

Therefore, it is only now, today that Srebnik can become a witness to the *impact* of the falling (and the burning) bodies,[17] only today that he can situate his witnessing in a frame of reference that is not submerged by death and informed solely by *Figuren*, by dead bodies. It is therefore only now, in returning with Lanzmann to Chelmno, that Srebnik in effect is returning from the dead (from his own deadness) and can become, for the first time, a

---

15. Bomba: "I tell you something. To have a feeling about that . . . it was very hard to feel anything, because working there day and night between dead people, between bodies, your feeling disappeared, you were dead. You had no feeling at all." (116).

16. Podchlebnik: "*What died in him in Chelmno?* Everything died" (6).

17. On the impact of the falling body, in conjunction with an innovative theory of reference, cf., Cathy Caruth, "The claims of Reference," in *Yale Journal of Criticism*, (Fall 1990), vol. 4, No. 1.

witness to himself, as well as an articulate and for the first time fully *conscious* witness of what he had been witnessing during the War.

The Return of the Witness

Urged by Lanzmann, Srebnik's return from the dead personifies, in this way, a historically performative and retroactive *return of witnessing* to the witnessless historical primal scene.

Srebnik recognizes Chelmno.

> It's hard to recognize, but it was here. They burned people here . . . . Yes, this is the place. No one ever left here again. . . . It was terrible. No one can describe it. . . . And no one can understand it. Even I, here, now. . . . I can't believe I'm here. No, I just can't believe it. It was always this peaceful here. Always. When they burned two thousand people—Jews—every day, it was just as peaceful. No one shouted. Everyone went about his work. It was silent. Peaceful. Just as it is now. [6]

Chelmno recognizes Srebnik. The Polish villagers remember well the child entertainer who "had to . . . [sing when] his heart wept" (6), and they identify and recognize the pathos and the resonance, the lyrics and the melody of his repeated singing:

> He was thirteen and a half years old. He had a lovely singing voice, and we heard him.
>
> > A little white house
> > lingers in my memory
> > Of that little white house
> > I dream each night. [4]

"When I heard him again," one of the Polish villagers remarks, "my heart beat faster, because what happened here . . . was a murder. I really relived what happened" (4).

Lanzmann places Srebnik in the center of a group of villagers before the church in Chelmno, which, at the time, served as a prison-house for the deported Jews and as the ultimate waystation on their journey—via gas vans—to the forest, where the (dead or living) bodies were being burned away in so-called ovens. The villagers at first seem truly happy to see Srebnik, whom they welcome cheerfully and warmly.

Are they glad to see Srebnik again?

> Very. It's a great pleasure. They're glad to see him again because they know all he's lived through. Seeing him as he is now, they are very pleased. [95]

Why does memory linger?, the inquirer would like to know. What motivates this livelihood of the remembrance?

Why does the whole village remember him?

They remember him well because he walked with chains on his ankles, and he sang on the river. He was young, he was skinny, he looked ready for the coffin. . . . Even the [Polish] lady, when she saw that child, she told the German: "Let that child go!" He asked her: "Where to?" "To his father and mother." Looking at the sky, [the German] said: "He'll soon go to them." [95–96]

When Lanzmann gets, however, to the specific subject of the role of the Church in the past massacre of the Jews, the Polish testimony becomes somewhat confused. The evocation of the memories becomes itself unknowingly tainted with phantasies.

They remember when the Jews were locked in this church?

Yes, they do . . .

The vans came to the church door! They all knew these were gas vans, to gas people?

Yes, they couldn't help knowing.

They heard screams at night?

The Jews moaned, they were hungry . . .

What kind of cries and moans were heard at night?

They called on Jesus and Mary and God, sometimes in German . . .

The Jews called on Jesus, Mary and God!

The presbytery was full of suitcases.

The Jews' suitcases?

Yes, and there was gold.

How does she know there was gold? The procession! We'll stop now. [97–98]

Like the Nazi teacher's wife (who only "sees things from outside," [82]), the Poles embody outside witness—present an outside view of the Jewish destiny, but an outside view which nonetheless believes it can account for the inside: in trying to account for the inner meaning of the Jewish outcry from inside the Church, and in accounting for the inner, unseen content of the robbed possessions of the Jews inside the confiscated suitcases, the Poles bear in effect *false witness*. Out of empathy in the first case, with respect to the imagined moaning of the Jewish prisoners of the Church, out of hostile jealousy and of competitive aggression in the second case, with respect to the imaginary hidden treasures and envied possessions, the Poles distort the facts and *dream their memory*, in exemplifying both their utter failure to imagine Otherness and their simplified negotiation of the inside and the outside, by merely projecting their inside on the outside. It is to their own phantasy, to their own (self-) mystification that the Poles bear witness, in attempting to account for historical reality. Their false witness is itself, however, an objective illustration and concretization of the radically delusional quality of the event.

The scene is interrupted by the silence—and the sound of bells—of the procession, a church ritual executed by young girls dressed in white, which celebrates the birth of the Virgin Mary.

This ritual celebration of the images of youth and the predominance of white in the religious ceremony connote the innocence of childhood, the pure integrity and the intactness of virginity, which the ritual is evoking as the attributes of the Holy Virgin. And yet, the presence of Srebnik at the scene reminds us of another kind of childhood, and the contiguity of this rather unvirginal and violated childhood (of the child who had to sing when his heart wept) with the immaculate virginity here enacted, of itself creates an almost sacrilegious, and desacralizing resonance, in an astounding, vertiginous and breathtaking cinematic condensation and juxtaposition of different dimensions, of different registers of space and time, of different levels of existence and experience. The sudden, unexpected superimposition of the Holocaust in which the church served as a death enclosure (as the antechamber to the gas vans) and of the present Christian celebration of the birth of the Virgin Mary, brings out a terrible and silent irony, of a church that in effect embodies a mass tomb, at the same time that it celebrates a birth, of a site whose history is stained with blood, at the same time that it is the stage of an oblivious celebration of an ethical virginity and of an intactly white immaculateness. Very like the whiteness of the snow covering the forests of Sobibor, Auschwitz, and Treblinka, the whiteness of the ritual itself turns out to be an image which, quite literally, covers up history, as the embodiment (and as the disembodiment) of a *white silence*.

Viewing the procession, one recalls Benjamin's discussion of contemporary art and, particularly, of photography and film as vehicles, specifically, of desacralization, as accelerating agents in the modern cultural process of the "shattering"—and of the "liquidation"—of the *cult-values* of tradition:

We know that the earliest art works originated in the service of a ritual—
first the magical, then the religious kind. . . [Now] for the first time in

world history, mechanical reproduction [photography and film] emancipates the work of art from its parasitical dependence on ritual. . . . The total function of art is reversed. Instead of being based on ritual, [art] begins to be based on another practice—politics.[18]

In a surprise translation, Lanzmann's camera converts, in the church scene, the religious and the artistic into the political. The church scene thus becomes the unexpected, sudden cinematographic exhibition of uncanny depths of political significance within the very ritual of the procession.

The Return of History

After the procession, Lanzmann—who does not forget—returns to the interrupted subject of the inside of the Jewish suitcases.

> *The lady said before that the Jews' suitcases were dumped in the house opposite [the church]. What was in this baggage?*
>
> Pots with false bottoms.
>
> *What was in the false bottoms?*
>
> Valuables, objects of value. They also had gold in their clothes . . .
>
> *Why do they think all this happened to the Jews?*
>
> Because they were the richest! Many Poles were also exterminated. Even Priests. [99]

Lanzmann's tour de force as interviewer is to elicit from the witness, as in this case, a testimony which is inadvertently no longer in the control or the possession of its speaker. As a solicitor and an assembler of the testimonies, in his function as a questioner but mainly, in his function as a listener (as the bearer of a narrative of listening), Lanzmann's performance is to elicit testimony which exceeds the testifier's own awareness, to bring forth a complexity of truth which, paradoxically, is *not available as such* to the very speaker who pronounces it. As a listener, Lanzmann endows the interlocutor with speech. It is in this way that he helps both the survivors and the perpetrators to overcome their (very different kind of) silence. Facing Lanzmann, the Polish villagers, in turn, exhibit feelings that would normally be hidden. But the silent interviewer and the silent camera urge us not simply to see the testimony, but to see *through* it: to see—throughout the testimony—the deception and the self-deception which it unwittingly displays, and to which it unintentionally testifies.

18. Walter Benjamin, "The Work of Art in the Age of Mechanical Reproduction," op.cit., 223–24.

Why do they think all this happened to the Jews?

Because they were the richest! Many Poles were also exterminated. Even Priests.

In response to Lanzmann's question, Mr. Kantorowski, the player of the organ and the singer of the church, finds his way out of the crowd which surrounds Srebnik and, pushing himself in front of the camera, overshadows Srebnik and eclipses him:

Mr. Kantorowski will tell us what a friend told him. It happened in Myndjewyce, near Warsaw.

Go on.

The Jews there were gathered in a square. The rabbi asked an SS man: "Can I talk to them?" The SS man said yes. So the rabbi said that around two thousands years ago the Jews condemned the innocent Christ to death. And when they did that, they cried out: "Let his blood fall on our heads and on our sons' heads." Then the rabbi told them: "Perhaps the time has come for that, so let us do nothing, let us go, let us do as we're asked."

He thinks the Jews expiated the death of Christ?

He doesn't think so, or even that Christ sought revenge. The rabbi said it. It was God's will, that's all.[19] [99–100]

Through the voice of the church singer which seems to take on the authority to speak for the whole group, and through the mythic mediation

19. On the generalizable historical significance of this passage, cf., Peter Canning's remarkable analysis in "Jesus Christ, Holocaust: Fabulation of the Jews in Christian and Nazi History": "The compulsive ritual of accusing the Jews of murder (or betrayal, or well-poisoning, or desecration of the Host) and attacking them is inscribed with bodies in history; it is not prescribed but only implicitly suggested in the New Testament, which preaches love and forgiveness. In the Gospel it is 'the Jews' who call down the wrath of God on themselves: 'Let his blood be on us and on our children!' (*Mt.* 27:25) Reciting this text, the Polish villagers whom Claude Lanzmann interviewed . . . excuse themselves, the Germans and God—all are absolved of responsibility for the Holocaust. Once again, 'the Jews brought it on themselves'. The Crucifixion was their crime. The Holocaust was the punishment which they called down on their own heads, and on their children.

The biblical myth functions as an attractor, not only of other narratives but of ongoing events which it assimilates. What I must risk calling the Holo-myth of Christianity—divine incarnation, crucifixion, resurrection—is not the one source or cause of the Holocaust, it 'attracted' other causal factors to it (the war, inflation, political-ideological crisis, socioeconomic convulsions), absorbed them and overdetermined their resolution. . . . Those other critical factors, and their resolution in a fascist syncretism, were not alone capable of turning antisemitism into systematic mass murder. Nazism reactivated the cliché it had inherited from the Christian Holomyth and its reenactment in the event of ritual murder, but transformed it into a regular, mechanized destruction process. (171–72). In *Copyright 1, Fin de siècle 2000,* (Fall 1987).

both of archetypal stereotypes of anti-Semitism and of the Christian story of the Crucifixion, the Poles endow the Holocaust with a strange comprehensibility and with a facile and exhaustive compatibility with knowledge: "It was God's will, that's all. . . . That's all. *Now you know!*" (100). It is by dehistoricizing the events of recent history, and by subsuming them under the prophetic knowledge of the Scriptures, that the Poles are literally washing their hands of the historical extermination of the Jews:

> So Pilate washed his hands and said: "Christ is innocent," and he sent Barabas. But the Jews cried out: "Let his blood fall on our heads!"
>
> That's all. Now you know. [100]

Thus the Poles misrepresent, once more, the Jews from the inside, and the objective nature of the Jewish destiny and slip, once more, across the boundary line between reality and phantasy; they unwittingly begin to dream reality and to hallucinate their memory. In testifying to a murder which they go so far as to call suicide, the Poles bear once again false witness both to the history of Nazism and to the history of the Jews.

But once again, this misrepresentation (this false witness) is itself attributed precisely to the Jews and represented as *their* inside story. Like the Nazis, who make the Jews *pay* for their own death traffic and participate— through "work details"—in the management of their own slaughter, the Poles pretend to have the Jews provide their own interpretation of their history and their own explanation of their murder. Kantorowski thus claims that his own mythic account is in fact the Jews' own version of the Holocaust.

> *He thinks the Jews expiated the death of Christ?*
>
> *He* doesn't think so, or even that Christ sought revenge. The rabbi said it. It was God's will, that's all. [100]

In forging, so to speak, the rabbi's signature so as to punctuate his own false witness and to authorize his own false testimony, Kantorowski disavows responsibility for his own discourse. In opposition to the act of signing and of saying "I" by which the authentic witnesses assume at once their discourse, their speech act and their responsibility toward history ("I found him in Israel and persuaded him to return . . . ," says Lanzmann; "I understand your role, I am here," says Karski; "I can't believe I'm here," says Srebnik), Kantorowski's testimony is destined to remain unsigned.

Mr. Kantorowski, after all, does indeed in some ways remain silent. Not only because, as he claims, it is the words of the dead rabbi that *speak for him*. But because what *speaks through him* (in such a way as to account for his role during the Holocaust) is, on the one hand, the (historic) silence of the

Church and, on the other hand, the silence of all given frames of explanation, the non-speech of all preconceived interpretive schemes, which dispose of the event—and of the bodies—by reference to some other frame. The
collapse of the materiality of history and the seduction of a fable, the reduction of a threatening and incomprehensible event to a reassuring mythic,
totalizing unity of explanation, is in effect what all interpretive schemes
tend to do. Mr. Kantorowski's satisfied and vacuous interpretation stands,
however, for the failure of all ready-made cultural discourses both to account
for—and to bear witness to—the Holocaust.

The film's strategy is not to challenge the false witness, but to *make the
silence speak* from within and from around the false witness: the silence
within each of the testimonies; the silence *between* various silences and
various testimonies; the irremediable silence of the dead; the irremediable
silence of the natural landscapes; the silence of the church procession; the
silence of the ready-made cultural discourses pretending to account for the
Holocaust; and above all, in the center of the film, Srebnik's silence in front
of the church, in the middle of the talkative, delirious, self-complacent
Polish crowd. The church scene is an astonishing emblem of the multiplicity and the complexity of layers which unfold between this central silence and the various speeches which proceed from it and encroach upon it.
Like a hall of mirrors, the church scene is a hall of silences infinitely reso-
nant with one another. "There are many harmonies," says Lanzmann,
"many concordances in the film. I knew very quickly that the film would be
built in a circular way, with a stillness at the center, like the eye of a
hurricane."[20]

The silence reenacts the event of silence. "It was always this peaceful
here," Srebnik had said, "Always. When they burned two thousand people—
Jews—every day, it was just as peaceful. No one shouted. Everyone went
about his work. It was silent. Peaceful. Just as it is now" (6).

Indeed, the church scene is not just a hall (a mirroring) of silences, but the
very stage of the performance—of the execution and the repetition—of an
act of silencing. Although Srebnik here personifies the return of the witness—the return of witnessing into the very scene of the event-without-a-
witness, what the church scene puts into effect and plays out, not in memory but in actual fact (and act), is how the real witness, in returning back to
history and life, is once again *reduced to silence,* struck *dead* by the crowd.
The scene is even more complex, since what the crowd points out as the

20. Quoted in "A Monument Against Forgetting," *The Boston Globe* 3 November
1985, 3. Cf., Lanzmann's remarks in his interview with Roger Rosenblatt, for channel 13
(Public Television WNET, USA 1987): "When one deals with the destruction of the Jews,
one has to talk and to be silent at the same moment. . . . I think there is more silence in
Shoah than words."

Jews' crime and as the reason for the Holocaust is the Crucifixion, or the Jews' murder of Christ. But the Polish villagers are not aware that they themselves are in turn acting out precisely such a *ritual murder story;*[21] they are unaware of the precise ways in which they themselves are actually *enacting* both the Crucifixion and the Holocaust in *annihilating Srebnik,* in *killing once again the witness* whom they totally dispose of, and *forget.*

What Kantorowski's testimony chooses to deny—*his* signature, *his* voice, the Poles' responsibility—it thus performs, reenacts before our eyes. What is not available in words, what is denied, what cannot and what will not be remembered or articulated, nonetheless gets realized. What takes place in the film, what materially and unexpectedly *occurs* and what returns like a ghost is *reference itself,* the very object—and the very content—of historical erasure.

I would suggest that what the film shows us here, in action, is the very process of the *re-forgetting of the Holocaust,* in the repeated murder of the witness and in the renewed reduction of the witnessing to silence. The film makes the testimony *happen*—happen inadvertently as a second Holocaust. The silent Srebnik in the middle of this picture—with his beautifully dignified and tragic mute smile, and with his mutely speaking face (a face signed by his silence) is in effect a ghost: a ghost which, as such, is essentially *not contemporaneous;* contemporaneous, in reality, neither with the voices of the crowd which surrounds him, nor even with himself—with his own muted voice. What the church scene dramatizes is the only possible encounter with the Holocaust, in the only possible form of a *missed encounter.*[22]

I would suggest precisely that the film is about the essence of this *missed contemporaneity* between Srebnik and the semicircle which surrounds him, between Srebnik's voice and his own silence, and fundamentally, between the Holocaust experience and the witness of the Holocaust experience.

Shoah addresses the spectator with a challenge. When we are made to witness this reenactment of the murder of the witness, this second Holocaust that appears spontaneously before the camera and on the screen, can we in our turn become *contemporaneous* with the meaning and with the significance of that enactment? Can we become contemporaneous with the

21. For an acute description of the functioning of the "ritual murder story" in history, cf., again, Peter Canning, "Jesus Christ, Holocaust: Fabulation of the Jews in Christian and Nazi History" (op.cit., 170–73).

22. Cf., Lacan's conception of "the Real" as a "missed encounter" and as "what returns to the same place." *Le Séminaire, livre XI, Les Quatre concepts fondamentaux de la psychanalyse* (Paris: Seuil: 1973); trans. Alan Sheridan, *The Four Fundamental Concepts of Psychoanalysis* (New York: W. W. Norton: 1978) chapters 3–5.

shock, with the displacement, with the disorientation process that is triggered by such testimonial reenactment? Can we, in other words, assume in earnest, not the finite task of making sense out of the Holocaust, but the infinite task of encountering *Shoah?*

III

The Return of the Song

If the church scene is thus punctuated, signed by Srebnik's silence, where is Srebnik's testimony, here lost, to be found? The film includes, indeed, an element through which the very silencing of Srebnik's voice can be somehow reversed, through which the very loss of Srebnik's testimony can be somehow recovered, or at least resist its own forgetting and itself be reencountered, in the repetition of the melody and in the return of Srebnik's "melodious voice" in his reiterated singing. In spite of his own silencing and of his silence, the return of the witness undertaken by the film nonetheless persists, takes over, and survives in the return of the song. In the absence—and the failure—of the contemporaneity between the Holocaust and its own witness, the song nevertheless creates a different kind of contemporaneity between the *voice* and the historical (revisited) *site* of the voice, between the song and the place at which the song is (and was) heard, between the *voice* and the *place* to which, at the beginning of the film, the song in fact *gives voice:*

> . . . it was here. . . . Yes, this is the place. [5]

The song creates, indeed, an unexpected contemporaneity between its reiterated resonance and the very silence of the place.

> It was always this peaceful here. Always. . . . It was silent. Peaceful. Just as it is now. [6]

At the same time, this contemporaneity between present and past, between the singing voice and the silent place, remains entirely incomprehensible to, and thus noncontemporaneous with, the witness.

> No one can understand it. Even I, here, now. . . . I can't believe I'm here. No, I just can't believe it. [6]

It is in hovering between the ways in which it is at once contemporaneous with the place and noncontemporaneous with the witness (with the singer), that the song returns to the inconceivable historical site of its own singing, and that the harmonies and the disharmonies of this return of the song provide an entrance, or a threshold, to the film. It is the song which is

the first to testify, the first to speak after the voiceless opening of the narrator. The song encroaches on—and breaks—at once the silence of the landscape and the muteness of the writing on the screen. Through Srebnik's
voice, the film introduces us into the soothing notes and the nostalgic lyrics
of a Polish folk tune which itself, however, dreams about, and yearns for,
another place.

> A little white house
> lingers in my memory
> Of that little white house
> each night I dream. [4]

The White House

Srebnik's voice inhabits his own song. But does anyone inhabit the "white
house" of which he sings? Who can enter the white house? Does the "I" of
Srebnik (the "I" who "can't believe he's here") inhabit what his voice is so
dreamily and yearningly evoking? What in fact is there inside the "little
white house"? What is there beyond the threshold, behind the whiteness of
the house?

The longing for the white house recalls the white virginity of the procession. The white house seems as safe, as wholesome, as immaculate in its
invitation and its promise, as the white procession of the youthful virgins.
And yet, we know that it is not only virginity, but an aberrant violation of
lives and of the innocence of childhood, that is implied ironically and silently by the juxtaposition of the church scene, and by the whiteness of the
ritual ceremony.

Virginity is what is not written upon. The white is, on the one hand, the
color of the virgin page before the writing—the white house sung before the
writing of the film—but also, on the other hand, the very color of erasure.[23]
For the viewer who has seen the film, and who has come full circle—like the
film, like the song—to start again at the beginning, the "white house"
brings to mind not just the snow that, whitely covering the peaceful mead-
ows, covers up the emptied graves from which the dead bodies were disin-
terred so as to be reduced to ashes, burned away, but similarly in a different
sense, the later image of white houses in the Polish village of Wladowa, a
village once inhabited by Jews but whose Jewish houses have been since
vacated (like the graves under the snow) by their original inhabitants (obliterated in extermination camps) and are now occupied, owned and inhabited

---

23. White is thus, for instance, the color of the blank page of forgetfulness on which
the ex-Nazi commissioner of the Warsaw ghetto, Dr. Grassler, claims to "take notes" to
"refresh" the total blankness of his memory about his Nazi past.

by Poles. The little white house yearned for thus turns out to be itself, ironically enough, a ghost house; a ghost house that belongs at once to dreaming ("Of that little white house / Each night I dream") and to memory ("A little white house / lingers in my memory").

Calling us into a dream, the white house, paradoxically, will also force us to wake up. Plunged into the dreamy beauty of the landscape and into the dreamy yearning of the melody of the white house, the spectator as a witness—like the witnesses of history—has to literally *wake up* to a reality that is undreamt of, wake up, that is, into the unthinkable realization that what he is witnessing is not simply a dream. We will be called upon to see the film—and to view perception—critically, to discriminate reality from dream, in spite of the confusing mingling of memory and dream, in spite of the deceptive quality of what is given to direct perception. On the borderline between dreaming and memory, the song—as a concrete, material residue of history—is that "small element of reality that is evidence that we are not dreaming."[24] The residue of an implicit violence (the unquantifiable ransom with which Srebnik has to keep buying his life) which at the same time is luringly soothing, the song incorporates the real both in its literal, and yet also, in its deceptive quality. As a purveyor of the real, the song invites us, at the threshold of the film, to cross over from the landscape and the white house into an encounter (a collision) with the actuality of history. It melodiously invites us to a crossing of the distance between art and reference. And no one can suspect that this melodious invitation was in history, and is now in the film, an invitation to the shock of an awakening; of an awakening to a reality whose scrutiny requires a degree of vigilance, of wakefulness and of alertness such that it exceeds perhaps human capacity. No one can suspect that what awaits us from behind the white house is not simply a nightmare, but the urgency of waking up into a history and a reality with respect to which we are not and perhaps cannot be, fully and sufficiently awake.

The place from which the song invokes us at the threshold of the film and to which it points, at the same time as the locus of the real and as the origin of singing, designates, I would suggest, the place of art within the film: the song becomes itself a metaphor for the whole film which is inaugurated by its melody, and which registers the impact and the resonance of its returns. Opened by the song, the film does not simply show itself, it calls us. It calls us through the singing it enacts. It is asking us to listen to, and hear, not just the meaning of the words but the complex significance of their return, and the clashing echoes of their melody and of their context. The film calls us

---

24. As Lacan puts it in an altogether different context. Cf., "Tuché and Automaton" (Chapter 5:2), in *The Four Fundamental Concepts of Psychoanalysis*, op.cit., 60.

into hearing both this clash and its own silence. It calls us into what it cannot show, but what it nonetheless can point to. The song inaugurates this calling and this act of pointing.

Yes, this is the place . . .

Shoah begins with the apparent innocence of singing, only to thrust us more profoundly and astonishingly into the discrepancy between the lyrics and their context, only to point us more sharply toward the ambiguity that lies behind that innocence.

A little white house
lingers in my memory . . . [4]

repeats sweetly the song. But another voice proceeds to speak over the resonance of the song:

When I heard him again, my heart beat faster, because what happened here . . . was a murder. [5]

Thus testifies, in Polish, the first voice-over—whose origin is not immediately identifiable, locatable—in the words of one of the bystanders, one of the Polish witnesses of history.

Then Srebnik's face in a close-up—the face that carries both the lightness, the enticing sweetness of the song and the weight, the outrage and the cruelty, of history—twists the silence of its pain into a smile and gazes vacantly, incredibly, incredulously through survival, death, and time, through piles of vanished burned bodies into the green trees, the brown earth, and the perspective of the blue horizon:

Yes, this is the place. . . . No one ever left here again. [5]

Darum, Warum

The contradictions riddling the very beauty of the first song are aggravated, underscored, and sharpened by the appearance of the second song which, narratively, is a singing replica—or a melodious counterpart—to the first song but which, rhetorically and musically, sets up a dissonance and a sharp contrast with the harmonies and with the innocence of the initial singing invitation.

He sang Polish folk tunes, and in return *the guard taught him Prussian military songs.* [3]

You, girls, don't you cry,
don't be so sad, for the dear summer is nearing . . .
and with it I'll return.

A mug of red wine, a piece of roast
is what the girls give their soldiers.

Therefore.—Why? Therefore.—Why?
  [*Darum.—Warum?, Darum.—Warum?*]
  [*Therefore—Wherefore?, Therefore—Wherefore?*]

When the soldiers march through the town,
the girls open their doors and windows.

Therefore. Why? Therefore. Why?
Only because of this [sound]
Tschindarrassa: Bum! [Cymbals, Drum]. [6][25]

The two songs sung by Srebnik are contrasted and opposed in many ways. Although they are both folk tunes and are both—by implication or explicitly—about returns, the dialogue between the tune in Polish and its counterpart in German is more than a mere dialogue of foreign tongues. Whereas the song about the white house concretizes a dream of arrival—an implicit dream of reaching, the Prussian military song is marked by a departure and a passage and is a ritual, not of arriving or of coming to inhabit, but of leaving. The act of leaving, at the same time, is disguised, denied, and masked by a discursive rhetoric of coming back and by a promise of returning. Apparently, the Prussian song is as sweet in its yearning and as harmless as the Polish song. And yet, the elements of lure on the one hand, and on the other hand of a subordinating force become (almost) apparent. By virtue of its function as a military march, and through the forceful beats of its percussions ("Tschindarrassa, Bum!"; "*Darum, Warum*"), the Prussian song[26] incorporates the latent rhythms of artillery and bombs. Hinting at both the malignancy of the deception and the violence to come, the song implicitly includes the military connotations—and the metaphoric, tactile contiguity—of war, of bloodshed ("a mug of red wine"), of brutality ("a piece of roast"), and of physical invasion ("the girls open their doors and windows"). The whole song, with the beats of its repeated rhymes between its questions and its answers ("*Darum, Warum*"), and with its metaphoric female gifts of drinking, eating, and of opening ("the girls open their doors and windows"), is a figure for a sexual interplay; but the interplay is one of conquest and of transitory military and sexual occupation. It is as though the enigma of the white house—the enigma of a space that is inviolate and intimate, sung in the first song—were, so to speak, invaded, cancelled out, forced open by the

25. Translation modified and expanded, transcribing all the German lyrics that are clearly audible in the film.

26. In my analysis of the Prussian song, I owe both gratitude and inspiration to Dr. Ernst Prelinger, who has provided me with a sophisticated explanation of the original German lyrics of the song, an explanation which informs my discussion of it here.

second. No wonder that, behind the lure of its enticing surface, the charm of the German song (which primarily plays out a sexual tease) turns out to be itself a sadistic tool by which the singing child becomes a hostage to the Germans, an instrument of torment and abuse through which young Srebnik is reduced by his adult spectators to a chained, dancing marionette transformed—playfully and cruelly—into a singing toy.

The Word of Our Commander

It is in this way that the shift between the Polish song and its German reply ("and in return, the guard taught him Prussian military songs") is accomplished at the threshold of the film, as a subtle—and yet ominous—transaction, an invisible—yet audible—exchange between the music of the victim and the music of (and from the point of view of) the perverse oppressor.

Another song which, later in the film, will mark Nazi perversity and Nazi violence much more explicitly and in which the victim, equally, will have to sing the point of view of the oppressor, is the song whose singers are today entirely extinguished and to which only the ex-Nazi Suchomel is able to bear witness, by singing it to Lanzmann. In much the same way as the singers of the song sang it in a voice that was not theirs—the voice of the oppressor—Suchomel, inversely, now reproduces the forced singing of the victims in the alien and jaunty voice of the ex-Nazi. It is thus that Suchomel repeats to Lanzmann the Treblinka hymn that the camp prisoners were forced to sing, for the guard's pleasure:

> Looking squarely ahead, brave and joyous, at the world,
> the squads march to work.
> All that matters to us now is Treblinka.
> It is our destiny.
> That's why we've become one with Treblinka
> in no time at all.
> We know only the word of our commander,
> we know only obedience and duty,
> we want to serve, to go on serving,
> until a little luck ends it all. Hurray!

"*Once more, but louder*," Lanzmann requests, in response to Suchomel's completed singing. Suchomel obliges Lanzmann. "We're laughing about it," he says with a mixture of complicity and condescension, "but it's so sad."

No one is laughing.

Don't be sore at me. You want history—I'm giving you history. Franz wrote the words. The melody comes from Buchenwald. Camp Buchenwald, where Franz was a guard. New Jews who arrived in the morning,

new "worker Jews," were taught the song. And by evening they had to be
able to sing along with it.

Sing it again.

All right.

It's very important. But loud!

> Looking squarely ahead, brave and joyous, at the world,
> the squads march to work.
> All that matters to us now is Treblinka.
> It is our destiny.
> That's why we've become one with Treblinka
> in no time at all.
> We know only the word of our Commander,
> we know only obedience and duty,
> we want to serve, to go on serving,
> until a little luck ends it all. Hurray! [105–06]

Having thus repeated once again the song, Suchomel, proud and bemused at
his own memory, concludes:

Satisfied? That's unique. No Jew knows that today! [106]

The self-complacency, the eagerness of Suchomel in obliging Lanzmann
suggests that he, too, in effect enjoys and takes implicitly sadistic pleasure
in the act of his own singing, in his own staged, imitative musical performance and in the inconceivable discrepancy of his own representation of the
victims. "You want history—I'm giving you history." Can history be *given?*
How does Suchomel *give* history, and what does the act of "giving"—the gift
of reality—here mean? Ironically enough, the song is literally history insofar as it conveys this historical discrepancy and this sadistic pleasure, at the
same time that it speaks through the historical *extinction* of the message
and the *objectification* of the voice. As a literal residue of the real, the song is
history to the extent that it inscribes within itself, precisely, this historical
discrepancy, this incommensurability between the voice of its sadistic author and the voice of its tormented singers. What is historically "unique"
about the song is the fact that it is a Nazi-authored Jewish song that "no Jew
knows today." "You want history—I'm giving you history." In the very outrage of its singing doubly, at two different moments (in the camp and in the
film, by the victims and by Suchomel) in a voice that is not, and cannot
become, its own, the song is, so to speak, the opposite of a signed testimony,
an *antitestimony* that consists, once more, in the absence and in the very
forging of its Jewish signature. Like Mr. Kantorowski's mythical account of
the Holocaust, the Nazi narrative of the Jews' victimization (both in the
camp song and in Suchomel's revoicing of it) is a speech act that can neither

own its meaning nor possess itself as testimony. "You want history; I'm giving you history." As the extinction of the subject of the signature and as the objectification of the victim's voice, "history" presents itself as anti-testimony. But the film restitutes to history—and to the song—its testimonial function. Paradoxically enough, it is from the very evidence of its enactment as an antitestimony that the song derives the testimonial power of its repetition, and the historic eloquence of its unlikely and ghostly return: "*Sing it again. . . . It's very important. But loud!*"

The Quest of the Refrain, or the Imperative to Sing

I would suggest that the imperative, "Sing it again," is the performative imperative that artistically creates the film and that governs both its structure and its ethical and epistemological endeavor: to make truth happen as a testimony through the haunting repetition of an ill-understood melody; to make the referent come back, paradoxically, as something heretofore unseen by history; to reveal the real as the impact of a literality that history cannot assimilate or integrate as knowledge, but that it keeps encountering in the return of the song.

"Our memory," writes Valéry, "repeats to us what we haven't understood. Repetition is addressed to incomprehension."[27] We "*sing again*" what we cannot know, what we have not integrated and what, consequently, we can neither fully master nor completely understand. In *Shoah*, the song stands for the activation of the memory of the whole film, a memory that no one can possess, and whose process of collecting and of recollecting is constantly torn apart between the pull, the pressure and the will of the words and the different, independent pull of the melody, which has its own momentum and its own compulsion to repeat but which does not know what in fact it is repeating.

The whole film, which ends only to begin again with the return of the song, testifies to history like a haunting and interminable refrain.[28] The function of the refrain—which is itself archaically referred to as "the burden of the song"—like the burden of the vocal echo which, as though mechanically, returns in the interviewer's voice the last words of the discourse of his interlocutors, is to create a difference through the repetition, to return a question out of something that appears to be an answer: *Darum, Warum* ("Therefore.—Why?") The echo does not simply reproduce what seems to

27. Valéry, "Commentaire de *Charmes*," in *Oeuvres* (Paris: Gallimard, bibliothèque de la Pléiade: 1957), vol. 1, 1510; my translation.
28. "*Shoah*," says Lanzmann, "had to be built like a musical piece, where a theme appears at a lower level, disappears, comes back at a higher level or in full force, disappears, and so on. It was the only way to keep several parameters together" (*Panel Discussion*, 44).

be its motivation, but rather puts it into question. Where there had seemed to be a rationale, a closure and a limit, the refrainlike repetition opens up a vacuum, a crevice and, through it, the undefined space of an open question.

> The flames reached to the sky.
> *To the sky . . . [6]*

The Singer's Voice

What gives this refrainlike structure of the film—the repetition of the song and of its burden, the return of the resonance of the refrain—the power not merely to move us but to strike and to surprise us, the power each time to astonish us and have an impact upon us as though for the first time? When Srebnik sings the two songs of the opening, and when the echo of the second song puts into question the apparent harmony and innocence of the first tune, what constitutes the power of the singing and the strength—the eloquence—of Srebnik's testimony through it, is neither the lyrics nor even the music (someone else's music), but the uniqueness of the singing voice. The uniqueness of the voice restores the signature to the repeated melody and to the cited lyrics, and transforms them from antitestimony into a compelling and unequalled testimony. What makes the power of the testimony in the film and what constitutes in general the impact of the film is not the words but the equivocal, puzzling relation between words and voice, the interaction, that is, between words, voice, rhythm, melody, images, writing, and silence. Each testimony speaks to us beyond its words, beyond its melody, like the unique performance of a singing, and each song, in its repetitions, participates in the searching refrain and recapitulates the musical quest of the whole film. Like Lanzmann, Srebnik facing an unspeakable event at thirteen and a half, and again at the beginning of the film—as a singer who remained alive because of his "melodious voice"—is in turn a sort of artist: an artist who has lost his words but who has not lost the uniqueness of the singing voice and its capacity for signature. What is otherwise untestifiable is thus transmitted by the signature of the voice. The film as a visual medium hinges, paradoxically, not so much on the self-evidence of sight as on the visibility it renders to the voice, and on the invisibility it renders tangible, of silence. The film speaks in a multiplicity of voices that, like Srebnik's, all transmit beyond what they can say in words. In much the same way as the singing crematorium witnessed and evoked by Philip Müller, the film resonates like a whole chorus of testimonies and of voices that, within the framework of the film, sing together:

> The violence climaxed when they tried to force the people to undress. A few obeyed, only a handful. Most of them refused to follow the order. Suddenly, like a chorus, they all began to sing. The whole "undressing

room" rang with the Czech national anthem, and the *Hatikvah*. That moved me terribly . . .

That was happening to my countrymen, and I realized that my life had become meaningless. Why go on living? For what? So I went into the gas chamber with them, resolved to die. With them. Suddenly, some who recognized me came up to me. . . . A small group of women approached. They looked at me and said, right there in the gas chamber . . . "So you want to die. But that's senseless. Your death won't give us back our lives. That's no way. You must get out of here alive, you must bear witness to . . . the injustice done to us." [164–65]

The singing of the anthem in the crematorium signifies a common recognition, by the singers, of the perversity of the deception to which they had been all along exposed, a recognition, therefore, and a facing, of the truth of their imminent death. The singing, in this way, conveys a repossession of their lost truth by the dying singers, an ultimate rejection of their Nazi-instigated self-deception and a deliberately chosen, conscious witnessing of their own death. It is noteworthy that this is the only moment in the film in which a community of witnessing is created physically and mentally, against all odds. Erasing its own witnesses and inhibiting its own eyewitnessing, the historical occurrence of the Holocaust, as we have seen, precluded by its very structure any such community of witnessing.[29] But this is what the film tries precisely to create in resonating with the singing chorus of the dying crematorium, whose many signatures and many voices are today extinguished and reduced to silence. The film, as a chorus of performances and testimonies, does create, within the framework of its structure, a communality of singing, an odd community of testimonial incommensurates which, held together, have an overwhelming testimonial impact.

The Disappearance of the Chorus

Müller wishes to die so as to belong, to be part of this community, to join the singing. But the dying singers have it as their last wish to exclude him from their common death, so that he can be not an extinguished witness like them, but a living witness to their dying and their singing. The singing challenges and dares the Nazis. The act of singing and of bearing witness embodies resistance. But for Müller, the resistance cannot mean giving up life; it has to mean giving up death. Resistance spells the abdication of suicidal death and the endurance of survival as itself a form of resistance and of testimony. Resistance signifies the price of the historical endurance—in

29. See above, in part I, the chapter entitled "The Occurrence as Unwitnessed," cf., p. 45.

oneself—of an actual return of the witness. As a returning delegate of the dead witnesses, Müller's act of testifying and his testimonial afterlife can no longer be, however, part of a living community. Facing his singing compatriots in the crematorium, Müller understands that the gift of witness they request from him, and his responsive, mute commitment to bear witness, leave him no choice but to stand alone, to step outside of the community[30] as well as of shared cultural frames of reference, outside of the support of any shared perception. The holding and the inner strength of the common singing empowers Müller and allows him to escape and to survive. But his survival cannot simply be encompassed by a common song, and his afterlife of bearing witness can no longer lose itself in a choral hymn. If his living voice is to speak for the dead, it has to carry through and to transmit, precisely, the cessation of the common singing, the signature of the endurance, the peculiarity and the uniqueness of a voice doomed to remain alone, a voice that has returned—and that speaks—from beyond the threshold of the crematorium.

Müller, Srebnik, and the others, spokesmen for the dead, living voices of returning witnesses that have seen their own death—and the death of their own people—face to face, address us in the film both from inside life and from beyond the grave and carry on, with the aloneness of the testifying voice, the mission of the singing from within the burning.

> Suddenly, from the part of the camp called the death camp, flames shot up. Very high. In a flash, the whole countryside, the whole camp, seemed ablaze. And suddenly one of us stood up. We knew . . . he'd been an opera singer in Warsaw. . . . His name was Salve, and facing that curtain of fire, he began chanting a song I didn't know:
>
> > My God, my God,
> > Why has Thou forsaken us?
> >
> > We have been thrust into the fire before
> > but we have never denied the Holy Law.
>
> He sang in Yiddish, while behind him blazed the pyres on which they had begun then, in November 1942, to burn the bodies in Treblinka. . . .

---

30. Cf., Rudolph Vrba's decision to escape, after the suicide of Freddy Hirsch that aborts the Resistance plan for the uprising of the Czech family camp: "It was quite clear to me then that the Resistance in the camp is not geared for an uprising but for survival of the members of the Resistance. I then decided to act . . . [by] leaving the community, for which I [was] coresponsible at the time. The decision to escape, in spite of the policy of the Resistance movement at the time, was formed immediately. . . . As far as I am concerned, I think that if I successfully manage to break out from the camp and bring the information to the right place at the right time, that this might be a help. . . . Not to delay anything but to escape as soon as possible to inform the world" (195–96).

We knew that night that the dead would no longer be buried, they'd be burned. [14]

A Winning Song

The entire film is a singing from within the burning of a knowledge: "We knew that night. . .". The knowledge of the burning is the knowledge—and the burning—of the singing. At the beginning of the film, Srebnik's song incorporates the burned bodies with whose death and with whose burning it still resonates. In singing, on the one hand, as he has been taught, about the girls "opening their doors" to soldiers who pass by, in the very way that he himself, uncannily, is commanded by the SS to "open the doors" of the arriving gas vans so as to receive—and to unload—the bodies to be burned; in singing also, on the other hand, his original melodious yearning for the sweetness of the white house, Srebnik's singing and his singular, compelling voice, is the bearer of a knowledge—and a vision—not just of the ashes but of the living burning, of the burning of the living—a vision of the half-asphyxiated bodies coming back to life only to feel the fire and to witness, conscious, their encounter with, and their consumption by, the flames:

> When [the gas vans] arrived, the SS said: "Open the doors!" We opened them. The bodies tumbled right out. . . . We worked until the whole shipment was burned . . .
> I remember that once they were still alive. The ovens were full, and the people lay on the ground. They were all moving, they were coming back to life, and when they were thrown into the ovens, they were all conscious. Alive. They could feel the fire burn them . . .
> When I saw all this, it didn't affect me. I was only thirteen, and all I'd ever seen until then were dead bodies. [101–02]

The deadening of the live witness, the burn of the silence of the thirteen-year-old child who is "not affected," passes on into his singing. The unique expression of the voice and of the singing both expresses and covers the silence, in much the same way as the unique expression of the face—of Srebnik's face at the opening of the film—both covers and expresses the deliberate and striking absence of dead bodies from *Shoah*'s screen. It is indeed the living body and the living face of the returning witness that, in *Shoah*, becomes a speaking figure for the stillness and the muteness of the bodies, a *figure* for, precisely, the *Figuren*. What the film does with the *Figuren* is to restore their muteness to the singing of the artist-child, to revitalize them by exploring death through life, and by endowing the invisibility of their abstraction with the uniqueness of a face, a voice, a melody, a song. The song is one that has won life for Srebnik, a life-winning song which, framed within the film and participating in the searching repetition of its refrain, wins for us a heightened consciousness and an increased awareness, by giving us the measure of an understanding that is not transmittable without it. As a fragment of reality and as a crossroad between art and history, the song—like the whole film—enfolds what is in history untestifiable and embodies, at the same time, what in art captures reality and *enables* witnessing. In much the same way as the testimony, the song exemplifies the power of the film to address, and hauntingly demands a hearing. Like Müller coming back to testify and speak—to claim an audience—from beyond the threshold of the crematorium, Srebnik, though traversed by a bullet that has missed his vital brain centers by pure chance, reappears from behind the threshold of the white house to sing again his winning song: a song that, once again, wins life and, like the film, leaves us—through the very way it wins us—both empowered, and condemned to, *hearing*.

> *When I heard him again*, my heart beat faster, because what happened here . . . was a murder. [5]

> He was thirteen and a half years old. He had a lovely singing voice, and *we heard him*. [4]

> > A little white house
> > lingers in my memory.
> > Of that little white house
> > each night I dream.

CLAUDE LANZMANN

Seminar with Claude Lanzmann
11 April 1990

Claude Lanzmann visited Yale University on 4–13 April 1990 at the invitation of the Department of Comparative Literature. The text that follows is an edited transcript of the second of two seminars on *Shoah* organized by David Rodowick.

Claude Lanzmann: I prefer that we avoid, if possible, generalities. Because I have spent my whole life fighting generalities and I think that *Shoah* is a fight against generalities. I prefer that we try to examine *Shoah* specifically, in a brotherly way. I am teaching you but you are also teaching me about some sequences of the film. As a matter of fact, it was very difficult for me to decide which sequences. If I had followed my taste, I would have said, "Let's look at the film in its entirety, because I don't see how one can extract excerpts." It would have been better for me because I would not have talked, because, after nine and one-half hours nobody has a desire to do so. It is not simply a joke. I made against myself some decisions which are arbitrary. It is a reason why I ask for your help. But it is my opinion, too, that one can enter into *Shoah* every way. If things are done well the core of the film is discovered and comes back.

I am not a decision-maker. More than anything I hate decision-makers with all my heart. I call them "decision-killers" because to decide is to kill. When I prepared my diploma in philosophy long ago, I wrote about the concept of possibility and noncompossibility in Leibniz's philosophy. What is noncompossible are two things which are not possible together at the same time. This means one has to dream and to imagine another life. If you choose one woman you cannot choose another one. Well, you can, but you are really in trouble. And when it is not only a question of one or two but of

YFS 79, *Literature and the Ethical Question,* ed. Claire Nouvet, © 1991 by Yale University.

several, it's even more difficult. It was like this for me during the making of *Shoah* and it is probably one of the reasons why it took me so long, because I examined all the possibilities. If I choose this one what will follow? Like when you play chess, you have to foresee many movements in advance. And I think that if one asks, as it was asked last time, "What is art," I would answer, too, that art for me is precisely to examine the possible and not to make hasty decisions.

It happened to me to be stuck for days, even for weeks, during the construction of *Shoah* because I am a stubborn man. When you climb a mountain, when it is a *première* on the north face, you have to invent the way because there is no way already made, and it happens that you are stuck and you cannot go on. It happened to me during the editing of the film, to be stuck and to decide that I would stop until I could find the proper way. And there were not several ways, there was only one. But in order to access this unique way, one had to examine all the possibilities and to give every possibility its own chance. This means that it was killing work, not only for the possibilities but for me, too.

I will give you an example. We will not see this sequence because it is very well known and it became emblematic of the whole film. The sequence was of the locomotive driver, of a Polish locomotive driver, when he drives the locomotive into the station of Treblinka. There is this discovery of the name "Treblinka" at the station which was something extremely important for me when I discovered it before shooting. I wanted to convey this and it had to be very important, too, for the future viewers of the film. I didn't expect that the man would suddenly do this gesture—of cutting the throat with the finger across the throat. I did not ask him to do this because I could not even imagine that he would do it, and I did not even know at this time that the gesture was made.

During the editing of the film, of course, I had the other gestures of the Polish peasants. Glazar, one of the survivors of Treblinka, does this too, and the real question was what to do with the gesture of the locomotive driver because there were other possibilities. One could start, for instance, with Glazar explaining this gesture. But there was something so strong in this scene with the locomotive driver that I decided that this would begin the second sequence on Treblinka. Of course, there is a whole development in the film before this precise scene takes place. But suddenly, at this very moment something starts to shift in the film. We are passing in another circle, call it whatever you want, of hell. And I was wondering: what will the viewer understand from this? It was not an easy decision to make but I made it, and this is the beginning of the Treblinka passages. We will not look at this because it is not necessary. I think that everybody who has seen the film has this very much in mind. But now, if David agrees, maybe we can go to

Glazar. This happens half an hour or three-quarters of an hour after the second scene where Glazar makes the same gesture. And after a while there is a *cascade* of the same gestures by the Polish peasants. This reintroduces some other themes which may be of importance.

[Here the seminar watches a clip from the first part of *Shoah*. The sequence is composed of ten shots, beginning with the testimony where Richard Glazar describes the train trip from Czechoslovakia to Malkinia. As Glazar speaks there are a series of subjective shots of the Polish countryside taken from a moving locomotive, then Glazar himself is shown demonstrating the "sign" of death. The sequence continues with description of the same events from the point of view of several tall, Polish farmers, followed by the account of Czeslaw Borowi, often referred to in reviews of *Shoah* as "pot belly." The oral testimony is recorded on pages 34–36 of the published transcript of the film.[1]]

Lanzmann: There are several things on several levels here. First of all, the Poles remember the Jews arriving in passenger cars, not in freight cars. The first peasant says that they were fat, which means that they were rich, nothing else. And the last one we saw, Borowi, who was really fat himself, explained that they were playing cards, that there were flowers in the wagons, and that they were drinking *orangeada*. It's a Polish word which I can't understand. But the question is: is it a lie or is it the truth? It is a question I ask to whoever wants to answer in the audience.

Amy Ziering: I would offer that it is a lie.

Lanzmann: You think that it is a lie?

Ziering: I think so, yes.

Lanzmann: Excuse me, you are wrong. Because if you had watched closely at the beginning, Glazar, the Czech Jew within the train, describes the trip and he says, exactly, "We were in passenger cars." Everybody was seated, nobody was standing, and the seats had numbers. Everyone had to sit in the right place which means that it is the truth. The construction of this film follows a logic. Nobody meets anyone in *Shoah*. I already said this, but there is a corroboration in spite of this—I make them meet. They don't meet actually, but the film is a place of meeting.

---

1. Claude Lanzmann, *Shoah: An Oral History of the Holocaust. The Complete Text of the Film* (New York: Pantheon Books, 1985). Readers should be forewarned that Lanzmann disavows the English transcript, which is plagued by inaccuracies and which differs substantially in form from the French text prepared by Lanzmann himself. The French text is published in Paris by Editions Fayard (1985).

Ora Avni: At the same time, when the Pole adds to the story the flowers, the cards, and the feeling of well-being in the cars, then you can imagine that this is how he wanted to perceive this. This is his perception and not necessarily Glazar's, for example. Maybe they were sitting but I doubt that there were flowers; but he perceived a picture of well-being . . .

Lanzmann: It is much more complicated than you think, because there were several periods in the deportations, several places of origin of the deportations, and the Polish Jews were not treated as the foreign Jews were. It is the reason why the Poles remember the foreign Jews very well. It happened, for instance, that they had shipped to Treblinka Jews from Germany. To proceed with order, and without panic, they had always said to these people that they were going to territories in the East to settle, to work, and to colonize. Some of them were, for instance, dentists. It happens that behind the passenger cars in which these people were shipped to their deaths—this is the truth and it is documented—all the equipment of several dentists followed. They were in the same train. They were following the owners of the equipment, the dentists themselves, in freight cars which were attached to the passenger cars. This means that the Nazis wanted to fool them, to deceive them.

And this happened too. It comes much later in the second part of the film when Glazar talks about the arrival of Jews from Salonika, the ones he compares to the Macabees. Why? Because they could have been fighters, because they were people in good physical shape, and they had not been rounded up for months in ghettos. They had just been rounded up, and in order to proceed smoothly these people had been shipped in passenger cars. But everything happened in this story. There were some rules and the rule was surely the freight cars for Polish Jews. The French were all shipped in cattle cars. There were rules, but there were also aberrations to all the aberrations that existed. It is the reason why when you are trying to "learn" (and I put the word to learn in quotations because I think that this can never be learned, and if you learn you forget), when you try to learn the Holocaust, when you think that you have completely mastered a particular episode of the extermination, it is an error. It is not true because you always have new things to learn.

Now to come back to the scene, what is the meaning of that gesture? When the Poles are walking around the freight cars, or passenger cars, standing in the station of Treblinka, waiting their turn to be driven into the camp which was six kilometers from the station, it lasts a long time. They had to wait because sometimes there were many trains. Because this man, this fat Borowi was twenty-five in 1942, he was conscious of what he was doing. And the two tall men, they were the same age, maybe a little bit younger. One has to imagine that they were kids, too, adolescents. They were boys of ten or fifteen and they were walking along the train, they were doing this. What do you think of the gesture? They said that it was a gesture of warning.

David Rodowick: What I find striking about that, is that along with this set of scenes with Glazar, is the repetition in the scenes with the peasants and with Borowi. First Glazar says, "They're doing this gesture, but I didn't understand, I didn't understand. . .". And the Poles repeat this. They say, "We made this gesture but *they* didn't understand, *they* didn't understand. . .". What is striking is that you bring these two points of view together, and that there is no communication between them. They can't transmit this sign from one to the other. It comes to mean many things. Could Jews on the train understand that it meant that they were to be killed? Did the Poles want them to understand really that they were to be killed?

Lanzmann: I think that this is really important. One has to put this in parallel with what is said several times in the film by the Jews of the *Sonderkommando*, of the special details. These Jews knew exactly what was at stake. If you take the barber, for example, if you take the barber scene when he describes the sisters, the friends, entering the gas chamber, he says: "What could you tell them?" Suddenly, at this very moment, he breaks. It is the same with Filip Müller.[2] Filip Müller says several times in the film, "For whoever had crossed the threshold of the camp it was too late. No one could be saved." And when he's talking about the description of the deaths inside the gas chamber, he says exactly that it was nonsense to try to warn the people in the yards; it could only make their deaths more difficult. Whether they accepted the information, whether they could understand the information or not, is another question. But anyhow, they could do nothing. And I think that one has to compare the deep humanity, the compassion of the Jews of the *Sonderkommando* towards the people who were about to die, with the gesture of the Poles, which I am utterly convinced is not a gesture of warning. What does it mean to warn people who are completely locked in sealed cars, to tell them you will die? Glazar shows precisely that he does not understand or that he doesn't want to understand. They are completely trapped.

Shoshana Felman: So, in other words, it's not a gesture that one could do for oneself. Even if one understood the Polish peasants, it has a completely different meaning when you do that about somebody else, and all the more so if that somebody else has no fear. And if you do that even to communicate

2. The barber referred to is, of course, Abraham Bomba. Filip Müller, a Czech Jew and survivor of the five liquidations of the Auschwitz "special detail," is also featured prominently in *Shoah*.

the meaning that you have understood in reference to yourself, it is just inconceivable. Even today Glazar can only repeat it as something that was not understood . . .

Lanzmann: I think that even today he does not understand. He understood after he saw the film.

Felman: But I find very striking in your editing something that I only noticed for the first time. He begins with voice-off, and he has no face until the moment that he does the gesture in the film. It is this gesture that brings his face to the screen. And it struck me that this almost gives him a face.

Lanzmann: Yes, except that he already appeared in the film.

Felman: Right. But still, seeing it just in the detail, it seemed very brilliant to do that, to bring the face along with the gesture of the murder that makes it, precisely, inconceivable.

Lanzmann: But what I wanted to say is that gesture opens the sequence of Treblinka with the locomotive driver, and what we have seen now is the end of the second scene of Treblinka.

Cyrus Hamlin: As I understand your description of the locomotive driver, he made the gesture in association with the place when you were with him. So that it was not specifically a repetition from the past, it was an association which surprised you, or which you were not expecting, and which seems to me for the viewer of the film different from a report of how it was either for the passengers on the train, like Glazar, or for the peasants who are remembering what they did back then. It's a curious conflation of the present with the past through a repetition of a gesture that seems to me, finally, to be an open sign—Treblinka.

Lanzmann: It's true. It *is* an open sign. Nobody knows at this moment the meaning of the sign. One can qualify this, but it was really extraordinary to attend the scene because I was there when he did this. I had a relationship with him, a friendly one. I told him, "We will shoot an arrival in Treblinka. I have rented the locomotive. It is the same locomotive as in 1942." I told him, "OK, you drive your locomotive?" There were no wagons behind the locomotive, but it is shot in such a way that one does not see that there are no wagons. We can imagine that this is a train, but he knew that it was only a locomotive.

Hamlin: Another question: when the camera shows the field from the train and we hear the voice of Glazar describing how he saw the boy in the field making a sign, we don't see the boy. We might expect the figure to appear suddenly, making the sign to us. Instead the camera shifts to the face of the one telling the story, and he then repeats the gesture and emphasizes . . .

Lanzmann: What you say is true. But actually we see the boy, because there is a boy with cows immediately after the gesture of Glazar. But we see the boy in another way because the two tall men were the boys that Glazar saw. There is no doubt about this. I don't know which one. But the locomotive driver took this completely out of himself. He took the responsibility on his shoulders to revive the scene completely. We pull into the station. He is looking behind. He has a twisted body, a twisted wrinkled face, and it's obvious that he is making an extraordinary effort of rememoration. And it comes to him: suddenly he invents that gesture.

Avni: He has not witnessed the discussion between you and the other two tall guys?

Lanzmann: No, not at all, and actually he was the first man I shot with in Treblinka.

Paul Galatowitsch: Was he driving the locomotive himself when you shot that scene? Because I had understood that gesture as purely mechanical . . .

Lanzmann: You are absolutely right to ask the question. There was another man on the other side of the locomotive, opening the place for the coal, turning manometers. He was not alone.

Galatowitsch: But the gesture that he made, it looked to me on the film like he was communicating with somebody at the back of the train, just to cut the brakes or something like that.

Lanzmann: No, no. At the back of the train there was nobody except on the tender—me, the cameraman, the assistant cameraman, and the sound man. But he was not looking at us. I told him, "You do whatever you want. We are shooting your arrival in Treblinka in the winter of 1942. You have behind you a train of fifty or sixty wagons loaded with Jews who will be killed right away, or in the two or three following hours." He was not looking at me. He is looking at these wagons, at these imaginary wagons behind him, and he invents this gesture. I had to do something with this afterwards, you know. It was what I call a pillar of the film. The question is where to place the pillar? It is the reason why I was talking about the difficulty of decision-making. I remember it took me days before deciding this.

Alfredo Monferré: I think it's interesting that the gesture that he makes is not how anybody died in Treblinka. And you see this associatively because this is how you kill an animal or how you used to kill an animal . . .

Lanzmann: You are right. It is a gesture of peasants. They are used to killing pigs like this.

Monferré: But they don't anymore. Just as you can tell that the locomotive is anachronistic, because today you have to rent the locomotive to use it in the film and the Polish railroad system no longer uses . . .

Lanzmann: When I filmed this in 1975, most of the railways in Poland had this type of locomotive. There were very few electric locomotives. But you are right, it is a gesture of animal killers.

David Phillips: But there is also one other time when the Jews are told they are going to die. One of the special detail people sees the wife of a friend, and he tells her, "You are going to die." And she tells other people the story. So they did want to tell people that "You are going to die."

Lanzmann: It's Filip Müller who tells the story of a woman who arrived in 1943, transported from Bialystok. A man in the working detail recognized her and told her, "You are going to die in two hours." She starts to tell this to the other women and they don't want to listen, and the men they don't want to listen. Müller has this very beautiful sentence, "Not that they thought that it was untrue. They had heard many stories" he says, "in the ghetto, in Grodno, in Bialystok. But who wants to hear such things?" This is again the question: to compare the sadistic gesture of the Poles. It is sadistic because nothing can come of this. There is no end, no possible end. It was too late and the real question is how and when all this started.

I remember when I was shooting the film, I was absolutely obsessed in Auschwitz. It is very obvious in Auschwitz. There is a big sorting station, with many rails coming from everywhere, and suddenly you have this unique one, this unique one which leads to the big gate of Birkenau, the bird of death. It was very difficult to film this. I remember I was walking without the camera, asking myself: "At which moment did it start to be too late?" Of course, when the gates of the camp are passed it is already too late. It is too late when the gates of the crematorium are . . . , but here it was already too late. When they were on the train it was already too late. When they boarded the train in Drancy or in Salonika it was already too late. When was it not too late? How will this story be helped? I know that I was obsessed with these questions. I was asking myself: "How to transmit these questions? How to transmit these feelings to the spectators, to the viewers of the film?" Between the main railroads and the gate of Auschwitz it is two kilometers. It's very difficult because you cannot make a "traveling" shot of two kilometers. If you make a panoramic shot it's also very difficult; it's too long. If you take a zoom it's very complicated too. It was very difficult to do this. But these were all the . . . , I don't want to say moral questions, but all the questions of content were immediately questions of technique and questions of form.

Maybe we will go on. I want to show you a moment where I was insin-cere, which is still weighing on me.

[Here the seminar watched a clip from the first part of *Shoah* where Henrik Gawkowski is interviewed on the locomotive. A dirt road is visible in the background of the first shot, turning off from the tracks. It is the former site of the sidetracks leading to the Treblinka ramp. The next shot is a subjective, *forward* travelling shot that follows the dirt road, eventually stopping at the ramp. In the following shot, Gawkowski and Lanzmann are shown looking at some papers. When Lanzmann summarizes the scene, saying that Gaw-kowski would arrive at the ramp with twenty cars behind him, the translator reports that Gawkowski contradicts Lanzmann. "No, they're in front of him. He pushed them." Therefore, if the preceding travelling shot is meant to recapitulate visually Gawkowski's point of view, it is impossible since Gawkowski could only have seen the wagons in front of him, not the arrival at the ramp. By the same token, Lanzmann explains below that he already knew this information from an earlier interview so that, in effect, he is "acting" in this sequence. The last shot depicts the arrival of a locomotive, coming directly toward the camera and eventually filling the frame. Gaw-kowski's testimony is recorded on pages 37 and 38 of the English transcript.]

Lanzmann: This is a travelling with the camera. I did it on foot; it was the only possible way. This is the very first moment we discover the camp. We never saw it before.

There. This is the point which will be my shame forever—where I am insincere because I know the answer. I say, "Here is the ramp." I am behind him, asking him to draw saying, "He is here with his locomotive and he has twenty wagons behind him." And he answers me, "No, not behind, they are in front." He did not pull them, he pushes them. Well, it's a trivial detail, maybe, but for me its very important.

Anyhow, I said that I am insincere here. One can see this in my face because I knew the answer. But it was very difficult. I met this man for the first time several months before the shooting of the scene, when I went for the first time to Treblinka. It was night. I awoke him and we started to talk. I discovered he was a gold mine for me. I would have liked to put him in a reserve in order to protect him so that nothing could happen to him before the shooting, because I was not prepared at all to shoot at this moment. I had the feeling immediately that if I went too far in my questions, something would be lost forever in the transmission of the truth. Because if I know these things, I will be acting, and this I did not want. With the Poles I did not want to know anything in advance. With the Jews it was the other way around. With the Jewish witnesses I wanted to know everything in advance. These are two different levels of interrogation, of ethics, I would say. Because not to know what the Jew of the *Sonderkommando* had to say would have been a crime. But to know what the Poles had to say in advance, this would have been a crime, too. But I had no choice because in this first meeting with him he told me he was not pulling the locomotive to go inside the camp. That he was pushing the locomotive, for me, was very important. There was more truth for me in this trivial confirmation, in this small detail, than in any kind of generalization about the question of evil. This is to tell you what I am interested in.

Hamlin: Let me ask, though, if the viewer of the film is in any way affected by your insincerity?

Lanzmann: This is the real question. In my opinion, if he is a good viewer he should be affected.

Hamlin: My question has to do with the perspective on the camp. We know that the railroad track has now become a dirt road and we're in a car. It is as if we're in the locomotive with the wagons behind us. But then when you hear from the man that the locomotive pushed them, the camera turns and you see the locomotive coming at you as if it were pushing you.

Lanzmann: The following scene?

Hamlin: Yes, so that the viewer discovers what you already know from the film.

Lanzmann: I am illustrating, but it is a turning point, too, because we are leaving Treblinka at this very moment to go into Sobibor. It's true that I was absolutely fascinated by the locomotive. This is something that has to be taken into account. I wanted to lie on the rail and it was very difficult, because I wanted to have this vision of this extraordinary mass of the locomotive arriving. The locomotive arrives and slowly the locomotive becomes the whole screen. There is no issue. You cannot get out; it's a wall. It is the same question of "When was it too late?" Everything is sealed at this moment. But it is a circling of the same thing. *Shoah* is a completely static, immobile film. We lay on the rail, and it was frightening to see this locomotive arriving, just stopping before the camera, which means just ahead of our faces. *Shoah* is also a physical film and it was necessary to feel the fear.

There is another shot in *Shoah* which comes in the second part of the film, after Raul Hilberg describes the scheduling of the routing of the trains for the camps, and when Filip Müller starts to explain that the life of the people of the working detail depended on the arrival of the transports. This means the death of the others, and one sees the wheels of the locomotive starting to move. It was extremely difficult to shoot, for the cameraman had to have his whole body completely outside of the locomotive. We were holding him, and there were belts, but one must have some fun, no? But look, you will see how insincere I am. Now you will see the lie. [Here the previous clip is shown a second time.]

Avni: In the scene where you are in the Polish village and people are in front of their houses, you compliment the lady on her house and eventually she tells you it is the house of Jews into which she moved. Weren't you lying there in the same way? Didn't you know the answer when you questioned her? I thought it was very clever of you to bring it in this way. Didn't you know they were Jewish houses when you eventually brought her to tell you the story?

Lanzmann: Yes, I compliment them on their house. If you notice exactly what she says here, she says it is "also" a Jewish house which means that actually I did not start the shooting with this couple, but with the last woman, the one who has educated children.[3] But this is a very small lie. I can be a very good liar, too. This lie I allow myself. The other one is more difficult, except that I had some justification because I knew, and I thought that it was extremely important, that in Treblinka the train was pushing the wagon. Some fifteen minutes or twenty minutes later, Rudolph Vrba describes the arrival of the trains in Auschwitz, and he says the locomotive was always at the front. Which means that at Auschwitz the wagons were pulled; they were not pushed. This is important for *Shoah* because it is true that I had moments of doubt where I was asking myself: "What is the importance of this? The end was the same whether the locomotive was pushing or pulling." But this is the film. There wouldn't be any film if for me these details were not so important. Everybody knows six million have been killed, which is an abstraction.

Pieter Lagrou: You just said that you thought it would be a crime to shoot the testimony of the Jewish witnesses without knowing beforehand what they were going to tell. What exactly did you know beforehand? Did you interview them before? Was it an interview with the camera or did you just do general research?

Lanzmann: No, I did meet them; I did talk with them. I did interviews, I tried to get everything out. But listen, it is comprehensible because for me the discourse of the Jews was sometimes very difficult to understand. Not only because of the barrier of the language. The language used between them

3. The scene in question begins on page 85 of the English transcript of the film.

and me was not their language, it was not my language. The only ones who use their mother tongue in the film are the Germans and the Poles. It was difficult for this reason. But it was difficult, too, because, don't forget, these were testimonies, the testimonies of the Jews, testimonies under terror. They are witnesses under terror because they lived under terror and what they remember is marked, stamped by this terror. The purpose was to communicate, to transmit. I wanted really to address the intelligence of the viewer more than the emotions. It's true when someone tells me, "I have seen your film and I am completely overwhelmed," it is not a joy for me because it is not what I aimed at. Shoshana Felman wrote beautifully about this question of intelligence in *Shoah* as narration in light.

Well, it was very obscure for me. For instance, Simon Srebnik. I didn't understand one word of what Srebnik was telling me. Srebnik was a boy thirteen and a half years old. He went through the most horrible things, which I have purposely not put in *Shoah*, because they were so horrible for this boy that I thought people would think that this was only a matter of sadism, that the killers were sadistic people and nothing else. The degree of horror was so high that this would have destroyed my purpose. My purpose was the transmission.

I can give you an example of what he told me. It was utterly difficult to understand. The Germans in Chelmno were a special killing squad. The boy knew them by name. Each one had a name: there was Beaumeister; there was Bottmann; there was Eufale, etc. Very often he added the word "Meister" before their name. All these names were pressing at each other in his head when he started to talk to me. It was a cataclysm. He told me the following story among many others. There was one SS, but I don't remember his name precisely. . . . Lenz, Meister Lenz. The boy told me that one morning Lenz was calling him, telling him, "Bring me a basin." He was calling one of the Jews of the work detail, a very weak one. Because he was weak he had to die. He said to the Jew, "Put your head on the basin." The boy was holding the basin, like this. Lenz said, "I want to know how much brains, *wie viel Gehirn*, a Jew has." He took his pistol and he shot the man, and the boy was receiving the brains and the blood in the basin.

There are hundreds of stories of this type, in Chelmno particularly, because Chelmno was something so horrible. For reasons of transmission I decided not to use this because it was ordinarily not the case, and the degree of horror would have been too unbearable. Chelmno is something very complicated. When I met Srebnik for the first time I had never been to Chelmno. In Chelmno you have a village. You have the church, you have the so-called castle, you have the forest. And in the forest you have the graves. But there were not only graves. There were the ovens, what he calls ovens, and there were other places, too. It was simply impossible to understand. Try to imagine what would have been the result if I started to shoot with him, to film without knowing. It would have been a disaster and a crime. When I went to Chelmno I started to understand a little bit more. I returned to Srebnik in Israel with my knowledge of Chelmno. I started to learn and to help him to tell me. This took several trips and I really didn't understand how I did this.

Now, how do you shoot all this in order to give an idea of the reality? For instance, how does one show the village of Chelmno? It is a village. You have a road and you have one house, another house—it's long. And there was the question of Mrs. Michelson who was living there, and the church was there. How to give the physical feeling of the village? Of the distance between the village and the forest? What is going on inside the forest, the church, the castle? All these parameters, which are the truth of Chelmno, which are the reality of Chelmno: how do you communicate this reality?

I remember I wanted to show the village of Chelmno and the cameraman told me there is only one way: by helicopter, to shoot from the sky. I said, "Never. There were no helicopters for the Jews when they were locked in the church or in the castle." This would have been a crime—a moral and artistic crime. What is the meaning of seeing things from the sky? This is a point of view of God, which is not mine. I remember that Jean-Paul Sartre wrote something very beautiful about Mauriac. François Mauriac had written one of his numerous novels, and Sartre (it was before the war) reviewed this book, a very sharp review, saying that there was no point of view in Mauriac's novels. At the end he says that Mauriac had, precisely, the point of view of God, because it was nowhere. And he offered, "God is not an artist, Monsieur Mauriac *non plus*, [neither is Monsieur Mauriac!"]

This question of using a helicopter to film Chelmno is exactly the same problem. To use a car to make a traveling shot inside the village of Chelmno: this was also a contradiction. Suddenly, I remember I was very happy. Because you have to think that one does such work and there are moments, very rare, where one feels creativity very strongly. There are moments where you have a *verum index sui*. I was sure. A horse! I hoped to cross the village of Chelmno by putting the camera on a cart, and to film from behind the horse. First of all you have the noise of the horse's hooves. You see it is interesting, because I have said with the Jews it would have been a crime. It is absolutely right to ask me why. I wanted to answer but I could have forgotten this, and we are again returning to the central issue of the film. The central issue leads us to the horse. I think the horse gave us a sense of the peasantry, of the primitive character of this little village.

[Here the seminar viewed the sequence where Mrs. Michelson, the wife of the Nazi schoolteacher in Chelmno, describes life in the village during the period of existence of the camp. The sequence begins and ends with a close-up of Mrs. Michelson as she recounts the "primitive" conditions of life in the Wartheland, the annexed section of Poland. The intermediary shot is a long take: a subjective travelling shot taken from horse cart. The rate of movement is rather slow, as befits the temporality of peasant life. Along the way, the camera marks the important reference points for her account: Mrs. Michelson's former house, the church, the "castle," etc. Mrs. Michelson's account is recorded on pages 80–82 of the English transcript.]

Lanzmann: I was happy when I found this. But with Abraham Bomba, the barber, it was the same. I discovered him in New York. I spent two days with him in the Catskills where he had a little cottage. We talked for two days. I had no camera, no film. He told me everything, even things which are not in the film. It was the only way; the shooting would have been impossible otherwise. I knew that this particular moment—the cutting of the hair in the gas chamber—was extremely important to me. It was the reason why I looked for this man specifically. He was the only witness. This is the reason why I rented the barber shop. I tried to create a setting where something could happen. I was not sure. You have to understand me, I did not know what would happen during the scene. But I knew what I wanted from him, what he had to say. There was a fantastic tension for him and for me. The tension was physical in this barber shop where nobody understood what was going on because all the other barbers were Hebrew-speaking of Moroccan or Iraqui origin. His customer, I think, spoke only Hebrew or Yiddish. The scene was going on in English. We were a kind of island in the middle of the barber shop, a kind of ghetto, with an extreme tension. When you shoot with a 16mm camera you have to reload every eleven minutes; you have to change the magazine holding the film. If you change, you have to cut the scene, you have to stop. We had only one camera. This is the same story of the point of view of God. Francis Ford Coppola is God with thirty-six cameras and a helicopter ballet in *Apocalypse Now.* But I had only one camera because I had no money. I felt that the tension was growing. I did not know; it was just a feeling. I did not know what would happen, and if *it* would happen, but I had an instinct. There was five or six minutes of film left in the camera, which is not much. I said "Cut." We reloaded immediately and we started again immediately. It was a good thing the change was made very quickly because it is after that he starts to break. It was very important. It would have been impossible to ask him, "Please cry again . . . ".

Kenneth Piver: Had Bomba told you previously the story about his friend, the barber, whose wife and sister he saw in the gas chamber?

Lanzmann: No, not that precisely. There were new things too. But in order to get new things, it was necessary to know much.

He said other things, for instance, which he did not say during the shooting of the scene. He told me this in the Catskills. After the war he came to this country, to America. He was a barber before the war, he was a barber in Treblinka, and he was a barber after the war, for women and men, in the basement of Pennsylvania station in New York. I asked him, "What was your feeling as you started your work, your profession, after the war?" He had this very strange answer. He told me something was missing. I asked him, "What was missing?" He told me everybody had clothes, wore clothes, which actually is not something missing, it's something added. But this is not in the film.

Karen Fiss: You told us about one story that wasn't included in the film. I'm wondering what you did with all the other information that you gathered? Was it recorded? Did you write about it or do you feel that it's not important? What are you doing with the film that wasn't included in the final . . .

Lanzmann: With what is not in the film? You want to know my deep wish? My wish would be to destroy it. I have not done it. I will probably not do it. But if I followed my inclination I would destroy it. This, at least, would prove that *Shoah* is not a documentary.

Susan Boyd-Bowman: Were there any places in the film where you were worried about what you would use for images?

Lanzmann: Yes there are. If you take, for example, this German, the man of the German railroads that I filmed with a hidden camera.[4] I don't know if you remember the images. It is absolutely *barbaque* [rotten] because we were not trained. The cameraman was not trained; I was not trained. He was very scared. I was scared, too. These people were never alone. They were the only ones to be seen on camera, but generally the family was around. They were never alone and with this one there were many difficulties, technical difficulties. We did not know that there was a television transmitter in the neighborhood interfering with the image. There are other moments where the image is like this because the cameraman tries to hide what we are doing because he is afraid. He is turning the bag with the camera inside. This was the reality and what Suchomel was saying was too important. One has to make another choice.

Boyd-Bowman: But were you ever tempted, even at that point to drop the minimalist esthetic and to go towards conventional illustrations or other ways around . . .

Lanzmann: To drop what?

4. Former SS Unterscharführer Franz Suchomel.

Boyd-Bowman: Well what I would call the minimal . . .

Lanzmann: You say esthetic? How dare you. How do you dare to talk about esthetic? I am just telling you that it was with a hidden camera in a bag and that the esthetic was really the last of my . . . . But one can see on the screen, it's horrible what's seen on the screen in this precise scene, it is not esthetical at all.

Boyd-Bowman: No you don't understand, I'm talking about the formalist style that's used throughout the film, you don't use archive material, you don't use a number of other conventional documentary devices and I'm simply asking if there were sequences that were so difficult for you to show that you were tempted to vary . . .

Lanzmann: To vary what?

Boyd-Bowman: To vary your method and include them.

Lanzmann: To illustrate? No never, no, no, no, never, this is out of the question.

Nico Israel: Could we return to the Bomba question? Did you say that Bomba after the war only cut men's hair or, did he cut women's hair and men's hair.

Lanzmann: That's what I said.

Israel: If that's the case, when you went back to stage the truth, as Dori Laub called it, in Israel, why did you use a setting of all-male customers?

Lanzmann: A men's shop, yes it's a good question.

Israel: Because obviously in staging the scene with the mirror in front, and having them enact a cutting, you're attempting to get at the repression through a kind of mimesis or a recollection. I was wondering why a male customer as opposed to a female customer?

Lanzmann: Yes, it's a good question. I asked this to myself. I think he would not have agreed to do this with women, and I think that I would not have agreed. I think that would have been unbearable. It would not have transmitted, I am sure. It would have been obscene.

Felman: It confirms the fact that what you're doing in the staging is not representational.

Lanzmann: Absolutely. The film is not at all representational.

Israel: I understand. But in order to get Bomba to talk about himself, it's a very effective technique to stage it in a barber shop. It's certainly one of the most striking scenes in the film. So in order to get him to talk about himself, he'd have scissors in his hands. It's not a matter of mimesis.

Lanzmann: He needs a distance, he needs a distance.

Israel: A distance and a closeness.

Lanzmann: This distance is even by the fact that the customers are men.

Monferré: Precisely the point in the testimony that is so difficult to transmit, and when he breaks down, is when he talks about the wife and sister of his friend. He says, "What could you do?" He caressed them. He says it in the most dead-pan voice because it's a scene of recognition in his story. It's the most painful moment, just as it is in Filip Müller's testimony.

Lanzmann: When they recognize, you're absolutely right. Therefore . . .

Monferré: Which would probably have been impossible if he had been cutting the hair of a woman. So what I'm saying is the truth. The mourned object that they can't really talk about are the women that they have lost, both of these men, because they survived. Each of the male witnesses has survived women. If you remember the scene with Filip Müller, when the convoy from his town in Czechoslovakia comes, and a group of women from that convoy comes up to him in the gas chamber. Woman is the irony of *Shoah.* Irony in the sense these women say to him, "You're in the gas chamber, we're already dead." He wants to die with them and they say, "No, you have to live to pass on our testimony." It's a group of women who speak collectively as women.

Stepping back, it seems extremely interesting to consider the question of what it would mean if no one testifies for the witness, on the one hand, but on the other hand, neither does the witness testify for himself? What is the impossible injunction in terms of gender where the man has to testify for the suffering of another, and when the difference there is precisely of a woman? Because all of these man are testifying *for* someone else, and *about* someone else, and figure centrally, so centrally that it's not there to be seen that there are no women. Think of Simha Rottem, that haunting final scene where he talks about the Warsaw ghetto. The last thing he heard is the voice. He said, "I passed half an hour looking for that voice and I thought I was coming near to the voice of a woman who was calling and crying out to be rescued, probably." And he said, "Finally I had to leave." He had to leave that voice of someone who is still alive, but who is going to die very soon, probably, and who is not rescued by him. So each of these man, in a way, pick up on leaving behind. It's extremely powerful.

Lanzmann: They are probably doing this in innocence. But you're right, it's an important point. You insist rightly on the women, but these are friends, too. They are compatriots in the case of Müller. It's very astonishing because this man had witnessed for a long time. He arrived in Auschwitz very early in the spring of 1942. He had seen thousands and thousands and thousands of people passing, going into the gas chamber without breaking. What I shot with him took a long time. Three days. That's long. And during the three days he did not break when he was telling this story. Why, suddenly, was there always a moment when they became absolutely sensitive: Bomba with the people of Czestochowa, the woman with the sister; Müller with the Czechs, his compatriots, at the Czech family camp. And there is another one, Glazar, when he sees there is a turning point, a breaking point for each of them. Glazar breaks when he sees the Jews of Salonika. They are not his compatriots, but suddenly, they are. They see, in my opinion, absolute innocence, and this awakens them.

I don't know if you remember the scene of Corfu, for instance. The Jews of Corfu have, in my opinion, a special function in *Shoah*. It is the reason why I say there are people who are more innocent than others. The Jews of Corfu are absolutely innocent, for me. I had a breaking point myself. I think this was the most difficult thing for me to do—to shoot and to edit the sequence on the Corfu Jews.

You were asking about archives. There are some archives in *Shoah*. These are the four pictures of the family of this beautiful old man, with this beautiful smile, Armando. They are the children of the old father. Suddenly there is a moment in *Shoah* when you see the photographs, the pictures, and suddenly you realize who are the dead. Because the survivors in *Shoah*, they are all people of the *Sonderkommando*, who testify for the dead. There is no doubt about this. They are spokesmen of the dead. But there is something deeper when the Corfu Jews arrive, and when this old man shows the picture. There is a kind of other truth that is very difficult to define, another truth which suddenly appears in the film.

But to come back to your question, I used to say that if there had been— by sheer obscenity or miracle—a film actually shot in the past of three thousand people dying together in a gas chamber, first of all, I think that no one human being would have been able to look at this. Anyhow, I would have never included this in the film. I would have preferred to destroy it. It is not visible. You cannot look at this. And if the customers of Bomba in the barber shop had been women, it would have been, for me, of the same kind of impossibility as that of the gas chamber.

Rodowick: It's getting late, after 10 o'clock. Do you have any final words?

Lanzmann: No. If I had a voice, we could go on.

Transcribed by Ruth Larson
Edited by David Rodowick

III.

CLAIRE NOUVET

An Impossible Response:
The Disaster of Narcissus

It seems we can no longer use the word "ethics" or engage in an ethical discourse without taking note of a certain reticence:

> What leaves me always more reticent, I am not saying in regard to ethics itself, or even to the word "ethics," but to the whole of the concepts, the values which generally determine or weigh down the ethical discourse, is that which, to my knowledge, until now—even in Levinas—presupposes values such as those of the person, the subject, consciousness, the self, the other as "self," as a conscious other, as a soul; that is, a network of philosophemes on which, I believe, the freedom of the question must be kept.[1]

The reticence to engage in an ethical discourse thus invokes another kind of ethicity, another and more imperative duty; the duty of a relentless questioning from which not even an "ethical" discourse should be exempted. Undertaken in the name of (in Derrida's words) an "ultraethicity," this questioning of "ethics" gives in fact priority to one question; the question of the other which becomes the ethical question par excellence. It is indeed in the name of the "other" that the reliance of the traditional modes of ethical discourses on the notion of subject comes under suspicion. It is to this other and to its coming that such an "ultraethicity" calls us to respond.

My purpose here is not to engage in a critical reassessment (however needed such a reassessment might be) of the strategies at work in a "traditional" ethical discourse. Instead I propose to rethink the coming of the other as well as our response to it (and responsibility toward it) through a

1. Jacques Derrida et Pierre-Jean Labarrière, *Altérités* (Paris: Osiris, 1986), 76. [My translation.]

YFS 79, *Literature and the Ethical Question,* ed. Claire Nouvet, © 1991 by Yale University.

close examination of a literary text: Ovid's Narcissus. Although this text has traditionally been canonized as one of the primary texts on subjectivity and even on "egoism," I will first remind the reader that it presents itself as a narrative about responsibility, a responsibility which it understands as it were etymologically (since responsibility comes from *respondere,* to respond), as the duty of responding to the call of the other. Narcissus is indeed punished because he failed to respond to the other; his drama is explicitly designated as the just retribution to a criminal unresponsiveness. While legislating the ethical duty of responding to the other, Ovid's text, however, significantly problematizes the status of this other thanks to a violent tension between narrative and text. As we shall see, the story of Narcissus stages an exemplary tension between text and narrative, the text inscribing a reading of the other in its relation to the self which the narrative never describes, which it even seems designed to forget and erase. It is this disruptive reading or "coming" of the other that I propose to examine, for it ultimately calls us to reassess the ethical imperative that the narrative legislated as well as the very possibility of a narrative which seems to maintain itself as narrative only at the cost of erasing this radically unsettling reading.[2] If literature gives a chance to the other, if it lets it come, it might very well be at the risk of facing its own narrative impossibility. But the necessity to negotiate with this impossibility might then itself define literature as both an incalculable risk and an unpredictable chance, as, maybe, another kind of responsibility than the one we were prepared to read.

ECHO OR THE CALL OF THE OTHER

Asked by Narcissus's mother if her son would live to be old, Tiresias, the blind seer, answered *"Si se non noverit,"* if he does not know/recognize himself. Although his answer seemed "vain" for a long time, it was, claims the Narrator, later confirmed by Narcissus's death which proved Tiresias's foreknowledge or, rather, his ability to utter "irreproachable answers." When he states that Narcissus will die *if* he recognizes himself, Tiresias preserves, however, the possibility of an escape; Narcissus can escape a premature death *if* he manages to avoid any self-recognition. In order to lead

2. Ovide *Les Métamorphoses,* texte établi et traduit par Georges Lafaye (Paris: Les Belles Lettres, 1966). vol. 1. Ovid, *Metamorphoses,* trans. Frank Miller (Cambridge: Harvard University Press, 1977), vol. I. One can even claim that the repetition of the Ovidian erasure need not be intended in order to be performed. As long as a narrative relies on the position of characters, as long as it puts into play a certain conception of the self, it is bound to cite Narcissus, willingly or not. It necessarily repeats the erasure which the Ovidian narrative exemplifies.

Narcissus to his death, the narrative must therefore provide a convincing motivation. This is done when it uses Narcissus's unresponsiveness to condemn him to an unavoidable and deadly self-recognition. The story of Echo, inserted between Tiresias's statement and Narcissus's death, functions as the example of this criminal unresponsiveness, Echo stands in for all the lovers that Narcissus left "unanswered."

Echo is a nymph condemned by Juno to repeat the last words of others.[3] Deprived of the power to originate speech, she can only speak as an echo. After seeing Narcissus hunting, she falls in love with him. From this moment on, she follows him waiting for him to utter words that she can repeat. One day, separated from his companions, Narcissus calls out. Echo uses his words to request his love. However, when she tries to embrace him, he rebukes her and flees. Abandoned and ashamed, she hides in the woods where, out of grief, she soon loses her body and becomes a pure echo.

As John Brenkman notes, Juno's punishment introduces a threat that the narrative tries to erase.[4] Turned into an echo, Echo is condemned to repeat the "sounds" uttered by others, sounds which might have nothing to do with what she intends to say. She is thus condemned to utter a speech which is precisely not a speech since it is severed from her intention, her consciousness. In order to restore Echo as a self, a speaking consciousness, the narrative makes Narcissus utter sentences that Echo can "use" to say what she means to say. Thanks to this elaborate manipulation, it transforms the repetition of "sounds" into "answers"; but for this transformation to occur, it must, however, endow Echo with a selective power that the very nature of her punishment deprived her of; it must, in other words, grant her the privilege of sometimes repeating the entire sentence, and at other times, only parts of it. Without this narrative inconsistency, the narrative could not turn Echo into a character. The echo could not become a speech attached to a consciousness.

Although the narrative strategy is designed to prevent the reduction of a character to a mere echo, in effect it exposes the opposite movement; it demonstrates how, thanks to a careful manipulation, a play of repetition and difference among signifiers can be turned into a character. As Brenkman puts it, the Ovidian text lays bare the very process through which a character is formed:

> the dissemination of signifiers in the play of repetition and difference
> between utterance and echo, is turned into a character's speech by linking

3. Let us note that in this story Juno is the agent of two punishments, one visual (Tiresias's blinding), one verbal (Echo's speech).

4. John Brenkman, "Narcissus in the Text," *Georgia Review,* (summer 1976), vol. 30. Henceforth cited in text.

a proper name "Echo," to a set of signifieds. The result is the crystalliza-
tion of a character and the representation of a voice-consciousness.
[Brenkman, *NT,* 309]

To reinscribe the echo in Narcissus's story means, then, to confront the
possibility that the two characters named "Narcissus" and "Echo" might in
fact not be characters at all. It entails reading a textual process which exposes the production of narrative characters as a necessary error, an error
which is nevertheless constitutive of any narrative. Presented as a dialogue
between two subjects, the exchange between Narcissus and Echo both exposes and occults the echo which destroys the very basis of the narrative.

In order to reinscribe the echo, the text, that the narrative inscribes but
cannot narrate, let us ask first of all the following questions: what does an
echo *do*? What is an echo? As we shall see, through a close examination of
the dialogue between Narcissus and Echo, an echo cannot be reduced to the
status of a simple repetition.

To Narcissus's first question *"Ecquis adest?"* (Is anyone near?), Echo
answers *"adest"* (he/she is near). In this instance the echo "transforms" the
question into an answer, a transformation which can still be accounted for
in terms of Echo's "intention." However, with Narcissus's second question,
the problem becomes more complex and it is Narcissus's intention which
becomes uncertain. Narcissus asks *"Veni!"* (Come!). This time the echo
does not transform the demand into an answer. It repeats the "same" demand. Narcissus's reaction is nevertheless quite surprising. Hearing *"Veni!"*
he turns around to see if anyone is coming!

> Voce "Veni" magna clamat; vocat illa vocantem
> Respicit et rursus nullo veniente: "Quid" inquit
> "Me fugis?" et totidem, quod dixit, verba recepit.
>
> [Ll. 382–84]

. . . and with loud voice cries "come!;" and "Come!" she calls him calling. He looks behind him and, seeing no one coming, calls again: "Why do
you run from me?" and hears in answer his own words again.

Although the echo repeats the same call he uttered, Narcissus hears the call
to come addressed to him as a statement that the other is coming to him. If
Narcissus can hear the demand "come" as if it were saying "I am coming"
(that is, as meaning exactly the opposite of what it seems to mean), we must
necessarily reassess Narcissus's utterance. What did Narcissus *mean* to say
when he uttered "Come!"? Did he invite the other to approach or was he
already stating his intention to approach?

With this question we must reevaluate our entire understanding of this
dialogue as the story of a distortion introduced by an echo into a stable,
original statement. Although Echo seems to send back Narcissus's utter-

ance with a different meaning than the one he intended (a meaning which would be "hers" and not "his"), we must now confront the possibility that this "other" meaning might already have been "meant" by the original statement. In other words, the statement "Come!" might mean "come" as well as "I am coming." The point is that we can no longer decide on its "true" intended meaning. The echo is not a distortion which affects the intended meaning of a statement. It marks the impossibility of determining any such intended meaning, that is, the impossibility of connecting a statement to the intention of a speaking consciousness.

With this in mind, we can now read the final misunderstanding on which the dialogue culminates. Narcissus says *"Huc coeamus,"* the echo sends back *"Coeamus."* It seems that Narcissus meant to say "let us meet." Echo repeats the "same" words but "helps" them by appearing with her arms stretched out in the beginning of an embrace. This gesture "helps" to comprehend what the echo is sending back. *"Coeamus"* now means "let us unite/copulate." But we can no longer simply say that the echo is making the original statement differ from itself, as if the utterance *"coeamus"* had a stable meaning. The echo calls our attention to the fact that the utterance might mean "let us meet," "let us come together," as well as "let us copulate"; and that no one, and certainly not the speaker of the utterance, can pretend to know what it truly means, can pretend to contain/comprehend this original and constitutive instability of meaning. At the very point where a demand of meeting might mean a demand of copulation, we are sent back to an original and confusing entanglement of meanings.

Although it is described as a dialogue between self and other, the exchange between Narcissus and Echo in fact *inscribes* another description, that of the echo which inhabits the voice as soon as it utters a sentence. This echo does not alter the utterance. It does not make it differ from itself. For this to be possible we would have to believe in the existence of a primary stable intended meaning which could be later altered by the echo. What Ovid's text suggests is much more radical: the echo does not affect an original utterance "afterward," it constitutes it from the very beginning. Although presented as coming "after" the sentence, the audible echo points in fact to the inaudible echo which affects the sentence in the present of its enunciation. As soon as it appears, language "echoes," that is, diffracts into a potentiality of alternative meanings without providing us with the means to decide on any true, proper meaning. Although presented as the "other side" of a dialogue, Echo remarks in fact the original lateral sliding of language into contingent meanings.[5]

As Ovid's text points out, this original diffraction of language into alter-

5. For an exploration of the question of the contingency of meaning, see Werner Hamacher's "Lectio: De Man's Imperative," in *Reading De Man Reading* (University of Minnesota Press: Minneapolis, 1989).

native meanings unsettles not only the notion of a reliable first meaning, but also the notion of a speaking consciousness. Programmed to read the story of Narcissus as a story of self-recognition, we indeed tend to forget that Narcissus never recognizes that which he believes to be the voice of another as, in fact, the echo of his own voice. He thus confronts us with the rather puzzling image of a speaker who does not hear himself speak. This failure to recognize his own speech is especially disconcerting since such a recognition seems to be the distinctive characteristic of a speaking consciousness. It is, indeed, the ability to recognize in the speech that comes back to him his own speech, that posits the speaker as an interiority closed onto himself. Far from insuring this proximity and presence to oneself through speech, far from confirming the enclosing comprehension of a consciousness, Ovid's text denies the privileged position of such a consciousness. The echo which inhabits language not only severs it from the control of a consciousness, it also defines this "consciousness" as covering the unrecognized otherness which, from the very beginning, speaks in place of "I." This otherness is not an other, another subject, but an Other, that is, the echoing of a language which deprives the "I" of its privileged status. And, indeed, if as soon as "I" speaks, language echoes, "I" *disappears* in a play of signifiers which generates an alternative of meanings that no consciousness can pretend to comprehend. As soon as "I" speaks, "I" loses a consciousness which it never had, and becomes the figure that we posit *in place of* a consciousness which is, from the moment we speak, lost. In that sense, the speaking, "I" marks the absence, the original disappearance of the subject. It is a figure of the subject put in place of a missing subject. It "stands" for a disappearance.

The Other which estranges "I" from what is abusively called its "own" speech therefore marks an original loss of speech, since when "I" believes it speaks, the echoing Other which speaks in its place in fact reduces it to muteness. Not only does "I" fall mute in the very act of speaking, but, by the same token, language itself falls mute. And, indeed, if language truly speaks when one true meaning can be assured, then the echoing language that Ovid's text stages can only be said to be endlessly "on its way to language."

It is at this point of our reading that the description of the echo as an "answer" must be reevaluated. To the call of Narcissus, the echo, we are told, "responds." It would be easy to dismiss this response as a mere delusion: Narcissus believes he hears a response because he is unable to recognize an echo. A demystified reader will not fall into this delusion and will keep separate the two terms that Narcissus confused: although it might "sound" like an answer, an echo does not constitute a "true" answer. This demystified reading might, however, be mystified to the extent that it refuses to consider the disturbing possibility that the Ovidian text opens: the possibility that an echo might not merely "sound like" an answer, but *be* an answer. Narcissus is certainly "deluded" to the extent that he believes that the answer proceeds from a subject, that is, to the extent that he believes himself to be engaged in a dialogue which takes place between two subjects according to the normal pattern of questions and answers. But it is precisely this model of dialogue which the Ovidian text disrupts by introducing the possibility of reading the echo as an answer, but as an answer which radically unsettles our common sense definition of "the answer," an answer which even points to the inherent fallacy of such an answer.

The echo, indeed, does not "answer" by providing a response to a question. It "answers" by sending back the question as "other." This does not mean that it sends back the question as "other than itself"; rather, it answers by underlining the otherness which, from the very beginning, diffracts the question into a potentiality of alternative meanings. From this it follows: first, that when we ask a question, we cannot possibly know what is being asked; second, that we can no longer believe that our question has one true signified that we could hope to unveil or restore, thereby preventing any further misunderstanding; third, that if a question is a question to the extent that it asks "something," we might not yet have begun to question: the more we ask questions, the more we might fail to ask them "once and for all."

When the echo "responds," it does not therefore pretend, like Tiresias's knowledgeable answer, to answer the question. It "answers" by noting the original lack of correspondence, the constitutive otherness, which inhabits the question. In that sense, its response displays the impossibility of even being able to respond *to* a question since such an answer would assume that which can no longer be assumed: that we know what is being asked, or that we hope to eventually determine such an original meaning. The echoing response that Ovid's text substitutes to the cognitive answer of the blind seer rewrites the answer as the echo which denounces the fallacy, the constitutive impossibility, of any cognitive, insightful answer.

Is it indifferent that the echoing answer substituted to Tiresias's cognitive answer should be marked as "feminine," as "her" answer substituted to "his" answer? We could again dismiss this feminine designation as one more example of Narcissus's "subjective" error. It seems, however, that we are confronting two mutually exclusive readings here. On the one hand, Ovid's narrative explicitly constitutes the feminine as an "other," a separate subject who can only speak by altering the language provided by another and, as it were, anterior subject. We recognize in this description the all-too familiar characterization of the feminine as derived and secondary, as an otherness added to a formerly unaltered entity. At the same time, however, Ovid's text proposes another reading of the feminine otherness. The feminine figures an otherness which can no longer be posited as simply another subject, or even as the "radically other," the "tout autre." Associated with the derivative and the secondary, the feminine is to be considered less as a being than as an operation: it is "other" to the extent that it "alters." Resisting the logic of the "tout autre" according to which the "tout autre" must remain unaltered in order to remain absolutely other, the feminine would name not an "other" exempt of alteration but instead an endless process of alteration.[6] This alteration does not affect language "afterward," but originally; it is not secondary, but originary. Moreover, this alteration puts language in motion, it initiates its endless drift, its endless lateral sliding: again, the "derived" marks in fact an original "*dérive.*" Redefined as the original process of alteration which diffracts language into latitudes of meanings, "she" can then be said to have already answered all the calls addressed to her. Her answers are, however, violent. To go back to the first question which inaugurates the "dialogue" between Echo and Narcissus "Is there anyone around?", this call is answered by the echo which alters it as soon as it is uttered. In that sense, we could say that the call "answers itself." The answer, however, is that there is no call "itself," no self-identity or self-coincidence of the call. The answer is that "I" does not know what it is calling for when it calls for the proximity of the other; that the Other speaks as soon as "I" calls out for the other, and in its place. And, indeed, the question "Is there anyone around?" immediately diffracts into alternative meanings: "Is there anyone around?" "Is there any other, any other subject?" but also "Is there anyone at all?" "Is the one that utters the call even here to utter it?"

The call "Is there anyone around?" thus proves to be the most pathetic call of all since in the very gesture of calling out for the proximity of an other, "I" is withdrawn from the call, dispossessed of what it believed to be its own speech by the unrecognized Other which echoes in its place. In the very gesture of calling, "I" is therefore deprived of the power to call, condemned to an apparently insurmountable muteness; "speaking, waiting to speak," calling and still not yet calling. The response to the question "Is there anyone around?" inhabits the question. To the question about the presence of an other, the Other has already answered in the question "itself." It has answered by violently altering the question and rendering uncertain the very presence of the caller; it is no longer certain that there is someone here as soon as "I" asks: "Is there anyone around?" In this respect, the Other has also answered Narcissus's second call: "Come." It has already come in the call to come, not, however, under the subjective guise of another subject, but as the process of alteration which initiates the original disappearance and muteness of the subject "itself." As the concluding scene of the "dialogue"

6. It would confirm Maurice Blanchot's suggestion that "L'Autre ne saurait accepter de s'affirmer comme Tout Autre puisque l'altérité ne le laisse pas en repos." *L'Ecriture du désastre,* (Gallimard: Paris, 1980), 59. *The Writing of the Disaster,* trans. Ann Smock (Lincoln, Nebraska: University of Nebraska Press, 1986). Henceforth both cited in text.

between Narcissus and Echo demonstrates, this coming of the Other constitutes a threatening violence which the fiction of an intersubjective dialogue both marks and covers.

Let us note, first of all, that this last scene apparently supports the assumption that the exchange between Narcissus and Echo takes place between two subjects. Narcissus has said *"Huc coeamus."* Echo repeats *"coeamus,"* and leaves the woods where she has been hiding during the entire exchange to appear in full visibility. The sudden vision of Echo's body gives credence to the fiction that Echo is to be considered as simply another character: she must be "somebody" if she is endowed with a body from which her speech proceeds. The status of Echo's body is, however, problematic. Although the narrative posits Echo as "some-body," the text has already undermined this position by exposing the gesture which turns an echo into "somebody." It has thus opened the possibility to read her body as an *embodiment.* This possibility is confirmed when we take note of the specific circumstances which surround her apparition. Echo's body appears in order to "help" Narcissus see the difference between his *"coeamus"* and her *"coeamus."* Her body, in other words, helps him *see* what he has been so far unable to *hear.* It "embodies" the echo in Narcissus's voice, that is, the otherness, the distance, the alien quality inherent in his speech. It brings to visibility, or, rather, to readability, that which one is prevented from hearing, one's own speech as an "outside" body of signifiers. What approaches under the subjective and corporal guise of Echo is then the embodiment of the distance which constitutes one's "own" speech as precisely anything but one's "own" speech. We can now begin to understand why the approach of this Other is so threatening, why Echo's visibility triggers Narcissus's violent refusal and withdrawal. When she approaches, when her body becomes visible, it is the embodiment of the alteration which inhabits language which appears.

Narcissus is nevertheless spared a full recognition of this otherness by a merciful subjective error. Although Echo embodies the otherness in one's own speech, Narcissus does not see this otherness as such. When Echo approaches, he sees a body, not the embodiment of a language which has ceased to be his own. The speaker is thus condemned to an unavoidable error; to see the otherness of/in language as if it were the voice of another, to embody the nonsubjective otherness which severs its speech from its consciousness in the figure of another speaking consciousness. In this perspective, any intersubjective dialogue can fall under the suspicion of being a necessary error: when we believe we are speaking to "somebody," the body of this other might merely be the screen which prevents us from seeing what we could not stand to behold, the image of our speech as the alien body that comes to us and deprives us of the power to both address and respond to an address. What approaches under the guise of Echo's body is indeed an image of the muteness of our "own" speech deceptively embodied as "somebody."

Although mistranslated in subjective terms, the fear that accompanies this coming of the Other leaves its trace in Narcissus's discourse. As Narcissus's reaction *"Emoriar quam sit tibi copia nostri!"* ("I would rather die than give myself to you!") points out, albeit in a deluded manner, the alteration which befalls language is deadly for the subject to the extent that it "kills" the very notion of a consciousness capable of comprehending what it says. There is indeed no "I," or "one" subject, but a *"copia nostri,"* "all of us," a prolific process of alteration which exceeds the "I" who pretends to contain it. To say that one would die rather than give the abundance that one "is" is to consign to the future a death which, although unacknowledged and unexperienced, has already taken place since the "abundance" that "I" speaks constituted "I" as "many" rather than "one," as dispossessed from the very beginning of "one"-self, as mute in the very gesture of speaking. Ironically enough, the subject who threatens to die does not know that it is already dead as soon as it speaks, nor does it know that it has already lost itself, that it "is" the loss that it fears.

With the sentence *"Emoriar quam sit tibi copia nostri!"*, Narcissus rejects Echo who soon, out of grief, loses her body and becomes an echo. In order to account for Narcissus's refusal to respond to Echo's request, the narrative invokes the notion of "pride." Supremely beautiful, Narcissus is desired by both sexes; supremely proud, he refuses to answer their love. However, what does "pride" mean in this context? Brenkman accurately describes its effect: pride interrupts the circuit of sexuality by intervening between desire and touching; it suspends desire by putting its aim out of reach. Although the effects of pride are quite clearly articulated here, a question remains unaddressed. How can Narcissus be proud? The very formulation of Tiresias's oracle presupposes, indeed, that Narcissus does not yet know himself. At the beginning of the narrative, Narcissus has never seen himself, he has never seen his own beauty. Pride cannot therefore proceed from an exalted self-image; Narcissus cannot be proud of a beauty which he has never seen. As the Ovidian text describes it, pride means only that Narcissus cannot be "touched:"

> multi illum juvenes, multae cupiere puellae;
> sed fuit in tenera tam dura superbia forma,
> nulli illum juvenes, nullae tetigere puellae.
>
> [Ll. 353–55]

Many youths and many maidens sought his love; but in that slender form was pride so cold that no youth, no maiden touched his heart.

If he cannot be touched, it is not simply because he rejects a touch which is "sexual contact"; his refusal to be touched proceeds rather from another, more profound, desire to be untouchable. Narcissus is afraid of being "touched" by the other in the metaphorical as well as the literal sense of the word. He does not want to be touched by the desire of the other, nor does he want to be touched by the beauty of the other. Pride, in other words, describes the peculiar predicament of a subject who can neither experience desire nor respond to desire because he undertakes to constitute himself as absolutely impervious to the other. This desire of impenetrability proceeds from fear. As the dialogue with Echo indeed demonstrates, Narcissus fears and shuns the approach of the other as a violent dispossession, a radical impoverishment, the scattering of an all-too fragile unity. If he were to be touched by the other, he would give to the other his *"copia nostri,"* his riches; the plenitude that he believes himself to be would become the other's.

Redefined as a sign of fear, pride can thus be said to define the position of any "self" which believes in the possibility of remaining uncontaminated by an otherness. It defines in fact the position of any subject which constitutes itself as a "self" by rejecting all otherness outside of "its-self"; indeed, it designates the belief in "selfhood" itself. At the same time, however, it essentially remains a delusion: "pride" names the delusive belief in the solitude of a self capable of maintaining the Other at a distance. This belief is indeed a delusion, for the original inscription of an unacknowledged otherness has, from the very beginning, "humiliated" the "proud" subject by shattering the self in the very process of its self-assertion.

Although delusory, this belief in selfhood produces deadly effects. It provokes Narcissus's refusal of Echo's love, a refusal which triggers her disembodiment. Out of pain, Echo loses her body and becomes an echo, or rather, as the text puts it: "there is a sound, which lives in her" *"Sonus est, qui vivit in illa;"* 1. 401. Narcissus's unresponsiveness disembodies Echo but does not kill her; at least not completely. The failure to respond provokes the death of the body, a death that Echo nevertheless survives as the *"sonus"* which goes on living after the body has evaporated. To all appearances, Ovid's text is here indulging in the rather classical representation of the voice as both live and unattached to the body. However, once again, it suggests another reading which contradicts the narrative description. With Echo's disembodiment it comes dangerously close to recognizing what must remain unrecognized if the narrative is to maintain the figure of a subject. By turning Echo into an echo, it indeed demonstrates that a subject can become a mere echoing "sound," that is, no subject at all. The metamorphosis of Echo into an echo thus both reverses and exposes the metamorphosis which generates the narrative: the transformation of an echo into the character. It is the threat of such a reading that Ovid's text tries to erase when it claims that the "sound" that Echo has now become "lives in her." This living sound is indeed trying to keep the subject alive; although Echo is now a sound, the text still posits her as a subject capable of containing a sound. But since Echo has lost her body, since there is "no-body" left, how can the sound be *in* her? The disembodiment "kills" Echo, the "other," by exposing the subjective other as the deceptive embodiment of an echoing Other.

What is thus "killed" is not merely one of the two "characters" posited by the story, but the very notion of character. By showing that what was believed to be a subject is in fact but an echo, the text "kills" the notion of subject. In that sense, when Narcissus's unresponsiveness disembodies Echo, it is already performing Narcissus's own disembodiment; it is already reading "Narcissus" as the proper name imposed on an echo, that is, on a play of repetition and difference among signifiers which takes on the deceptive figure of a subject speaking to another subject.[7]

AN OPEN RESPONSIBILITY

> (la responsabilité dont je suis chargé n'est pas la mienne et fait que je ne suis pas moi.)
>
> —Maurice Blanchot

Immediately following Echo's disembodiment, the law appears on the narrative stage. An anonymous youth, whom Narcissus rejected as he rejected all other loves, utters the following prayer:

> "Sic amet ipse licet, sic non potiatur amato."
> Dixerat; adsensit precibus Rhamnusia justis.
>
> [Ll. 405–06]

> "So may he himself love, and not gain the thing he loves!" The goddess, Nemesis, heard his righteous prayer.

---

7. In that sense, the embodiment of Narcissus's voice in Echo figures the disembodiment of Narcissus's voice as well. Narcissus's voice is disembodied to the extent that it falls outside of Narcissus's body without even coming back to this body as if to its source. The body of the echo, the body of signifiers, dispossesses the speaking "I" of the body as the container, the source of "his" speech.

As Brenkman remarks, this prayer sets the explicit meaning ascribed by the narrative to Narcissus's drama of self-recognition: "The narrative thereby situates the pool as the place where Narcissus's transgression will be answered. It is the scene of a punishment" (Brenkman, *NT,* 301). In order to make Narcissus's deadly recognition *signify* the deserved punishment for the crime of being "proud," the Ovidian narrative posits, however, a surprising principle: the moral obligation of responding to a demand of love. According to this moral principle (which is legislated without any explanation or justification), the story of Narcissus becomes the story of a criminal unresponsiveness justly punished. Ovid's narrative thus presents itself as a narrative about responsibility, a responsibility which it understands (etymologically, as it were, since responsibility comes from *respondere,* to respond) as the duty of responding to the request of the other. But, how does the self-designation of the narrative as an exemplary "lesson" about the ethical duty of responding articulate itself with the reading of the self that the text has consistently inscribed?

It seems, indeed, that the moral law legislated by the narrative invokes a notion that the Ovidian text has systematically denounced: the notion of a responsible subject. As we have seen, Narcissus is guilty of a crime, "pride," which consists in believing in one's own status as a subject untouched by any otherness. To the extent that the law seems to address a subject, it is then paradoxical, it addresses a subject in order to make him pay for the crime of believing he is indeed a subject. Moreover, when it qualifies Narcissus's lack of response as "criminal," the law seems to presuppose not only the presence of a subject but also the very possibility of response. The possibility of responding, insured as long as we read the dialogue between Narcissus and Echo as an intersubjective dialogue, is, however, problematized when we read this dialogue as the inscription of an original echo. By superimposing the description of a dialogue and the inscription of the echo which inhabits language, Ovid's text has indeed staged an unresolvable contradiction. While the subjective dialogue posits the possibility of responding, the description of the echo challenges such a possibility. Since the echo that speaks as soon as "I" speaks dispossesses "I" of its "own" voice, removes it from its "own" utterance, how, indeed, can "I" ever respond to a call? And more pointedly, how can "I" ever respond to the call that it uttered, "Is there anyone around?" There is no one there to respond to, or for, an utterance. There is no one there to be "responsible."

We could easily use this impossibility to escape from the ethical imperative imposed by the Ovidian narrative. Since a response is shown to be impossible, we can ignore the meaning ascribed to the narrative: that of a punishment for the crime of not responding. The constitutive irresponsibility attached to the play of the signifier would entitle us to discard altogether the problem of responsibility. In short, in the name of a constitutive inability to respond, we could consider ourselves as forever innocent of the crime of unresponsiveness. It is apparently such a gesture that Brenkman both prescribes and performs. According to him, we must "deprive" the drama of Narcissus of its designation as a punishment in order to read it as a drama of the self. Such an active ignorance will enable us to describe the "true" relation self/other that the narration cannot write. It will in effect liberate the text from its narrative containment. It will enable it at last to be written.[8]

Apparently our own reading is coming close to prescribing and justifying a similar gesture. It is at this point, however, that the power of Ovid's text might have to be measured. Far from depriving the drama of the self of its ethical dimension, if forces us to reassess the naive assumption with which we started our reading: that the designation of Narcissus's unresponsiveness as "criminal" was grounded in the belief in the *possibility* of such responsiveness. It is this assumption that the Ovidian text shatters. As the text makes clear, the ethical imperative to respond does not need to concern itself with the possibility of its fulfillment in order to remain an imperative. Impossible to follow as it might be, it still stands as an imperative.

The apparition of the ethical imperative indeed brings the imperative already at work in language to thematic visibility. Immediately following Echo's story, the moral law can be read as the translation, the echo, of the *imperative* quality of the echo. As we have seen, "I," speaking, disappears in echoes which speak in its place and turn it into a mere "figure of speech." This echoing language, however, does not ensure a peaceful disappearance of the "I." The echo which answers my call by remarking my originary absence from "my" call "comes back" as a prayer addressed to "me." An answer which is also a demand, it enigmatically addresses "me," commands me to respond while, at the same time, condemning me to unresponsiveness. Language thus obliges *me* to respond to and for the Other that dispossesses me

8. Brenkman's analysis purports to read a "drama of self and other" which "is never thematized as such; indeed, it is what is excluded from the thematic structure of the narrative. Or, rather, it is what the narrative would exclude by limiting its force, by containing it within a limit that denies its originality. We have already traced the process of that exclusion and that limitation: the pool as the scene of a punishment in which the image is but the source of an illusion that carries within itself the necessity of its own disappearance; Narcissus's death, the terminal point of his aberration and his delusion. When the Narcissus episode is read by actively ignoring its designation as a punishment, it does not simply fall outside the narrative system. The reading in which we are engaged, can now disclose an altogether different textual activity." op.cit.,320. Later, this reading which "deprives" "Narcissus's drama" "of its designation as a punishment," claims to "allow the text to transgress itself in order to liberate the productive force of that text," 321.

of my "own" speech. The "me" that emerges from this imperative (or supplicatory) linguistic twist is therefore both "innocent" because unable to fulfill the commandment and "guilty" because still accountable in regard to a commandment which cannot be put to rest by the simple virtue of its impossibility.

Read as the translation, the "echo," of the linguistic predicament which befalls the "I" as soon as it speaks, the ethical imperative cannot be ignored or discarded. Far from enabling us to move out of the ethical question, by escaping the issue of responsibility, Ovid's text legislates in effect what appears to be the impossible law of an echoing language: to respond when it is impossible to respond, when we, like Narcissus, can only fail to respond and are already failing to respond to the Other at the precise moment when we call out for the other to approach.

I will suggest that here Ovid's text is anticipating the problematic that Maurice Blanchot explores in *L'Ecriture du désastre*, a text which, by including a reading of Ovid's Narcissus in a reflection on "disaster," implicitly gives rise to a question of capital importance for our purposes: what is "disastrous" in Narcissus's story?

Maurice Blanchot summarily dismisses Echo in his reading of Narcissus; according to him, when Narcissus encounters Echo, he encounters speech as:

> l'entente répétitive d'une voix qui lui dit le même sans qu'il puisse se l'attribuer et qui est précisément narcissique en ce sens qu'il ne l'aime pas, qu'elle ne lui donne rien à aimer d'*autre*. [195]
> . . . save the repetitive sound of a voice which always says to him the self-same thing, and this is a self-sameness which he cannot attribute to himself. And this voice is narcissistic precisely in the sense that he does not love it—in the sense that it gives him nothing *other* to love. [127]

In spite of this dismissal, it seems, however, that a very different but unacknowledged reading of Echo is taking place whenever the question of the other, and especially of the other as constitutive of the self, is addressed.[9] Among all the threads that Blanchot's text weaves in unpredictable knots and interruptions, we can indeed single out a recurrent reflection on the other explicitly inspired by the reading of Emmanuel Levinas's works. This description of the other reads that which was left unread in Narcissus's story: the violence of the otherness which, under the name of "Echo," originally "opens," de-constitutes the self.

The approach of the other is indeed consistently described as initiating a withdrawal which is nevertheless constitutive of the "self:" the other "me

9. The reading of Echo would thus be displaced and, as such, acknowledged, a displacement which would deserve critical attention that exceeds the limits of this article.

fait sortir de mon identité, me retire le privilège d'être en première personne"; "C'est par l'autre que je suis le même, l'autre qui m'a toujours retiré
de moi-même" (Blanchot, 35). ["the Other relates to me as if I were the Other
and thus causes me to take leave of my identity. . . he withdraws me, by the
pressure of the very near, from the privilege of the first person" (18).] Although all these formulations seem to presuppose the prior constitution of a
self which would be "itself" before the intervention of the other deprives it
of its-self, this chronology is implicitly denounced as fallacious. What must
be thought (in spite of language inherently resistant to such thinking) is
precisely the simultaneous constitution and deconstitution of the self as
self by the other. The other constitutes a "moi sans moi," a "moi comme
autre que moi," a "moi" as an "éternelle absence, ce que nulle conscience ne
peut ressaisir" (Blanchot, 42).

The subject thus acquires the status of an enigma: it is a subject without
subjectivity since "the other in place of me" constitutes a "moi sans moi," a
subject "qui se fait absence" (Blanchot, 51) a simulacrum which stands in
place of an originally missing subject. This enigmatic subject is placed under
a no less enigmatic responsibility. Although "sans moi" and therefore "sans
réponse," the "moi" is nonetheless, like Narcissus, called to respond when
it is impossible to respond. Displaced outside of the explicit reading of
Ovid's Narcissus, the following description succinctly describes Narcissus's
predicament as we must now read it: at the very point where the self
emerges as that which is destroyed by being reduced to the status of a
simulacrum, "je suis contraint à une responsabilité qui non seulement
m'excède, mais que je ne puis exercer, puisque je ne puis plus rien et que je
n'existe plus comme moi" (Blanchot, 37) [I am at the same time pressed into
a responsibility which not only exceeds me, but which I cannot exercise,
since I cannot do anything and no longer exist as myself (20)]. I will suggest
that it is this enigmatic responsibility which the Ovidian law invokes when
it presupposes a responsible subject at the very moment when both the
subject and his capacity to respond cannot possibly exist. The responsibility
that it legislates can thus be called "disastrous": it asks an "I" turned into a
"me" to answer for the impossibility of answering, it assigns to this "I" an
"identity" which it has from the very beginning lost.

Narcissus must respond for the impossibility of responding. This is the
impossible justice that the Ovidian text stages, a justice which is itself
impossibly invoked. We should indeed pay attention to the fact that the
justice of the law appears in the text as an answer to a call: Narcissus's "just"
punishment "answers" the prayer of an anonymous youth who stands in for
all the lovers that Narcissus rejected. This youth demands revenge in their
place, especially in Echo's place who by definition is unable to originate
such a demand. However, since Echo has been chosen as the privileged

example of Narcissus's lovers, she implicitly defines these lovers as deprived of the power to invoke justice. Supplementing Echo's lack of voice, the youth therefore figures the invocation of justice as an impossible call. For the law to appear and rule the text, a voice endowed with the power to address and originate speech must supplement a voice quite unable to address this original call. The prayer of the youth thus redefines the nature of a prayer: a call which must be uttered when it is impossible to call, when one is dispossessed of the power to call. His prayer in fact echoes the prayer that the echo is.

Nemesis decrees the prayer to be "just." From this point on the narrative becomes an exemplification of the work of a law which punishes Narcissus by designing a punishment which "fits" the crime. The punishment seems, at first, to be a mirror image of the crime, based, like all mirror images, on a reversal of places. The law responds to the crime and makes one respond for it by constructing a specular structure of reversed symmetries. Narcissus is thus punished by experiencing the fate that he inflicted on others. Because he failed to respond to love, he is to experience a similar lack of response.

Although the punishment seems to be in perfect symmetry with the crime, the law undoes the neatness of this specular structure by introducing a major displacement; whereas the perpetration of the crime relied on verbal repetition, the punishment responds to the crime by relying on visual repetition. This displacement from speech to vision provokes other significant displacements which ultimately call into question the "just" symmetry of the law. If the law was symmetrical, Narcissus should indeed encounter another Narcissus who would, as he did, refuse his love.[10] Instead, Narcissus encounters his image. The displacement from speech to vision allows the text to replace the relation between two subjects (since Echo is assumed to be a self like Narcissus) with a relation between a subject and a nonsubject, a reflected image. Thanks to this replacement, the refusal to respond becomes the impossibility to respond. The outcome of his confrontation both repeats and significantly alters the outcome of this confrontation with Echo. The disembodiment that he inflicted on Echo is "answered" by the disembodiment which he experiences. The disembodiment that he inflicted on Echo, however, did not kill her: when Echo's body disappears, she survives as a pure "sound," an echo. This "survivable" disembodiment becomes a deadly disembodiment in Narcissus's case: when his body evaporates, he dies. The penalty for the crime of not responding is death by liquefaction.

Although it seemed at first "just," because "symmetrical," the law now appears to be unjustly excessive: it punishes Narcissus for the crime of not

10. Brenkman notes this inconsistency in op.cit.

responding by confronting him with the impossibility of responding; it condemns the subject whose unresponsiveness disembodied the other to experience a similar but lethal disembodiment. But this cruel excess in fact constitutes a precise reading of Echo's story. When the law replaces a refusal with an impossibility and a survivable disembodiment with a lethal one, it is in effect reading the crime, it is bringing to thematic visibility what remained unrecognized and unrecognizable in the crime. What the law reads is the impossibility inscribed in the crime; it reads the refusal of a response as the impossibility of responding, it reads the possibility of a survivable disembodiment as a lethal disembodiment. At the same time, the law reads the crime *as a crime.* It designates the impossibility of responding as "criminal," a designation which was already implicit in Echo's story.

Although the narrative uses the emergence of the law in order to clearly demarcate the "before" of the crime from the "after" of the punishment as two distinct moments in a chronological sequence, the intricate "correspondence" that it weaves between crime and punishment undermines this chronological sequence. Echo's story and Narcissus's drama of self-recognition "correspond" as two versions of the "same" scene. The punishment repeats the "crime," a repetition which is however "different" to the extent that it reads the first version of the scene, that makes explicit what remained implicit in this version. By substituting the impossibility of responding for the refusal to respond, the mere image of a self for a self, and a lethal disembodiment for a survivable one, Narcissus's "visual" drama *reads* that which remained unacknowledged and "unexperienced" in the "linguistic" drama: the "disastrous" constitution of the self, the death which marks its "birth."

THE FIGURE OF INFANCY

A reading of Echo's story and Narcissus's drama as two versions of the "same" scene must account for an obvious difference: the explicit shift from an audible repetition to a visual repetition. Confronted with an echo in the first scene, Narcissus is, in the second one, confronted with an image. The opposition between sight and speech is not, however, as clear-cut as the narrative would have us believe. Although characterized as "visual," Narcissus's drama reinscribes speech is significant ways. To begin with we should remember that the stage of Narcissus's punishment, the pool, is surrounded by the forest where Echo—now transformed into an echo—is hiding. Surrounded and covered by the forest where the echo resides, the pool is thus surrounded and covered by a voice. The visual repetition of the first scene takes place, as it were, in the shadow of a voice. Moreover, far from being a silent scene, the drama of Narcissus's "self-recognition" makes an extensive use of speech. Narcissus indeed speaks; first to the woods, and then to his *umbra*, his reflection.

This speech constitutes the first step of his "punishment." The law condemned Narcissus to experience the fate that he inflicted on the other: the pain of a rejected and therefore unfulfilled love. In order to make him experience this pain, the law puts Narcissus in Echo's place: as she did, he is now compelled to love, that is, to speak, to "humiliate" himself by requesting another's love. Although "like Echo" to the extent that he articulates a demand of love, Narcissus is, however, "unlike her" to the extent that his demand is not an echo. The narrative thus implicitly distinguishes two types of demand. The first one, Echo's demand, points to the contingency of an inscription. It demonstrates that language can always inscribe "love" even in the most indifferent discourse; an echoing language can make the propositions of the unloving Narcissus "sound" like a demand of love. Singled out as the most interesting case of linguistic echo, the demand of love is thus made to exemplify the drift of a language which can always mean something other than what the speaker meant to say. The second one, the demand of love which Narcissus utters in front of the pool, proceeds, in contrast to the first one, not from an echo but from a speaker presumably endowed with the power to originate a speech which says what he means to say. This nonechoing speech is, however, characterized by a curious lack of echo. As we noted earlier, Narcissus speaks to the woods where the echo resides before speaking to his image. The slide from a rather foolish address to the woods to a no less foolish address to the *"umbra"* highlights a narrative inconsistency. Although Echo is hiding in the trees that Narcissus addresses, the echo does not send back Narcissus's voice.[11] Echoless and therefore soundless, Narcissus's voice is thus implicitly defined as the mere shadow of a voice, a mute voice. This strange muteness in fact points to the inaudible echo which inhabits his demand of love.

Narcissus's demand is indeed addressed to his *"umbra,"* "his own image," an *"umbra"* which echoes in an undeterminable play of substitutions. When Narcissus loves the "umbra" he believes he sees another. Is his love then addressed to the self or addressed to the other? Furthermore, Narcissus loves an "umbra," a reflection, but a reflection which is a resemblance, a similitude. Is Narcissus's love then addressed to the self or to the self as a resemblance to the self? Finally, this reflection is an *"umbra,"* that is, a figuration, an empty form, the form given to a nothingness. Is Narcissus's love addressed then to the image of the self as the form given to a nothingness? To what is Narcissus's love addressed? To the image of the self as self? To the image of the self as other? To the image of the self as a resemblance to the self? To the image of the self as nothingness? Of what "insatiable" thirst is he the victim? Thirst of selfhood, the otherness, of both selfhood and other-

11. This lack of echo is quite inconsistent with the end of the sequence, where Echo suddenly appears to echo Narcissus's last cry before he dies.

ness in a resemblance, thirst of nothingness? The text does not allow us to decide between these alternatives. In front of the pool, Narcissus's demand of love echoes into an unresolvable alternative of meanings which severs the speaker from his "own" demand. Although apparently opposed, Echo's demand and Narcissus's demand are in fact two versions of the same muting echo. If the voice of an "unloving" Narcissus can unknowingly echo into a declaration of love, the loving Narcissus who "declares" his love has not yet begun to speak it; in other words, the echo which inscribes love in an "unloving" discourse prevents a "loving" discourse from ever saying the love that it means to say; it even prevents it from knowing what it means to say when it says "love."

No wonder, then, that Narcissus's voice is "echoless." The demand of love that he utters is a demand that he cannot *"entendre"* in the two meanings of the word; that he cannot *hear* and that he cannot *understand*. The demand of love is therefore a demand that cannot be fulfilled since such a fulfillment would presuppose that which the originary alteration of the echo precisely hinders: the determination of one single meaning. Speaking love, the speaker confronts the painful suspension of a language oriented toward a meaningful fulfillment that its originary alteration prevents it from ever reaching.

Although already problematized, Narcissus's speech nonetheless plays an essential role in the ensuing drama. As we shall see, it is speech, and speech alone, which distinguishes Narcissus as a live subject from the "imago" that he confronts in the pool. We all know that in front of the pool Narcissus falls prey to an error. But what is the nature of this error? Contrary to what is commonly assumed, Narcissus does not love himself, but what he sees in the mirror of the pool: a body, somebody, "another." However, to claim that Narcissus simply mistakes himself for another is still to reduce the complexity of the deception; or rather, it is to focus on the consequence of the error and not on the error itself. Narcissus believes he sees an other because he mistakes an image for a body; that is, because he cannot tell the difference between an *"imago"* and a *"corpus."* Standing in front of a pool, he fails to recognize the reflexive property of the water which he merely considers as an obstacle between himself and the desired body of the other. Unaware of the existence of mirror effects, he takes for a body precisely that which is not a body but a reflection.

Narcissus must then be initiated to the secret of representation. He must learn to differentiate between the representation and the thing that it represents. His error illustrates the difficulty of such an initiation. According to the Ovidian text, we do not know our face until we see it represented. However, in order to know that we are looking at our own face, we must first know that we are looking at a mirror image. But how do we gain such knowledge? How do we recognize a mirror effect?

The Narrator privileges the body as the main differential trait between the representation and what it represents. Addressing Narcissus, he enjoins him to turn away from the *disembodied* image, the elusive *simulacrum*, the *"unbodied* hope", *"spem sine corpore,"* that he loves. From this description, we could expect the body to play an essential role in Narcissus's recognition of the mirror effect. However neither the fact that the body he believes he sees cannot be touched nor the fact that it simultaneously duplicates his gestures is sufficient to trigger Narcissus's recognition. Although the Narrator insists on the polarity *imago/corpus*, the recognition does not make any reference to the *corpus*. As Brenkman notes, Narcissus recognizes himself because he *speaks* to the imago:

> Spem mihi nescio quam vultu promittis amico,
> cumque ego porrexi tibi bracchia, porrigis ultro,
> cum risi, adrides; lacrimas quopque saepe notavi
> me lacrimante tuas; nutu quoque signa remittis
> et quantum motu formosi suspicor oris,
> verba refers aures non pervenientia nostras!
> iste ego sum: sensi, nec me mea fallit imago. . . .
>
> [Ll. 457–63]

Some ground for hope you offer with your friendly looks, and when I have stretched out my arms to you, you stretch yours too. When I have smiled, you smile back; and I have often seen tears, when I weep, on your cheeks. My becks you answer with your nod; and, as I suspect from the movement of your sweet lips, you answer my words as well, but words which do not reach my ears.—Oh, I am he! I have felt it, I know now my own image.

Narcissus realizes that what he believed to be "somebody" is but a representation because he fails to hear the sounds that the mouth in front of him seems to form. When he cannot hear the sounds that the "other" seems to utter, he recognizes the only trait that constitutes him as a "self": an audible speech. It is language which differentiates the human subject from a mere imago. It is language, and language alone, which assures him of his substance, of his ontological status in contrast to the figural status of the imago.

Although peculiar, this mode of recognition does not disturb a rather classical definition of the subject. Narcissus's self-recognition can be easily reinscribed in the familiar pattern according to which Narcissus would be an already constituted self, endowed with body, life, speech, and consciousness, who gains knowledge of his own body and face when he sees them represented in an imago which, not being a self, a subject, is itself deprived of body, life, speech, and consciousness. Ovid's text would merely illustrate the predicament of a self-representation which is unable to represent the speaking "I" as such; it can represent the movement of his lips but cannot reproduce the sounds of his voice. According to this reading, Narcissus's self-recognition would preserve a clear separation between the self and its representation. It would in fact comply to the Narrator's order which enjoined Narcissus to turn away from the imago, that is, to separate the self from the *simulacrum*. Moreover, it would enable the text to dispose conveniently of the problem of the other; since what Narcissus believed to be another self "like himself" is not a self, this other can be evacuated as a mere delusion.

Narcissus's self-recognition allows, however, for another reading than the one already outlined. Read literally, the sentence "*Iste ego sum*" does not reduce the problem of the other but instead brings it to the foreground in a rather provocative manner. The sentence "I am that one," "the ego is that one" indeed defines the ego as the other, an "other" which is not, however, another subject, a subjective otherness, but the mute and unresponsive imago that the water reflects. It thus recognizes that which was left unrecognized in the "dialogue" between Echo and Narcissus: the muteness of language, a muteness which Narcissus's echoless demand of love already indicated. The "ego" is "iste" to the extent that it is the image of the echoing and nonsubjective Other that language is, an Other which condemns the "I" to muteness.

It is therefore highly appropriate that Narcissus should see in the pool the figure of a child. Although he addresses this child as "puer," a term which designates the speaking child, he is forced to recognize that the child is in fact an "*infans*," i.e., the child is mute or, rather, not-speaking. Let us note, moreover, that the Ovidian text has used the term "*infans*" once before. Narcissus's mother, Liriope, gave birth to an "*infans*" whom she called "Narcissus." The "*infans*" that Narcissus confronts in the pool does not, however, refer to the past "*infans*" that he was before becoming a speaking "*puer*"; instead, it denounces as fallacious the belief that one can simply move from the muteness of infancy to the speech of childhood, thus disposing of infancy as a mere phase in the development of the self, a past which can once and for all be revoked. What Narcissus sees in the pool is not the "*infans*" that he was but the *infans* that the speaking self is. He sees the infancy of language, an infancy which cannot be appropriated as one's own past muteness.

While the Ovidian narrative singles out language as the only distinctive trait of the human subject, as the only mark capable of differentiating a substantial self from an unsubstantial figure, Ovid's text denounces the fragility of this differential mark at the same time. Far from functioning as a reassuring demarcation, capable of keeping separate the two "opposite" terms of a polarity such as "speech" and "muteness," language entangles them as it entangles the two terms of that other polarity, "self"/"imago." The sentence "*Iste ego sum*" does not, indeed, only state the muteness of the speaking self, it also identifies this self as an originary simulacrum, a mere figure. And here again, we confront two mutually exclusive readings. On the one hand, the narrative description of the recognition maintains a clear separation between the self and the simulacrum; the self is to be conceived of as the live model later represented in a lifeless, bodyless simulacrum. This version of Narcissus's self-recognition reassures us that Narcissus was indeed mistaken when he confused an imago for a self. It eliminates the threat that this confusion introduced: the threat that the supposedly substantial subject might in effect be mere imago, a simulacrum, a disembodied hope. On the other hand, Narcissus's statement, taken literally, gives credence to his confusion: the self can be confused with an imago because it is "itself" an imago. When he says "I am that one," Narcissus unknowingly defines the self as a nonself, an image deprived of subjectivity. He recognizes the figural status of a subject which is nothing more than the fragile human figure imposed on the "infancy," the muteness of the language.

No wonder, then, that when he recognizes the self as a simulacrum, Narcissus begins to "die." To recognize the self as an originary simulacrum is to recognize that the constitution of the self coincides with its decomposition, that the self "appears" as originally missing, a simulacrum referring to no "original." It is in that sense that the self "dies" in the very process of constituting "itself." Although the narrative presents Narcissus's death as the future event toward which he is "heading," this death has indeed already occurred.

Presented as two different events, Narcissus's recognition and his subsequent death constitute in fact the narrative unfolding of a single moment which escapes the chronological frame of any narrative. And, indeed, if in the very process of recognizing "himself," Narcissus recognizes the self as the figure put in place of an originary missing self, the self as such "dies" in its emergence. The narrative recounting of Narcissus's "death" thus reenacts a death which the narrative cannot narrate because it "takes place" in the very constitution of a self which appears as born dead or, rather, as not yet born, not yet alive.

The specificity of the narrative relation of Narcissus's death should, however, be taken into account, for it highlights a distinctive feature of his recognition. Narcissus does not properly "die," he *liquefies*. Moreover, the liquefaction of his body is initiated by another form of liquefaction: the tears that he spills when he recognizes his "self" in the figure of an *infans*. These tears blur the water and provoke the disappearance of the imago which floated on it, a disappearance that Narcissus mourns by tearing his garments and beating his breast, two gestures which signify the grief of mourning.[12]

12. It has been noted that Narcissus mourns in the manner of women.

Narcissus, then, mourns his death before it actually takes place in the narrative; or, rather, the dissolution of an imago into water already enacts the death which the narrative only describes afterward. When the waters clear again and reflect his lacerated body, Narcissus begins, indeed, to dissolve in a liquefaction which recalls the drowning of the imago into the water of the pool, its liquefaction:

> . . . when the water has become clear again, he can bear no more; but, as the yellow wax melts before a gentle heat, as hoar frost melts before the warm morning sun, so does he, wasted with love, pine away, and is slowly consumed by its hidden fire. No longer has he that ruddy color mingling with the white, no longer that strength and vigor, and all that lately was so pleasing to behold; scarce does his form remain which once Echo had loved so well . . .

The puzzling liquefaction of Narcissus's body exposes what has been suggested all along; the self which turns into water is itself water turned into the image of a self. The death by liquefaction indeed concludes a narrative which has entangled the two apparently antithetical terms of "body" and "water" from the very beginning. We should remember that Narcissus proceeds from a mother, Liriope, who, being a naiad, figures precisely that which is not figurable: the water which dissolves shapes and figures. This water gives birth to a child through a violent generation; Narcissus is the outcome of the rape of one water, Liriope, by another water, Cephisus. The sexual copulation of these two waters could be read as the description of a perfect sexual union, which melts one term into the other, thus achieving a perfect fusion. This, however, is not the case. When he rapes Liriope, Cephisus imprisons her in his sinuous, curving embrace; in other words, the rape violently imposes a sinuous shape on a shapeless water. This violent imposition of a shape of the shapeless produces a "child" which can now be reassessed as the figure imposed on a liquefaction, a figure nonetheless endowed with a beauty which likens him to gods and statues:

> Spectat humi positus geminum, sua lumina, sidus
> Et dignos Baccho, dignos et Apolline crines
> Impubesque genas et eburnea colla decusque
> Oris et in niveo mixtum candore ruborem
> Cunctaque miratur quibus est mirabilis ipse.
>
> [Ll. 420–24]

> Prone on the ground, he gazes at his eyes, twin stars, and his locks, worthy of Bacchus, worthy of Apollo; on his smooth cheeks, his ivory neck, the glorious beauty of his face, the blush mingled with snowy white: in all things, in short, he admires for which he is himself admired.

This godlike beauty is explicitly designated as the mother's legacy. "Gifted with a rare beauty," Liriope gave to Narcissus a beauty which is, however, never described, since the only descriptive detail provided by the narrative is precisely not descriptive: Liriope is *"caerula Liriope,"* *"caerula"* meaning "blue azure," an epithet which can be applied to both water and sky. Liriope's beauty is thus defined by a color which renders the differentiation between two distinct elements, water and sky, uncertain. It is, it seems, the beauty of indeterminacy. When Narcissus looks at the beautiful child reflected on the water, he is therefore looking at that which should not be seen: the self as Godlike, as an imago which gives shape to a shapeless indeterminacy. As Ovid's text implicitly reads it, the self is "watery." It is the "embodiment" of that which precisely has no body and no form, water. It gives form to a liquefaction; to the very process which dissolves form and figure. In that sense, it gives a shape to its constitutive and ongoing dissolution.

Narcissus's death by liquefaction brings to thematic visibility the liquefaction initiated by the simple sentence "Iste ego sum." By defining the self as a mere imago floating on water, this sentence recognizes the figural status of the self; a recognition which "dissolves" the assumed substantiality of the human figure defining it as precisely nothing more that a figure floating on the watery, nonhuman, nonsubjective Otherness of language. The notion of a substantial self "dissolves" in its emergence as a mere figure of Speech. It is this figural status of the self that the conclusion of the narrative once again points to. Narcissus's story does not end, as is commonly assumed, with a metamorphosis, but with a substitution: a flower *takes the place* of his liquefied body. By taking the place of the missing Narcissus, this flower implicitly reads Narcissus as being a substitutive figure himself. It reads the self as a figure put in place of an originally missing subject, "a funeral flower or a flower of rhetoric" (Blanchot, 196). It thus retroactively redefines the site of Narcissus's recognition as the place of an originary and lethal inscription. There, on the mirror, the self "dies" in the very process of "inscribing" its self as an imago, a figure, a rhetorical flower. This originary inscription constitutes an original fall, an original reversal. Although the Ovidian text distinguishes itself from other versions of the myth by not making Narcissus drown in the pool, his fall is nonetheless implicit in the literality of his self-recognition. Narcissus falls in the pool when he recognizes the self as being nothing more than the image reflected/inscribed on the surface of the pool; the self literally falls into its image. This image is, like all mirror images, an inverted image, an image which indeed occasions the inversion, the reversal, the "falling," of the very notion of a substantial, ontological self.

The story of Narcissus thus points to, without ever being able to narrate, a disastrous scene of writing. The mirror of the pool is the site of a self-inscription which is indeed "disastrous" to the extent that it "kills" the self by reducing it to the status of a figure. This death, which marks the birth of the self, cannot be undergone as a conscious experience or remembered as a past event. Like Narcissus unaware of his own liquefaction, the self unknowingly and unconsciously dissolves in its inscription. This inaugural "death" therefore has the uncertain status of a past which cannot be recaptured as a remembrable historical fact since it was never present. As the title given by Maurice Blanchot to his reading of Narcissus, "*Une scène primitive?*" [A Primal Scene?], suggests, the story of Narcissus might revolve around a primal scene; that is, an event which cannot be lived by an "I" in/as a present since it generates the very figure of this self; an event which therefore cannot be recalled as having ever "taken place."

NARCISSUS: A PRIMAL DISASTER

> —Rien au monde ne peut nous enlever le pouvoir de dire je. Rien, sauf l'extrême malheur.
> —Le péché en moi dit "je."
>
> —Simone Weil

The story of a subjective disaster, the story of Narcissus, might then have to be read as the story of the primal disaster which all subsequent "malheurs" (to use a term to which Simone Weil gave all its weight) reenact. Reenacting the forgotten and primal disaster which generated the self, the "malheur" deprives the "I" of its self-assurance, that is, of its assurance of indeed being a self. Depriving the self of its self, it therefore cannot be experienced by an "I" since it ruins the very notion of a self by deporting "me" outside of the substantial and ontological self that "I" believed to be. In that sense, the disaster de-humanizes its victim by stripping him of the privilege (on which the humanity of the "human subject" relies) of being a first person. Dispossessing me of my self, it sends me back to the original dispossession which marked the appearance of the self, and thus to an unbearable self-knowledge. If the "malheur" initiates self-knowledge, it is indeed Narcissus's literal and deadly self-knowledge: to recognize the self as a simulacrum, that is, as something other than a self, as precisely not a self but a figure; to acknowledge, in other words, the fragility of the human figure which can always be shown to be a mere figure.

More precisely, the "malheur" forces its victim to recognize its "self" in the figure of an *infans*, it forces it, in other words, to recognize that the self is no more that the figure given to an infancy, a nonspeaking. This infancy cannot be reduced to the status of a silence which would preserve the possibility of saying what it silences; it points instead to the nonspeaking which inhabits any speaking, to the muting echo which prevents language from ever fulfilling itself in the determination of one, true, final meaning. And, indeed, if language fulfills itself only when it becomes meaning-ful, then the muting echo which diffracts it as soon as it articulates itself prevents it from ever achieving itself and reduces it to an endless project, to an endless infancy. It is this unbearable linguistic predicament that the "malheur" does not allow us to escape; it gives all its acuteness to the predicament of a language which cannot articulate itself without echoing, without failing to become a "true" language. Confronted with the task of speaking a "malheur," we are therefore confronted with the task of speaking an infancy which we can only fail to speak in the very process of speaking it. The confrontation with this failure does not, however, exempt us from speaking. As the story of Narcissus demonstrates, the infancy comes back as a reproach, an accusation, a prayer, a questioning echo which demands the impossible: to speak when we cannot but fail to speak, when we can no longer speak as a self-assured first-person.

To the extent that it deals with language, literature seems destined to confront its infancy. It is, as it were, haunted by the calling infancy of language and thus placed under the obligation of responding to this call. Its response, however, cannot be a cognitive answer. If it responds, it can only be through a writing which endlessly foreshadows that which forever remains to be said, which delineates, as it were, the contours of an irreducible infancy:

> Nous parlons sur une perte de parole—un désastre imminent et immémorial—, de même que nous ne disons rien que dans la mesure où nous pouvons faire entendre préalablement que nous le dédisons, par une sorte de prolepsie, non pas finalement pour ne rien dire, mais pour que le parler ne s'arrête pas à la parole, dite ou à dire ou à dédire: laissant pressentir que quelque chose se dit, ne se disant pas: la perte de parole, le pleurement sans larmes . . . [Blanchot, 39]

> It is upon losing what we have to say that we speak—upon an imminent and immemorial disaster—just as we say nothing except insofar as we can convey in advance that we take it back, by a sort of prolepsis, not so as finally to say nothing, but so that speaking might not stop at the word— the word which is, or is to be, spoken, or taken back. We speak suggesting that something not being said is speaking: the loss of what we were to say; weeping when tears have long since gone dry . . . [21]

> Responsabilité d'une écriture qui se marque en se démarquant, c'est-à-dire peut-être—à la limite—en s'effaçant . . . [Blanchot, 58]

And such is the responsibility of writing—writing which distinguishes itself by deleting from itself all distinguishing marks, which is to say perhaps, ultimately, by effacing itself [34]

This writing which unwrites itself, in order to point to an infancy which cannot ever be uttered, erodes any self-certainty, any self-assurance. In fact it exposes the self to the subjective disaster that the name of "Narcissus" designates. If "tous les poètes sont des Narcisse," as Schlegel is supposed to have said, this statement echoes in two different and mutually exclusive readings which exemplify both the incalculable risk and the unpredictable chance that the term "literature" might have come to name. It exemplifies its risk since it can give rise, as Narcissus's story does, to a "humanist" interpretation, which Maurice Blanchot summarizes thus:

la création—la poésie—serait subjectivité absolue, le poète se faisant sujet vivant dans le poème qui le reflète, de même qu'il est poète en transformant sa vie de telle manière qu'il la poétise en y incarnant sa pure subjectivité. [Blanchot, 205]

creation—poetry—is absolute subjectivity and the poet a living subject in the poem that reflects him, just as he is a poet by virtue of having transformed his life into poetry by incarnating in it his pure subjectivity. [135]

Although it seems innocuous enough, this humanist interpretation entails a violent reduction of the question of the other. Defined as a process of self-assertion or of self-creation, literature would reduplicate the violent constitution of a self which generates itself by excluding the other outside of "its-self." First posited as the outsider, the foreigner, the other can later become, in a gesture no less violent, another self "like" the self, that is, an "other" which is always thought in reference to a prior and domineering self. To this self-assurance the story of Narcissus gives the name of pride; the subject who believes himself to be a self closed onto himself and uncontaminated by any otherness, is "proud." This pride, however, is criminal to the extent that it denies the original humiliation inflicted on the self, its original victimization. The self is indeed originally invested by a nonsubjective Other which "victimizes" it, first by reducing it to the status of a mere figure, and secondly by placing it (as a simulacrum) under the obligation of fulfilling a task which this Other has rendered impossible: responding. Constituted as a simulacrum, the self is thus made responsible for the wound inflicted onto it: it must respond to and for the impossibility of responding. It is this original victimization that a proud self-assertion forgets and, above all, denies. The "criminal," in other words, would fail to recognize his original status as a "victim," his original humiliation. He delusively asserts his self by rejecting the Other outside of his self in the figure of a subjective "other." This other can then be made to incarnate the threat of the unrecognized Other. Feared as a threat to the integrity of the self, the subjective other embodies the threat to the very notion of self that the Other indeed represents. Ironically enough, the fear of the other, the rejection of the other, the killing of the other, are all accomplished because a human subject tries to assure himself of both his selfhood and his humanity; they result from a proud self-assertion which, unwilling to confront the hypothesis that the self might be a mere figure, is therefore all too willing to reassure itself by projecting this figural status onto the "other," and the other alone.[13] According to this implacable logic, the self can assert itself as a human subject only by positing an other with it deprives of both humanity and subjectivity, which it reduces to the status of the mere simulacrum of a human subject, a simulacrum which it can then dispose of once it has fulfilled its function: to reassure the self, by being positioned as the opposite term, that the self is not "itself" a simulacrum. The characterization of the other as a mere simulacrum allows the self to ignore its own figural predicament and to believe in the possibility of a world cleansed of the threat of figurality. In this perspective, a "humanist" reading can be suspected of grounding the most "inhuman" acts precisely by being too self-assured, that is, too easily assured of both the substantiality and the humanity of the "human subject." If literature constitutes an incalculable risk, it is to the extent that it can always, like Ovid's text, give credence to this proud and "self-confident" humanist reading; that it can be disposed of as belonging unquestionably to the "humanities."

Literature, however, can *also*, like Narcissus's story, allow for another kind of reading, the kind of reading that Maurice Blanchot opposes to the humanist interpretation of the sentence "Tous les poètes sont des Narcisse." This "other" reading responds to an obligation, to an impersonal imperative marked in the following sentence by "il faut:" "*il faut* sans doute l'entendre encore autrement" (Blanchot, 205) [One ought, no doubt, to understand (Schlegel's) statement in another way too (135). The tone of this sentence is ambiguous. One could "hear" in it a self-assured imperative, a commandment: "Read otherwise!", an injunction to work harder, to summon one more effort: "Encore un effort . . ." However, the "sans doute," which seems to evacuate all doubt, reinscribes it, or rather acknowledges that the imperative quality of "il faut" proceeds in fact from a relentless and

---

13. In this context we might note the fact, mentioned by a Jewish concentration camp survivor in Claude Lanzman's Shoah, that "The Germans even forbade us to use the word "corpse" or "victim." [. . . They] made us refer to the bodies as *Figuren*, that is, as puppets, as dolls. . . ." [Translation mine.] Claude Lanzman, *Shoah* (New York: Pantheon Books, 1985), 13. On this question see Shoshana Felman's article in this issue, 44–45.

demanding uncertainty. It is this uncertainty which demands another reading another "entente," an "entente" which could maybe give a chance to the other. According to this other reading that we *must* also perform, Narcissus's story denounces the fallacy of the humanist hope:

> c'est que dans le poème où il s'écrit il ne se reconnaît pas, c'est qu'il n'y prend pas conscience de lui-même, rejeté de cet espoir facile d'un certain humanisme selon lequel, écrivant ou "créant", il transformerait en plus grande conscience la part d'expérience obscure qu'il subirait: au contraire, rejeté, exclu de ce qui s'écrit et, sans y être même présent par la non-présence de sa mort même, il liu faut renoncer à tout rapport de soi (vivant ou mourant) avec ce qui appartient désormais à l'Autre ou restera sans appartenance. Le poète est Narcisse, dans la mesure où Narcisse est anti-Narcisse: celui qui détourné de soi, portant et supportant le détour, mourant de ne pas se re-connaître, laisse la trace de ce qui n'a pas eu lieu. [Blanchot, 205]

> in the poem, where the poet writes himself, he does not recognize himself, for he does not become conscious of himself. He is excluded from the facile, humanistic hope that by writing, or "creating," he would transform his dark experience into greater consciousness. On the contrary: dismissed, excluded from what is written—unable even to be present by virtue of the non-presence of his very death—he has to renounce all conceivable relations of a self (either living or dying) to the poem which henceforth belongs to the other, or else will remain without any belonging at all. The poet is Narcissus to the extent that Narcissus is an anti-Narcissus: he who, turned away from himself—causing the detour of which he is the effect, dying of not re-cognizing himself—leaves the trace of what has not occurred. [135]

The literary text functions like Narcissus's mirror because it repeats the originary inscription, that is, the originary *fall* of the self into an image of the self. The text/mirror does not reflect/inscribe a self, a subject endowed with life and consciousness, but instead denounces the inherent fallacy of this "subject," its ghostlike quality. Writing itself, the self writes itself out, thus repeating the disastrous self-inscription that "Narcissus" names, his dissolution, his falling into a mere simulacrum deprived of subjectivity. Writing therefore cannot provide the comfort of any self-recognition. Writing, "I" does not not recognize itself nor does it approach a greater "consciousness" of itself. The story of Narcissus's self-recognition is also the story of the impossibility of any "self"-recognition: "I" can only fail to recognize "itself" since there is no recognizable "self," since there is precisely no self. It is in that sense that Narcissus is *also* anti-Narcissus. Narcissus dies because he cannot re-cognize "himself" but only a nonsubjective

Other in place of the missing self, an Other which dispossesses him of his self, an Other to which he therefore cannot relate as a self to another self. This nonsubjective Other kills the very notion of a self in an original murder which cannot, however, be remembered as ever having taken place, as a present to which "I" could ever have been present. Writing leaves the trace of an original disaster which was not experienced in the first person precisely since it ruined this first person, reduced it to a ghostlike status, to being a "me without me." This "me without me," this simulacrum which has lost its self-assurance, can then "entendre" that which the self-assured ego is bound to ignore: the reproachful call of an infancy which obliges "me" to respond while depriving "me" of the possibility of responding. This "me without me" is both "innocent" because assigned an impossible task, and "guilty" because the impossibility of the task still does not exempt "me" from fulfilling it:

> La responsabilité, ce serait la culpabilité innocente, le coup depuis tou-
> jours reçu qui me rend d'autant plus sensible à tous les coups. C'est le
> traumatisme de la création ou de la naissance. [Blanchot, 41]

> Responsibility is innocent guilt, the blow always long since received
> which makes me all the more sensitive to all blows. It is the trauma of
> creation or of birth. [22]

This reading of Narcissus as the paradigmatic victim must nevertheless ignore Narcissus's prior designation as the paradigmatic "bourreau" [execu-tioner]. When he claims that Narcissus rejected Echo because "elle ne lui donne rien à aimer d'*autre*," Blanchot in effect exculpates Narcissus from the crime of having rejected the other, that is, from the crime of having denied the Other. Having disposed of this primal crime, he can then dis-regard the ethical reversal of places inflicted on the proud "criminal." It is, indeed, because Narcissus is guilty of the crime of pride, that is, of self-assertion, that he is later punished by re-living precisely that which he cannot "live:" the humiliation originally inflicted on the proud subject. His "later" victimization can then be read as repeating an original yet un-acknowledged and even violently denied victimization.

With the reversal of the humanist executioner (who asserts his self by relegating the other outside of his self) into a de-humanized victim (who recognizes his self as the figure imposed on a nonsubjective Other), Ovid's text opens a dangerous question: if a humanist self-assertion is "criminal," can we ever hope to avoid this crime? Can we ever claim to be innocent of it? If the fault resides in taking a position of self-assurance, this fault might indeed designate an original fall: in the very process of "falling" into its image, the self would at the same time "fall" into the delusion of being a self.

The "malheur" which later befalls the self would then constitute a violent reminder of this "original fall," a violent return of that which was left unrecognized. By reminding the self of its original wound, of its fragility, of its highly uncertain status, it revokes from the start any attempt to think it from the height of a self-assured subject. It even revokes any attempt to think it as long as thinking presupposes the stability of a thinking "I." It is by definition "incomprehensible" since it revokes the very notion of a self. We therefore cannot pretend to comprehend it, but can only expose our "selves" to its questioning, a questioning which can only disturb the comfort of our "good conscience" by confronting us to the uncertain status of our "subjectivity," of our "selfhood," and even of our "humanity."

JILL ROBBINS

Visage, Figure: Reading Levinas's *Totality and Infinity**

What would it mean to face what Derrida has called "the ethics of ethics"? That is to say, to confront the very opening of the question of ethics—the grounds of both its possibility and impossibility—prior to the production and elaboration of all moral rules or precepts? According to Emmanuel Levinas, the face of the other [*le visage d'Autrui*] is the very site and privileged figure for such an opening. In the face-to-face encounter, responsibility in its most original form of response, or language-response, arises. The pages that follow will consider both the specificity of the ethical and the specific otherness that Levinas identifies in the face-to-face.

Yet if the face is the privileged figure for the opening of the question of the ethical, the question of the textual status of the face remain to be asked. Can there be a figure for the ethical? a figure for the face? The very question is problematic in that rhetoric, as a (derivative) science of figures, is incommensurable with the more originary level of Levinas's description. Could

*Abbreviations
TI   Emmanuel Levinas, *Totality and Infinity*, trans. Alphonso Lingis (Pittsburgh: Duquesne University Press, 1969, 1979). *Totalité et infini* (The Hague: Martinus Nijhoff, 1961).

FC   Emmanuel Levinas, "Freedom and Command," in *Collected Philosophical Papers*, trans. Alphonso Lingis (Dordrecht: Martinus Nijhoff, 1987). "Liberté et commandement," *Revue de métaphysique et de morale* 58 (1953).

DL   Emmanuel Levinas, *Difficile liberté: essais sur le judaïsme* (Paris: Albin Michel, 1963, 2d ed. 1967, 1974).

EI   Maurice Blanchot, *"L'Entretien infini* (Paris: Gallimard, 1969).

I would like to thank Rebecca Conway for her helpful comments on an earlier version of this essay.

YFS 79, *Literature and the Ethical Question*, ed. Claire Nouvet, © 1991 by Yale University.

the opening of the question of the ethical be marked with a certain figurality? And supposing that one can speak about an alterity that is rhetorical or textual, can the alterity of the other and textual alterity be even addressed in one breath? Here again, the question of ethics and the question of language come into their closest possible proximity.

THE FIGURE OF THE FACE

"The alterity of the other," writes Levinas in his 1961 *Totality and Infinity*, "is not 'other' like the bread I eat, the land in which I dwell, like, sometimes, myself for myself" (*TI*, 33). A relation to this latter, finite alterity characterizes what Levinas calls the work of identification, that is, my ability to absorb otherness "into my identity as thinker or possessor" (*TI*, 33). (He also calls it the economy of the Same, and it refers to the habitual exchanges that make up the self's concrete relationship with the world.) But the alterity of the other is *infinite*. Encountered neither as a phenomenon nor as a being (something to be mastered or possessed), the other is encountered as a face. It is in the encounter with the face of the other [*le visage d'Autrui*] that the other's infinite alterity is revealed.

The first reference to the face in *Totality and Infinity* reads as follows:

> For the presence before the face, my orientation toward the Other can lose the avidity of the gaze only by turning into generosity, incapable of approaching the other with empty hands. This relationship, established over the things hereafter possibly common, that is, susceptible of being said, is the relationship of discourse [*discours*]. The way in which the other presents himself, exceeding the idea of the other in me, we here name face [*nous l'appelons, en effet, visage*]. [*TI*, 50]

Levinas "names" the face here according to the formal structure of infinity as he has previously described it, "an *ideatum* that surpasses its idea" (*TI*, 49), a thought that thinks more than it can contain.[1] But although he names the face here, he will also insist that the primordial relationship to the face is *not* one of naming: "*Autrui* is not only named, but invoked. To put it in grammatical terms, the other does not appear in the nominative, but in the vocative" (*DL*, 21), or as he also says, "in the dative."

These grammatical terms, which are only provisional and which will later be abandoned, do indeed seem to illuminate the passage above, in

---

1. The Cartesian idea of infinity is a guiding notion of Levinas's work and one of the privileged moments in his history of philosophy. The first reference to the face in *Totality and Infinity*, cited above, introduces it as "a deformalization or the concretization of the idea of infinity."

particular the transformation that vision undergoes in the encounter with the face. For in "the presence before a face," the avaricious gaze *turns into* generosity ["l'avidité du regard se muant en générosité"] and language ["discours"]. The (ethical) necessity for this transformation stems from Levinas's assertions that vision is a violent way of relating to the other. It "immobilizes its object as its theme." As a form of adequation (*TI*, 34), it is unable to respect what is infinitely other. It seeks to absorb that alterity, to draw it into the play of the Same. In this way, vision is just one instance of the self's *habitual* economy, an economy that always fails to do justice to the other. Other possibilities within this habitual economy include representing the other, recognizing him, knowing him, understanding him, or any form of the theoretical relation. All would be unjust, for they would attempt to appropriate the other, to reduce him to the (self-) Same.

That is why, in the passage above, vision, a relationship of adequation, turns into generosity and a certain kind of language, relationships of nonadequation. This transformation that the gaze undergoes is, precisely, ethical in the sense that Levinas gives it: "we name this calling into question of my spontaneity by the presence of the other ethics" (*TI*, 43). Thus the (ethical) encounter with the other interrupts the self's habitual economy and its tendency to conceive of the world as a space of possibilities and power [*pouvoir*].[2] It interrupts the play of the Same. And let us also note in passing: the ethical transfer is a figural transfer as well. The turn from vision to generosity and language, and ultimately, to voice, resembles a synesthesia, a crossing of sensory attributes. Moreover the verb *se muer*, "to turn, to moult, to metamorphose," implies a break, within the figural turn, in phenomenality. We will come back to these reflections. For now, suffice it to say that in Levinas's account, the primordial relationship to the other that one faces is "discourse." The nontotalizing relationship to the face of the other is accomplished "in a discourse, in a conversation [*entre-tien*] which proposes the world. This proposition is held between (*se tien entre*) two points which do not constitute a system, a cosmos, a totality" [*TI*, 96]. Thus, discourse is a relationship with the other that maintains the distance of infinite separation "yet without this distance destroying this relation and without this relation destroying this distance: (*TI*, 41). And thus, as Alphonso Lingis

2. Throughout *Totality and Infinity*, Levinas plays on *pouvoir*'s interchangeable senses of possibility and power, as part of an ongoing polemic with Heidegger's description of the world as a space of possibilities for *Dasein*. This reading is problematic insofar as it seems to confuse possibility, an *Existential*, with power (a relation between already constituted entities). By contrast, Levinas's use of the term, "spontaneity" is not ontic and not at all psychological: it is part of his reading of the Heideggerian "being-in" as joyous possession of the world which ignores the other. See the reading of Levinas and Heidegger by Jacques Derrida, "Violence and Metaphysics," in *Writing and Difference*, trans. Alan Bass (Chicago: University of Chicago Press, 1978), 134ff. Henceforth cited in the text.

comments: "To face someone is both to perceive him and to answer to him."[3] One faces the other as interlocutor. One faces the other in language.

Yet let us not take for granted that we know what we mean here by language. For the *parole* that ensues in response to the face of the other cannot be understood according to hermeneutic models of "conversation" or "dialogue." It is a founding "conversation," a discourse before discourse, which is, Levinas says, "established over the things hereafter possibly common, that is, susceptible of being said." A conversation rigorously without communality, it makes *lieux communs* possible. Rather than being a searching together for consensus, it is what makes possible the difference between consensus and disagreement.

Nor is this to be mistaken for any form of communication. It is "prior" to language understood as an exchange of signs. The face signifies in a distinctive manner which Levinas calls expression *kath' auto,* ["according to itself"], or that which signifies only relative to itself. Expression is the way in which the face, which is not reducible to my vision, exceeds and breaks out of the phenomenon. It breaks through what Levinas calls the form, the plastic image with *its* look:

> This way for a being to break through its form, which is its apparition, is, concretely, its look, its aim. There is not first a breakthrough, and then a look; to break through one's form is precisely to look; the eyes are absolutely naked. A face has a meaning not by virtue of the relationships in which it is found, but out of itself; that is what expression is. [FC, 20]

> The life of expression consists of undoing the form in which the existent, exposing itself as a theme, in this way dissimulates itself. The face speaks. The manifestation of the face is already discourse. [*Le visage parle. La manifestation du visage est déjà discours.*] [TI, 66]

We will not enter into the extent to which Levinas's discussion of expression *kath' auto,* "over and above the disclosure and dissimulation proper to forms," is part of a polemic against Husserl and Heidegger. What concerns us here is, first of all, that "my" gaze undergoes not just a transformation in the encounter with the face, but also a reversal. The face, which is not reducible to my vision of it, looks back. It talks back [*le visage parle*]. To see a face means that the face looks and talks back. (This reversal was already implied in the word *visage. Visage—* from the Latin *visum,* "a thing seen"—is not just a thing seen or intended. It is also that which intends me, as Levinas etiologizes it: "Regarder un regard, c'est regarder ce qui ne s'abandonne pas, ne se livre pas, mais qui vous *vise:* c'est regarder le *visage,*" DL, 21.) Sec-

3. Alphonso Lingis, Translator's Introduction to Emmanuel Levinas, *Collected Philosophical Papers,* op. cit., xxx. Henceforth cited in the text.

ondly, in the transformation plus reversal that constitutes the (ethical) encounter with the face, it is not just that my look becomes discourse and that
I face the face in language, but also, the face, which breaks through its form,
looks back at me, and speaks. As Alphonso Lingis also remarks: "the face
faces in language" (Linguis, xxx). To encounter a face is to encounter a
speaking face. As Levinas writes above, "the face speaks" [le visage parle].

Derrida has remarked in "Violence and Metaphysics" that it may be
"tempting" to consider this discourse on the face a prosopopeia (Derrida:
Violence and Metaphysics, 101). It is tempting particularly for literary critics, because when Levinas gives the face as voice here, he in a sense de-faces
it, gives it a figure. At times it is as if figuration performs the desired (ethical)
break in phenomenality, the turn away from the optical. Yet while this, like
the earlier transformation or ethico-figural transfer ["l'avidité du regard se
muant en generosité"] seems tropological, prosopopoeia or any other rhetorical term is simply inapplicable here, again because of the level of Levinas's description, which is written both within and against the tradition of
Husserlian phenomenology and Heideggerian ontology, and because, in
short, of the founding status of the encounter described. Perhaps one would
want to speak of the tension between the figural transfers operating within
the sequential narrative of Levinas's description and the anteriority of the
founding experience that is described. In the passage above we read: "The
face speaks. The manifestation of the face is already discourse." While the
sequential narrative proceeds forward, the (quasi-transcendental) description proceeds backwards. The "already" here belongs to an immemorial past
that is accessible to no present.

The face, as Derrida remarks, is given as "the original unity of glance and
speech" (Derrida: Violence, 100). At stake in Levinas's discussion of expression (which seems very much grounded in the experience of actual faces)
is the way in which, in contradistinction to other modes of signification,
facial expressions signify only themselves. They do not refer to something
other, even to states of mind or feeling.[4] Their autosignification is prior to
language conceived as a system of signs or as knowledge that could be
available to a consciousness. It is a primordial speaking that is an invitation
to speak. Levinas writes:

> For expression does not consist in presenting to a contemplative con-
> sciousness a sign which that consciousness interprets by going back to
> what is signified. What is expressed is not just a thought which animates

4. Compare, in this context, Augustine's account of how the face signifies in Confessions 4:8. There is coincidence between "the movement of the heart" and "the signs
revealed in the face," and thus these signs have, in effect, a necessary rather than arbitrary
link to their referent.

the other; it is also the other present in that thought. Expression renders present what is communicated and the one who is communicating; they are both in the expression. But that does not mean that expression provides us with knowledge about the other. The expression does not speak about someone, is not information about a coexistence, does not invoke an attitude in addition to knowledge; expression invites one to speak to someone. The most direct attitude before a being *kath' auto* is not the knowledge one can have about him, but is social commerce with him. [*FC* 20–21]

Derrida and Blanchot have both pointed out the phonocentric moments of Levinas's description and thus its complicity with what Derrida has called the metaphysics of presence. Such turns of phrase as "expression renders present what is communicated and the one who is communicating," or as we can read elsewhere in his work, that expression means "being behind the sign," or that "he who manifests himself comes, according to Plato's expression, to his own assistance" (*TI*, 66), all seem part of a privileging of oral discourse as "plenitude" (*TI*, 96), as a presence to oneself (Derrida: *Violence*, 101–02). As Blanchot remarks, it is at just these moments that the discourse, the *entretien* that Levinas describes "becomes a tranquil humanistic speaking again" (*EI*, 81). This is largely a result of the privileging of oral discourse in Levinas. (For Levinas rarely uses the word "man." The *visage*, as we recall, is defined as the way in which the other presents himself, exceeding the idea of the other in me. The *visage* is man in his infinite alterity, man insofar as he is infinitely other. *Visage* is not a description added on to the conception of "man"; it is prior to it.) But that the Levinasian *entretien* would revert to a humanistic conversation is also due to a fault of the language ("our" language), which is weighted towards the hermeneutical and the dialectical. (We might recall again, that the face's speaking, which belongs to the "already," does not take place in the present and is accessible to no present.)

Thus let us not forget the radicality of the Levinasian *entretien*, of the language relation with the other, especially as Blanchot has elaborated it in *L'Entretien infini*. In this encounter, the asymmetry between discussants is absolute. The other is described alternately by Levinas as the Most-High and the weak one. At times he seems the overlord, and at times the utterly helpless and destitute. He is, as we shall see, the one who commands me and the one to whom I am infinitely obligated. Thus, despite the seeming symmetry of the exchange of glances and speech, despite the formal symmetry of the phrases "face-to-face," and despite, in Blanchot's phrase, "l'affrontement de deux figures" that it invariably suggests, the face-to-face encounter has nothing symmetrical about it. Blanchot comments: "I never face the one who faces me. My manner of facing the one who faces me is not an equal confrontation of presences. The inequality is irreducible" (*EI*, 89). And this is why at the close of *Totality and Infinity*, Levinas offers a formulation to describe the relation to the other that both Blanchot and Derrida have picked up on, namely, "the curvature of intersubjective space which inflects distance into elevation," or simply, "the curvature of space" (*TI*, 291).

The speaking relation to the other in the face-to-face is not, then, "l'affrontement de deux figures"; it is, as Blanchot comments further, "the access to man in his strangeness by speech" (*EI*, 89). How can such a speaking maintain "the strangeness of this strangeness" and not "repatriate it"? (*EI*, 97). As in the Levinas passage cited earlier, this will be a kind of speaking that is not a knowledge about or speaking about the other, but rather a speaking *to* him, an invocation. And a question that surely haunts much of Levinas criticism, and that has been treated by both Lyotard and Derrida, is, how to speak about this invocation of the other without neutralizing the relation, transforming it into a form of knowledge? How to speak about Levinas's discourse without rendering its performative dimension constative, assimilating it to the denotative language of the same? How, for that matter, to speak *to* the other without comprehension (a form of "repatriation")? Would this not occasion the grossest of misunderstandings?[5]

If this speaking to the other is "to maintain the strangeness of this strangeness," it must be characterized by nonreciprocity and noncomprehension. "Parole sans entente et à laquelle je dois cependant répondre" (*EI*, 92), writes Blanchot. Such a speech, is thus, in an important sense, impossible. *Parler sans pouvoir* is what Blanchot calls it, that is, to speak without power (for the other has interrupted my *pouvoir de pouvoir*), to speak without being able (to speak), to speak without ability.[6]

This is a strange speech, this speech that is "the access to man in his strangeness." It is a founding speech, not speech between two already constituted entities, but speech that founds the rapport, and that *is* the rapport (without rapport). In this *entretien*, as Blanchot writes, the *entre* designates an interval held up over a void, as abyss. This speech with the *visage* is a speech with the outside (although Levinas generally uses the term "exteriority"), for *Autrui* is "always coming from the outside" (*EI*, 80). A speech with the outside, it is speech with, the "stranger, the destitute, the proletarian" (*TI*, 75), or, in the Biblical locution that Levinas frequently invokes, "The stranger, the widow, the orphan." The other is "always, in relation to

5. See Jean-François Lyotard, "Levinas's Logic," in *Face to Face with Levinas*, ed. Richard A. Cohen (Albany: State University of New York Press, 1986): 117–58, and Jacques Derrida, "En ce moment même dans cet ouvrage me voici," in *Textes pour Emmanuel Levinas*, ed. François Laruelle (Paris: Editions Jean-Michel Place, 1980): 21–60

6. For a discussion of the *in*ability in responsibility, see Ann Smock, "Disastrous Responsibility," *L'Esprit Créateur* 24 (1984): 5–20.

me, without country, stranger to all possession, dispossessed and without dwelling, he who is as if 'by definition' the proletarian . . . " (*EI,* 80).

AND CAIN SAID TO ABEL

The being that expresses itself, that faces me, says *no* to me by his very expression. (*FC,* 21)

[The Other] opposes to me not a greater force . . . but precisely the infinity of his transcendence. This infinity, stronger than murder, already resists us in his face, is his face, is the primordial expression, is the first word: "thou shalt not kill." [*TI,* 199]

The face, it is inviolable; these eyes absolutely without protection, the most naked part of the human body, offer, nevertheless, an absolute resistance to possession, an absolute resistance in which the temptation of murder is inscribed: the temptation of an absolute negation. The Other is the sole being that one can be tempted to kill. This temptation of murder and this impossibility of murder constitute the very vision of the face. To see a face is already to hear: "Thou shalt not kill." [*DL,* 22]

Levinas had described expression as an autosignification and as an invitation to speak, within the originary language encounter with the face of the other. It is only in his analysis of murder that the face's speaking is given a particular content, albeit negative. In the passages above we discover that the expression "says no," that the "primordial expression," "the first word" is a prohibition, "thou shalt not kill," that "to see a face is already to hear: 'thou shalt not kill.'" How are we to understand the "primordial expression"? Does it mark the fact that the (im-)possibility of murder inhabits the language relation to the other at its origin, as Blanchot would have it? "Such would be the speech that measures the relation of man face-to-face with man, when there is no choice but to speak or to kill. A speech as grave, perhaps, as the death of which it is the detour. The speech/murder alternative is not the tranquil once and for all between good speech and bad death . . . in this situation, either to speak or to kill, speech does not consist in speaking, but first of all in maintaining the movement of the *either/or*; it is what founds the alternative" (*EI,* 88).

Just as this *parole* is precisely not part of a dialogue in the usual sense, not a humanistic word that keeps the peace, but a "grave" word—in both senses—a word which maintains the very violence of the alternative, so too the primordial expression which Levinas describes is not a mere speaking, for it takes place on the level of distress, nudity, and exposure to violence. In the above descriptions, the face is both utterly defenseless—"naked," that is, "without covering, clothing, or mask" (FC, 21), naked because of its eyes, its look which breaks through form, and causes it to be "divested of its form" (FC, 20)—and also that which challenges my powers, "inviolable," saying "no," opposing me, offering resistance. We have seen this double aspect of the face before, at once as the destitute one and as overlord. We have seen this challenge as well when the encounter with the face of the other is said to interrupt the self's habitual economy and its *pouvoir de pouvoir*.

These powers are, at the limit, murderous. Vision is a violence; it would possess the other; it is even "by essence murderous." The face resists possession insofar as it is not reducible to my vision; it breaks out of the form that would encapsulate it. Yet to the extent that the face does present itself as form, the temptation of murder is "inscribed" there. The temptation of murder is inscribed in the face's phenomenalization, inscribed in the sensuous moment of expression (*ex-primere*, to press out). Expression thus invites both speaking and murder. The very ambiguity of the face's presentation, as that which lodges itself within form and is also beyond form, renders it absolutely vulnerable. In Levinas's account, it renders it absolutely resistant as well: "This temptation of murder and this impossibility of murder constitute the very vision of the face." This ambiguity of the face's presentation is one of the reasons why murder is, as Levinas says, "impossible": "Murder exercises a power over what escapes power. It is still a power, for the face expresses itself in the sensible, but it is already impotency, because the face rends the sensible" (TI, 198). Murder wants to kill the other, who is beyond the sensible. Yet in murdering the other, it arrives only at the sensible. In this way, murder always misses its mark. No doubt it effects an annihilation of the other in his being. But it thereby misses the genuine alterity of the other, namely that which in him goes beyond the sensible (and that which in him is beyond being).

If the face is vulnerable to violence insofar as it expresses itself in the sensible, and resistant to violence insofar as it is beyond the sensible, how are we to understand Levinas's assertion that the face offers "an absolute resistance *in which* the temptation of murder is inscribed," namely, that the resistance itself is the temptation? As Levinas explains the nature of this resistance, the face is "total resistance without being a force" (FC, 19). In murder, however, "one identifies the absolute character of the other with his force" (FC, 19). In other words, one mistakes the other's resistance *for* a force.[7] Or as Blanchot puts it, murder takes the infinity by which *Autrui*

7. "Violence consists in ignoring this opposition, ignoring the face of a being, avoiding the gaze, and catching sight of an angle whereby the *no* inscribed on a face by the very fact that it is a face becomes a hostile or submissive force. Violence is a way of acting on every being and every freedom by approaching it from an indirect angle" (FC, 19).

presents himself as if it were a property of *Autrui* and wishes to reject it absolutely. Thereby it misses *Autrui;* "it changes him into absence, but does not touch him" (*EI*, 87). Thus the one who murders is caught in a substitutive structure; he is like a man who must aim at his target (infinity) over and over again, and always miss it. (That is why he cannot kill his victim enough times.) The infinite alterity of the speaking face is "incommensurate with a power exercised"; there is a "disproportion between infinity and my powers" (*TI*, 198). And it is in this sense that while murder is a real possibility, it is what Levinas calls an "ethical impossibility."[8]

But by ethical impossibility Levinas also means the cessation of my murderous powers, of my *pouvoir de pouvoir.* This cessation of *pouvoir* is inaugurated and marked by the face's primordial expression, which "says no," whose "first word" is "thou shalt not kill." "To see a face is already to hear: 'thou shalt not kill.'" The encounter with the face of the other interrupts the "imperialism of the same" (*TI*, 39). This interruption is emblematic of the ethical movement. At times Levinas calls it a "conversion" or "reversal" of our nature.[9] At stake is the very birth of ethics or responsibility.

As we have seen elsewhere in Levinas's work, this interruption is marked by an ethico-figural turn of speech, a quasi-synesthetic turn from my vision to the other's voice, or from the sense of seeing to that of hearing: "to see a face is already to hear 'Thou shalt not kill.'" But is this a matter of hearing, with its connotation of self-coincidence, at all? The face's primordial expression is a *citation*, that is, it is characterized not by phenomenality, but by the structure of the mark, with the constitutive absence that that implies. Moreover, the "voice" delivers a commandment from an immemorial past, accessible to no present: "To see a face is *already* to hear: 'thou shalt not kill.'" This "already" ruptures self-coincidence. Thus when Levinas gives the face as voice here, again he gives the face as (nonphenomenal) figure. He gives the face as a figure for, one might add, the literal, for the originary donation of the law. But that the face (*visage*) could be a figure (*figure*) was always possible within the semantic destination of the word. And if the face can indeed be a figure, are we sure that we know what we mean by "figure"? Is not "figuration" itself transformed by such a usage?

How are we to evaluate the fact that the commandment that the face

8. "If the impossibility of killing were a real impossibility, if the alterity of the other were only the resistance of a force, his alterity would be no more exterior to me than that of nature which resists my energies, but which I come to account for by reason; it would be no more exterior than the world of perception which, in the final analysis, is constituted by me. The ethical impossibility of killing is a resistance made to me, but a resistance which is not violent, an intelligible resistance" (*FC*, 21–22).

delivers to me is, after all, one of God's commandments, the sixth commandment, "thou shalt not kill"? First, let us remark on the basis of Levinas's 1953 essay, "Freedom and Command," that there is a general way of understanding commandment that is more or less independent of any theological context. In that essay, Levinas explains that the "no" that the face opposes to me is "not the *no* of a hostile force or threat . . . it is the possibility of encountering a being through an interdiction" (*FC*, 21). Unlike repression, interdiction signals a positive possibility, or better, an ethical relationship. Interdiction is inseparable from the asymmetry which characterizes the face-to-face encounter and from the distinctive way in which the face signifies. The very fact that expression breaks through form is, in effect, its imperative:

> The being that is present dominates, or breaks through its own apparition, it is an interlocutor. Beings which present themselves to one another subordinate themselves to one another. This subordination constitutes the first occurence of a transitive relation between freedoms, and, in this very formal sense, a command. (*FC*, 21]

And as he concludes a few pages later, "speech in its essence, is commanding" (*FC*, 23).

But the question concerning the nature of this commandment remains. Does its presence imply that Levinas's ethics are dependent on the revealed morality of positive religion? Apparently not, for Levinas's sense of religion is as removed from ordinary understanding as is his sense of ethics. In *Totality and Infinity* he writes, "we propose to call religion the bond that is established between the same and the other without constituting a totality" (*TI*, 40).

Yet Levinas does, nevertheless, cite one of the ten commandments, which are at the center of the revealed morality of the Judeo-Christian tradition. In this context, one would have to note that while Levinas respects many aspects of the Christian religion, he is not concerned with a unitary Judeo-Christian tradition. His concern is primarily with the Judaic, and

9. Emmanuel Levinas, Interview with Richard Kearney in *Face to Face with Levinas,* ed. Richard A. Cohen (Albany: State University of New York Press, 1986), 25. Robert Bernasconi describes it as an intentionality in reverse in "Levinas and Derrida: The question of the Closure of Metaphysics," in the same volume. See also Bernasconi's, "Deconstruction and the Possibility of Ethics," in John Sallis, ed. *Deconstruction and Philosophy: The Texts of Jacques Derrida* (Chicago: University of Chicago Press, 1987): 122–39, and "Fundamental Ontology, Metontology, and the Ethics of Ethics," *Irish Philosophical Journal* 4 (1987): 76–93.

particularly, with the rabbinic tradition as a "source" for his ethics. More-over, Levinas distances the Judaic from the interpretation it has received within the unitary Judeo-Christian tradition, an interpretation that is often negative and privative. He offers instead a reinscription of the Judaic. For example, as he states in a recent interview,

> It is often said 'God is love'. God is the commandment of love. 'God is love' means that He loves you. But this implies that the primary thing is your own salvation. In my opinion, God is a commandment to love. God is the one who says that one must love the other.[10]

At work here is a critique of the Christian economy of salvation with its habitual ignoring of the other. The legalism of the Judaic religion, its preoc-cupation with 613 commandments, is here reinterpreted as a fundamental orientation toward the other. This reinscription of the Judaic in Levinas's work is found primarily in what he calls his "non-philosophical" or "confes-sional" writings, his readings of the Talmud and his essays on Judaism.[11]

Although such an explanation would seem to make Levinas's ethics de-pendent, once again, on the revealed morality of a positive religion, in this instance Judaism, this is not the case. For one thing, the explicit references to Judaism in Levinas's work are found mostly in the nonphilosophical writings. Secondly, we cannot take for granted that we know what we mean by "Judaism" in Levinas's work. The Judaism in question is a reinscribed "Judaism" that is equivalent neither to the determinations it has received within the dominant "Greco-Christian" conceptuality nor to Judaism as a historical or positive religion, although it necessarily takes off from there.[12]

Finally, and still with reference to positive religion, when Levinas writes that the face commands me, "thou shalt not kill," he seems to suggest that the law is revealed not by God, as in the Biblical claim, but in the face of the other (man), and that this relationship is prior to any relation between man and God. This is indeed the case, but it need be the case only if that rela-tionship between man and God is conceived of as a theology, a discourse on God's attributes, or a thematization. As Levinas implies in the interview cited above, the relationship to God is, however, not a *credo*, nor is it any kind of ontological assertion. It is the primacy of doing for the other. That is

---

10. Levinas, "The Paradox of Morality: an Interview with Emmanuel Levinas," trans. Andrew Benjamin and Tamra Wright, in *The Provocation of Levinas: Rethinking the Other*, ed. Robert Bernasconi and David Wood (London: Routledge, 1988), 177.

11. See, in addition to *Difficile liberté*, Levinas's *Quatre lectures talmudiques* (Paris: Minuit, 1968), particularly the reading of Sabbath 88a–88b there.

12. I develop this in a chapter on Levinas in my *Prodigal Son/Elder Brother: Interpretation and Alterity in Augustine, Petrarch, Kafka, Levinas* (Chicago: University of Chicago Press), forthcoming.

the sole relationship between man and God. In many ways this "Judaism" is closer to an atheism.

But one might still ask, what is the "religious" meaning of the commandment "thou shalt not kill?" Within historical Judaism, according to one commentator, the concept of murder is "enlarged" to include even "the omission of any act by which a fellow-man could be saved in peril, distress or despair."[13] With all due caution, such a reference may help to illuminate the spirit of Levinas's murder analysis.[14] But Levinas's phenomenological descriptions of the relation to the other already make the "religious" meaning (in his sense) of the commandment quite explicit, without further reference to religion in the traditional sense. Its "religious" meaning is the imperative of response or responsibility that arises in the encounter with the other, who faces, in language.

What did Cain say to Abel immediately before he murdered him? In Genesis 4:8, there is a lacuna in the text (preserved in the Masoretic tradition), where the verse is incomplete: "And Cain said to Abel his brother . . . ". "The Hebrew vayommer means not 'told' or 'spoke to' but 'said unto', and the words said ought to follow."[15] The text of Genesis 4, verses 3–8, in Everet Fox's translation, reads,

> It was, after the passing of days that Kayin brought, from the fruit of the soil, a gift to YHWH, and as for Hevel, he too brought—from the firstborn of his flock, from their fat parts. YHWH had regard for Hevel and his gift, for Kayin and his gift he had no regard. Kayin became exceedingly enraged and his face fell. YHWH said to Kayin: Why are you so enraged? Why has your face fallen? Is it not thus: If you intend good, bear-it-aloft, but if you do not intend good, at the entrance is sin, a crouching-demon, toward you his lust—but you can rule over him. Kayin said to Hevel his brother . . . But then it was, when they were out in the field, that Kayin rose up against Hevel his brother and he killed him.[16]

In numerous versions of the Bible (such as the Samaritan, Greek, Syriac, Old Latin, and Vulgate), and consequently, in most translations, the missing phrase is supplied: "let us go outside." This metonymic response seeks to provide a bridge to the place of the action that follows. The midrashic re-

---

13. *Pentateuch and Haftorahs*, ed. J. H. Hertz (London: Soncino Press, 1978), 299.

14. That the murder situation should be "paradigmatic" at all within Levinas's ethical discourse has to do with the difficult sense in which the ethical becomes *visible* through the violation of the ethical.

15. Harry M. Orlinsky, ed. *Notes on the New Translation of The Torah* (Philadelphia: The Jewish Publication Society, 1969), 68.

16. *In the Beginning: A New English Rendition of the Book of Genesis*, trans. with Commentary and Notes by Everett Fox (New York: Schocken, 1983).

sponse to this lacuna in *Bereshith Rabbah* 22:16 is freely embellishing. It interpolates an extended discussion between Cain and Abel. This response, like that of Philo, assumes that the brothers had a *quarrel*. Philo even writes: "the plain is a figure of contentiousness."[17] And although the midrash explains alternately that the two quarreled about material possessions, religious ideology, and sexual jealousy, the face of the quarrel seems more important than its content.[18]

Considering the episode as a whole, the contemporary commentator André Neher remarks Cain's silence in response to God's question, "Why has your face fallen?"[19] This silence is not entirely unreasonable, given the notorious obscurity, indeed, the near unintelligibility of the admonitory verse that follows, "If you intend good, bear-it-aloft . . . ".[20] But, writes Neher, "in place of God, he chose his brother as the recipient of his answer: 'Cain said unto Abel his brother . . . '."[21] And thus, as Elie Wiesel remarks, he turned his quarrel against God against his brother instead.[22] What did Cain say to Abel here? For Neher, the initial "rupture in communication" between Cain and God underscores the failure of dialogue that is central to the episode as a whole: "Abel does not speak, whereas Cain speaks all the time" ("incessantly," as Wiesel notes). "Thus dialogue was swallowed up in silence and death." Neher concludes: "it is as if the obliteration of the dialogue were the cause of murder" (Neher, 95). The "dialogue" of which Neher speaks, based on an ideal of symmetry and an understanding of language as communication, is derivative of the Blanchotian "speech or death," the asymmetrical *parole* that founds not only the possibility of "dialogue" in such a sense, but also the very speech/murder alternative. Yet Neher's comment gives pause: it is as if the textual gap or lacuna in its very materiality were the cause of the murder the episode recounts.

---

17. *Philo*, vol. 2, with an English trans. by F. H. Colson (Cambridge, Mass.: Harvard University Press, 1929), 205.

18. See the discussion by Nehama Leibowitz in *Studies in Bereshit Genesis*, trans. Aryeh Newman (Jerusalem: World Zionist Organization, 1972), 38–45.

19. As Claus Westermann notes, "J" understands Cain's reaction to the rejection of his gift as "psychosomatic." "He became inflamed . . . his face fell." *Genesis 1–11: A Commentary*, trans. John J. Scullion (Minneapolis: Augsburg Publishing House, 1984), 297. Everett Fox reminds us that "the text is punctuated . . . by changing connotations of the word 'face.'" *In the Beginning*, 19.

20. Commentators agree that the Hebrew of this verse is obscure, and its textual difficulties irresolvable.

21. André Neher, *The Exile of the Word: From the Silence of the Bible to the Silence of Auschwitz*, trans. David Maisel (Philadelphia: The Jewish Publication Society, 1981), 97–98. See also the related discussion by Neher in *L'Existence juive: solitude et affrontements* (Paris: Seuil, 1962), 34–36. Henceforth cited in the text.

22. Elie Wiesel, *Messengers of God: Biblical Portraits and Legends*, trans. Marion Wiesel (New York: Pocket Books, 1977), 54.

What did Cain say to Abel? Perhaps, as Neher suggests, he simply repeat-ed God's words to him "in all their fearful ambiguity." These words were not only obscure, but as Elie Wiesel comments, "cruel": "Repudiated by God, Cain sank into a black depression. Whereupon God, with a cruelty as star-tling as it was unprovoked, asked why he looked so crestfallen, why he was so depressed. As though He did not know, as though He was not the cause!: (Wiesel, 58). Perhaps, Wiesel continues, Cain wanted to unburden himself to Abel, who did not listen.

And Cain said to Abel, "Let us go outside." Why did he direct him toward the outside?" "Outside, where there were no witnesses," says one commen-tator (Westerman, *Genesis* 1–11, 302). Blanchot writes, "as if he knew that the outside is the place of Abel, but also as if he wished to lead him back to that poverty, to that weakness of the outside where every defense falls away" (*EI*, 87).

KEVIN NEWMARK

Ingesting the Mummy: Proust's Allegory of Memory

Je suis le ténébreux,—le veuf,—l'inconsolé,
Le Prince d'Aquitaine à la tour abolie
—Gérard de Nerval, "El Desdichado"

If the line of filiation that connects Nerval to Mallarmé and both of them eventually to Proust can be described as a genealogy, it would have to be a curious pedigree indeed, riddled as it is with dead ends, discontinuities, disinheritances, and generally unfinished or abolished constructions. On the level of a genetic imagery that is recurrent to the point of the obsessional, for instance, there seems to be little chance for the identification, much less the survival, of a family tree threatened in Nerval's case by the chimerae of youth, in Proust's by the disillusionments and sterility of old age, and in Mallarmé's by the improbability of even being born. But this appears to be an insoluble problem only as long as we remain stuck at the naively elementary level of the image or theme. For once the question is enlarged enough to include the specifically textual moment of writing that is implied in the constitution of any theme, no matter how negative or barren, things begin to assume a somewhat different and more promising shape. It can be argued, and some of the most productive readings of these authors have in fact argued, that it is precisely by writing out those images of chimerae that Nerval's text passes beyond them into its maturity, and that by writing about the impossibility of being born that Mallarmé's text can overcome this same obstacle in exemplary fashion. In a similar way, *A la recherche du temps perdu* could be said to constitute in its very existence as text the discovery or recovery of that which is stated as lost and in need of search throughout: the moment of its own conception and birth. The apparent concatenation of theme and structure that results is both circular and complementary, the beginning of the writing of the text we have before us coinciding with the end of the thematic search contained and recounted

YFS 79, *Literature and the Ethical Question,* ed. Claire Nouvet, © 1991 by Yale University.

150

within it, the actuality of the text responding to and fecondating the thematic statement of lack articulated by it.

This specular system of relationships established between beginning and end as well as between structure and statement effects at the same time a figural and temporal balance that helps to restore the picture of a symbolist family of writers or a genealogy of symbolism that would include the branch running from Nerval to Proust. By insisting on the various moments of negativity that must be faced in order to be overcome in the necessary passage and return from birth to youth and from youth to maturity, death, and rebirth, Nerval, Mallarmé, and Proust make of the symbolic correspondence between theme and statement, or image and text, a task that is to be effectuated across time rather than something that is given as immediately accessible. "The only paradises worthy of the name," Proust reminds us near the end of his *recherche*, "are ones we have lost."[1] Hence the ambivalence of the critical interpretations with which this brand of symbolism tends to be assessed: when the negativity inherent in symbolist poetics is seen as the turning back, by means of a mere aesthetic representation, to what by definition remains buried in the past, it is considered a formalism and a flight from objective reality; but when it is seen as the prelude to an act of understanding that recuperates all the discrepant levels of lived experience by bringing to light the synthesis of a universal meaning, it is considered a necessary step within an ongoing engagement with social and historical realities. In any event, whether they are seen as regressive or prophetic, "symbolist" writers like Nerval, Mallarmé, and Proust become in this way corresponding moments in a larger family history that includes romanticism as its immediate predecessor and our own postmodernity as its heritage.

In the case of Proust, one can begin to appreciate the stakes of this genetic scheme more clearly by focussing on the debate that gets played out around the question of "memory" in *A la recherche du temps perdu*. What is the role of memory in Proust's text, with its concomitant stress on questions of time and especially on time past? Although the general tendency in the first part of this century was to emphasize those aspects of the Proustian *oeuvre* that tied it firmly to a past seemingly closed off to everything but nostalgia, of late we have begun to distinguish ourselves from precisely these first readers of Proust by situating the *Recherche* at the furthest possible remove from this sort of nostalgia.[2] Such changes in the barometric readings of literary masterpieces help to remind us that rather than compos-

1. Marcel Proust, *A la recherche du temps perdu*, ed. Pierre Clarac and André Ferré, (Paris, Bibliothèque de la Pléiade, 1954), 3 volumes, 3:870. Further references in text, all translations are my own unless otherwise noted.
2. For the archetypical reading of Proust as nostalgic recounting of a lost past, see Edmund Wilson's essay in *Axel's Castle* (New York, W. W. Norton & Co., 1931), 189, 190.

ing a fixed universe of transcendental meanings, the literary canon is itself part of a dialectical narrative whose meaning is not given in advance but produced historically, in large part by way of the evolving sequence of its successive interpretations. Thus Gilles Deleuze, with his avowed interest and investment in the postmodern condition of the contemporary age, seems anxious to align Proust as closely with us as possible by distancing him from a lopsided orientation toward the past when he says that, "no matter how important its role, memory only occurs here as the means of an apprenticeship that exceeds it both in goal and principle. The Search is turned toward the future, not toward the past."[3] The future the *recherche* is turned toward starts to sound very much like our own present when Proust is later credited with having found a truth capable of "displacing" the age-old Platonism of the Logos by turning thought itself into a form of creation, a mode of "production," or a kind of "machine" to be put into public "service" (134, 177, 184). Despite significant differences of emphasis, we find once again the familiar pattern in which the origin or beginning—doubly present in Deleuze's counterreference to the Platonic conception of reminiscences or "memory"—is only a *means*, a necessary, and necessarily negative detour towards the goal or *end* of a historical process in progress, and of which we would be the latest avatars.

The question remains, however, whether any simply temporal scheme can do justice to the complexity of a text that is constantly attempting to articulate the passage of time with the simultaneity of a multiplicity of points in space. Memory in Proust is never simply a matter of the before and after, or past and future, of a completed entity, it always includes at the same time the necessary reference to a spatial structure constituted around the mutually dependent elements of an inside/outside relationship. The locus of this differential relation between interior and exterior is of course nothing other than the self-conscious subject itself, which is in turn composed of the delicate interplay between mind and empirical reality. A great deal is at issue in passages such as the one where Marcel claims that, "at last, by continuing to follow from inside to outside the states of mind simultaneously juxtaposed within me, and before reaching the actual horizon enclosing them, I can discover pleasures of another kind. . ." (1:87). The pleasure that is intimated at here proleptically would itself be the subject's ultimate discovery in the work of art of a perfect adequation between temporal duration ("continuity") and spatial extension ("simultaneous juxtaposition"). Drawing attention to the nature and importance in *A la recherche du temps perdu* of this spatializing process of juxtaposition that

3. Gilles Deleuze, *Proust et les signes* (Paris, Presses Universitaires de France, 1964), 10. Further references in the text.

eventually overtakes even the sequential movement of time itself, Georges Poulet has helped to return the problem of following or rediscovering the identity of the self through time to the more fundamental question of constituting it as a spatial relation between inside and outside in the first place.[4] The emergence from a merely "local" and superficial existence to the more "fundamental" mode constitutive of a genuine subject, according to Poulet, is "the act by which the mind transports whatever it sees, thus effecting the passage of objective reality into the imaginary" (34). But when Poulet then goes on to quote the reference to Elstir's painting— "Elstir was incapable of looking at a flower without immediately transplanting it into that interior garden where we are forced to remain forever" (2:943)—we can see that things are considerably more complicated than a one-step process. For despite the narrator's tone of discouragement or despair at this point, it is not simply a case here of bringing the outside inside, unilaterally transporting or transplanting objective reality into the imaginary, even and especially if this segment of the movement first appears as life imprisonment. Unlike Swann, then, Elstir can become a model for the narrator precisely because he refuses to be confined within this prison that seems to separate empirical experience once and for all from the ideal space of a mind.[5]

Clearly, what is of most consequence in this passage, and even emblematic for the novel as a whole, is not just the bringing of the flowers into an interior garden—which can always appear as a defensive strategy of security and protection as well as a form of alienation—but rather the indisputable fact that in the act of painting they have in some way been put *back out* into the world again. It can only be by "bringing whatever [has been] experienced *back out* of the shadows," the narrator reminds us at the end of the novel, that we can ever hope to have access to anything like our "true life, a life finally discovered and illuminated." And the sole means of achieving this exteriorization, of course, is through the "production of a work of art" (3:879,895). The passage in question on Elstir's painting, in fact, goes out of its way to emphasize the importance of just such an outward turn of thought. It stages a mock confrontation in Mme Verdurin's dining-room between the living roses that once provided the painter's model and Elstir's portrait of them. Whereas the "real" flowers are available now only through

4. Georges Poulet, *L'Espace proustien* (Paris, Gallimard, 1963). Further references in the text.

5. Claudia Brodsky's interpretation of the *Recherche* is interesting for the way it suggests the inadequacy of the model of memory presumed by most readers of Proust, but by using Swann in order to do so it remains overly tied to the binary structure of experience/recollection it seeks to displace. It may be true that the *Recherche* never manages to recapture anything, but that is not to say it does nothing to the idea that there was something out there to capture in the first place. See, "Remembering Swann," in *The Imposition of Form* (Princeton, Princeton University Press, 1987).

Mme Verdurin's passive recollection of them, Elstir's portrait, actually there and propped against a chair, serve to bring *la Patronne* and her idealized reminiscences face to face with something that is neither natural nor imaginary, but which nonetheless "almost resembles them." What functions as the tablepiece for the luncheon in question, then, is neither the objective reality of the flowers, long gone, nor Elstir himself, who has fallen from favor, but rather this portrait of objectified thought. As such it is "almost," but not quite, equal to both sides of the inside/outside relationship, and so is finally identified by the narrator as an unheard of flower, "a new variety with which the painter, like an ingenious horticulturist, had embellished the family of Roses" (2:943).

Taking a hint from the narrator's own horticultural comparison, it could be argued that the process which is first described as simply "transplanting" a rose from one soil to another when it goes from objective reality to the imagination next resembles the insertion of an entirely foreign "transplant" when the inner rose is put back out to enhance, embellish, and transform the family of Roses—both empirical and ideal—it also serves to replace. It would hardly be an exaggeration at this point to say that the operation engaged in by the self when it transplants between inner and outer gardens is at least twofold: it is both an interiorization that transports the self-same flower from one place to another, from world to mind, for instance; and an exteriorization that leaves its mark on both regions in such a way that neither inside nor outside would ever be able to remain the same.[6] This passage on Elstir's paintings seems merely to confirm in the language of flowers, or rhetorical figures, what we have known all along, or will be reminded of once again later on by Proust. The transfer from outside to inside is a grafting operation as well as a simple transplanting. In other words, the painting of ideal ressemblances must also be supplemented by a kind of nonmimetic graphesis, or writing, in which the subject will have to participate if it is to survive at all. But if the result of such grafting is the production of a truly unheard-of variety of flower, "a new variety of roses which without him would have never been known," then how can we still call that a survival, and who or what would be the "identity" that is thus preserved as something totally different?

One of the most comprehensive readings of the *Recherche* from this point of view is undoubtedly that of Gérard Genette, which is scattered through a number of essays written at various times and for differing con-

6. The narrator himself is not wholly unaware of the complexity of this double movement when he dubs the transplanting operation of his own writing "translation": "I realized that the essential book, the only true book, is not something a great writer has to create, since it already exists in each one of us, but rather it has to be translated. The task and duty of a writer are those of a translator" (3:890).

texts, but which aims above all at refining and complicating the terms of
Poulet's original insights.[7] Thus, Genette is able to retain the basic focus on
the subjective phenomena of time and space while also accounting for the
additional complexity introduced into this dual scheme by the passage in
the novel to an overtly written dimension. By translating slightly what
Poulet sees as a rivalry between experiences of time and space into the
complementary rhetorical structures of metaphor and metonymy through
which these experiences are articulated textually, Genette is able to accom-
modate the sequential and diachronic movement of a narrative to the jux-
tapositioning within it of simultaneous layers of subjective consciousness.
Rather than forming mutually exclusive experiences, time and space are
necessarily related to each other in a unified system of textual connections
produced by the narrative itself between spatiotemporal analogies (metaphor) and spatiotemporal proximities (metonymy). The key to this system is
the writing subject, who is nothing but the sequential narrative, or temporal
unfolding, of the cumulative analogies that can finally be revealed to exist
between all the spatial relations of outside to inside that constitute the
experience of a self.

The obvious model for this totalizing coordination of spatiotemporal
identities and proximities is provided of course by Proust's "petite
madeleine." According to Genette, the madeleine is both metaphorical and
metonymical since it functions both as a temporal identity and a spatial
proximity: "the true Proustian miracle is not that one madeleine steeped in
a cup of tea would taste the same as another madeleine steeped in tea, and
would awaken its memory; it is rather that this second madeleine resuscitates along with it a bedroom, a house, an entire town . . ." ("Métonymie
chez Proust," 57–58). The only thing that is missing in this excellent description of the miracle of resuscitation is the recognition that when the
temporal metaphor and the spatial metonymy that constitute this
madeleine are then swallowed and taken into the body of the narrator, there
is produced at the same time—but "where?" is the question—the supple-
mentary analogy between inside (madeleine) and outside (madeleine) as
well as an unexpected proximity between before (youthful experiences) and
after (adult vocation). Obviously, the confused exclamations of the narrator
himself at this point—"the essence was not *in* me, it was me. . . . Clearly,
the truth I am seeking is not *in* [the steeping madeleine], but *in* me" (1:45)—
do not begin to do justice to the complexity of this operation. Where is the
truth, then, in relation to the subject that experiences it—in him, with him,

7. Gérard Genette, "Proust Palimpseste," in *Figures 1* (Paris, Seuil, 1966); "Proust et le
langage indirect," in *Figures 2* (Paris, Seuil, 1969); *Figures 3* (Paris, Seuil, 1972); "L'Age des
noms," in *Mimologiques* (Paris, Seuil, 1976). Further references in the text.

or through him? Had he recognized the answer to this question at this point, the narrator would not have needed the following three thousand pages of stumbling around in the dark to understand his vocation as author. Closer to the truth than the simple miracle of the madeleine, perhaps, is Genette's characterization of the "auto-illustrative" structure of the novel. Such a structure would, like the madeleine, combine analogies and proximities, but it could only be said to come into being when the narrator has passed from the status of mere personage to that of self-conscious author. This moment would constitute, according to Genette, "the Text, in the full sense of the term."

Still, the question would seem not so much whether there is something like a "text," for the existence of the *Recherche* is as undeniable as it is productive of endless critical commentary, but rather to document with as much analytic precision as possible what the text *is* in the full sense of the term. This would entail looking for the actual constitution *by* the text of the claim *for* the text that the dimensions of time, space, and the self can appear in their "truth" ["la vraie vie"] only by means *of* the completed text. And it would further require an examination of the consequences of such an auto-illustrative claim by the text for the text in order to determine whether the resulting "life" in it is produced as a continuous identity or a mutant and unrecognizable species. Such, at any rate, is the reading strategy adopted by Paul de Man when, with respect to slightly different claims made in the novel, he tests the aesthetic and metaphysical statements made in the text on reading against the literary practices illustrated by the text read and finds an irreducible discrepancy between them.[8] Such a discrepancy could in fact be said to account as well for Marcel's befuddlement when he tastes the madeleine in "Combray." It could be that this moment of confusion, the overcoming of which constitutes the thematic development of the rest of the novel, is of interest for more than just its thematic role.

Rather than forming the first step in the successfully completed search for self-identity recounted in its wake, this unresolved split in the narrator between what he is and what he can say he is may be the only legitimate thing the text can ever do about what it is saying. If this were to be the case, and only a detailed analysis of specific passages can be used either to contest or to bear out such a hypothesis, then considerable care would have to be taken in reading not only the self-assured pronouncements made by the narrator at the end of his vocational itinerary, but also in reading those critics who, like Genette, take these truth claims at face value.[9] The binary

8. Paul de Man, "Reading (Proust)," in *Allegories of Reading* (New Haven: Yale University Press, 1979).

9. See "Héros/narrateur," in *Figures 3:* "the narrator not only, in a wholly empirical way, knows *more* than the personage; he *knows*, absolutely, he possesses the Truth . . ." (260).

opposition that is finally to be overcome between narrator and personage, or at a different level between narrator and author, may not suffice to locate the odd voice that finally says: "There is a critical uncertainty whenever the mind finds itself exceeded by itself; when it is at one and the same time the investigator and the land to be investigated" (1:45). There could be no better description than this, in fact, for the autoillustrative writing of the *Recherche*, which, as text, is both the writing self and the means of access to this self. That there should be not only a grave uncertainty about the outcome of this search, but an uncertainty as well as to who or what (self) could ever write about the uncertainty of its (own) coming into being, deserves to be taken seriously, seriously enough, at least, to return once again to the supposed source of the journey.

It was Harry Levin who pointed out the link between the singularity of the madeleine experience and the figural pattern through which it operates.[10] This pattern, which does not remain unchanged by its rearticulation in Proust's novel, is basically that of Biblical exegesis: "the name and shape of that little tea-cake are traceable to the shells that pilgrims wore on their hats as badges of their vocation. Let us make no mistake; we are at the commencement of a religious pilgrimage" (390). Whatever one thinks of the etymological gesture that attempts to link the name as well as the shape of the madeleine directly back to the shell and emblematized pilgrimage it stands for, it would be difficult to deny the structural affinity which the madeleine scene in the novel exhibits with certain easily recognizable topoi of the Biblical tradition. Thus M. H. Abrams is wholly within the spirit of the text when he suggests that the *Recherche* is actually "a displaced and reconstituted theology, or else a secularized form of devotional experience."[11] Even French critics, preoccupied as they are with local historical, thematic, and formal concerns, have had to note the obvious ritual subtext for the tea-soaked madeleine: "allowing for the numerous religious connotations. . . . I am tempted to compare this gesture to the Christian rite of communion: the infusion and madeleine replacing the bread and wine; the aunt officiates and holds out the host: 'this is my body, this is my blood.' "[12] It becomes an easy matter at this point to reestablish all sorts of historical and generic connections between Proust's text and the rest of the literary canon, constituting in this way a comprehensive system of classification in which the individual text communicates with the universality of the tradition and the unique moment with an entire history. By conforming to the

10. Harry Levin, *The Gates of Horn* (New York, Oxford University Press, 1963). Further references in the text.

11. M. H. Abrams, *Natural Supernaturalism* (New York, W. W. Norton & Co., 1971). See especially, 65–70, and 80–83.

12. Philippe Lejeune, "Ecriture et sexualité," *Europe*, (February/March 1971); 121. See also Serge Doubrovsky, *La Place de la madeleine* (Paris, Mercure de France, 1974).

tripartite model of divine creation, paradise lost, paradise regained, the *Recherche* can be seen to participate in an impressive lineage, transforming it along the way by means of stylistic and thematic innovations. Such innovations and displacements would include the formal devices of the auto-biographical voice and the figural language used to constitute it which are analyzed by Genette, as well as the highly complex and untraditional forms of sexuality that are suggested by both Lejeune and Doubrovsky. Finally, though, that the madeleine can function simultaneously as an original psychic symbol for Marcel's (or Proust's) repressed sexuality, as a derived metaphysical symbol for the possibility of rediscovering life after death (that is, the transcendence and redemption of meaning), and as a formal symbol for the "symbolist" program of its author, merely confirms the symmetrical dynamic of exchange that mediates here between the individual work and its place within a historical and generic continuum of aesthetic forms.

Such intertextual schemes of coordination of thematic statement and poetic structure are already familiar to us from their implication on the intratextual level of the *Recherche* as well, and they always manage to by-pass the essential question regarding the status of this totalizing system within a given text. They do so by assuming its unproblematic completion within any given text in order to compare with it a number of other texts in the same tradition, thereby establishing a coherent system of classification out of the similarities and differences that are constituted between them. The question, once again, is not whether writing the *oeuvre* is possible for the subject—since clearly this writing has occurred—nor whether such writing can communicate across differences of time and geography with all the versions of the same model (in this case, the liturgical rite of the eucharist)—since clearly it does—but rather to test the claim that the passage leading from individual experience to writing, from death-in-life to "the true life," which is accomplished by the structure of the symbol, can be made accessible to the subjects whose ultimate definition and identity depend on it. In other words, does the beginning communicate, or commune with the end of the work in such a way that the initial question, "what does it mean?" (1:45), can be fully accounted for without disturbing the voice that would consume and reverse it in the final assertion, "and I now understood that my past life was nothing but the material for a literary work" (3:899)?

As Genette aptly notes, the function of the madeleine is precisely that of providing connections, and first of all a connection from the incomprehensible and obsessional stutter of the first section of the novel to the three-thousand pages that spread out along symmetrical axes from it and eventually redeem it. Until the moment Marcel, now a full-grown man, and at the invitation of his mother, tastes once again the madeleine drenched in tea, his past is restricted to the repetitive scene of bending to the paternal law by climbing the stairs at Combray to his bed and the separation this means from his mother. Even though there is in the nightly ritualistic kiss he receives from his mother a prefiguration of a "communion of peace," these opening pages stand clearly under the sway of an arbitrary and inexplicable law of the father. At that terrible moment on the staircase when Marcel is all but lost in the eyes of his mother as well as in his own, the father who grants a last-minute stay is compared to Abraham himself: "I stood there without daring to make a move; there he was before us . . . with the same gesture Abraham is making in the Benozzo Gozzoli print that M. Swann had given me . . ." (1:36). And like the old testament law represented by Abraham, the law that speaks to Marcel through his own father is like the dead letter separated from its spirit, since the boy remains as blind to its ultimate meaning as he does to the source of its power, for "when [his] anxieties had been assuaged, [he] was no longer able to understand them" (1:43). To be saved like Isaac, then, is to be condemned at the same time to a formalistic, ritualistic repetition of an empty law that awaits its fulfillment in the incarnation, the word made flesh, the transcendence of meaning.

The economy that regulates this fulfillment is a dialectic of loss, or sacrifice, and redemption; and as we have already noted, in Proust, the model for this economy is the eucharistic feast. In addition, though, this eucharistic model, which remains to some extent a filial ritual, displaces the tradition of paternal authority by mediating it through a maternal figure: in Proust there is no access to the recovery of lost meaning without taking into account the place of the mother. The madeleine and the tea, then, are the transposition of the mechanics of transcendence into a nontheological code whose meaning would be conditioned by the place occupied by the mother within it. The reason for this maternal transposition or displacement from the eucharistic ceremony to the partaking of the madeleine seems perfectly clear, moreover, since it is a direct result of the narrator's theory of the symbol. The fundamental distinction between the eucharist and the madeleine is that the eucharist, worn down through age-old layers of habit, has become a merely conventional symbol, an ideal object that is totally exhausted in its hypothetical meaning for the intelligence, and for this reason it cannot give access to the truth as it actually exists. The madeleine, on the other hand, a material symbol that has been experienced independently of its eventual meaning, always preserves some of the reality it originally shared with what Proust will call the "essence" of reality. Obviously, the distinction here between conventional and material, which is also a question of sexual difference as well as "essence," can be operative only from the point of view of the thinking subject that is in the process of constituting itself thanks to such "symbols."

For, to judge by the wholly conventional link that now obtains between the madeleine and Proust's *Recherche*, there is nothing inherently more "material" (or maternal) about the madeleine than there is about the eucharist, except in the consciousness that registers it as such. This process of registration is described near the end of the novel as the writing out of a book whose pages are accessible only to those truths that leave a material trace on them: "This book, the most difficult of all to decipher, is also the only one that has been dictated to us by reality, the only one whose 'impression' has been made in us by reality itself. Whatever idea is left in us by life, its *material figure*, the trace of the impression it has made on us, remains the token of its *necessary truth*. Ideas formed purely by the intellect can only have a logical truth, a hypothetical truth . . ." (3:880, emphasis added). Far from being an aesthetic idealism, then, Proust's symbolism is a materialism at the furthest remove from the merely abstract truths of logic and speculation. Truth, as it is being described here, is not simply the formal beauty of an aesthetic object or the logical beauty of a proposition, but is in addition the literal truth of what actually happens, what intervenes in reality with the necessity of a material event that leaves it mark on the world.[13] For this reason, the means of recovering the truth and thereby tasting the joys of what the narrator will refer to as "the celestial food" has itself to achieve materiality, "even if the simple taste of a madeleine seems logically unable to contain the basis for this joy" (3:873).

The way the madeleine achieves materiality and is allowed to write the truth in the book the narrator will eventually have to decipher as his very own is through the repeated communion services Marcel attends on the Sunday mornings of his boyhood in Combray in tante Léonie's bedroom. The scene, in which Marcel is the acolyte and tante Léonie the celebrant, ends with Marcel's receiving the bit of madeleine steeped in tea from the outstretched hand of his aunt. But because, just as with the eucharistic service, the preparation of the sacrament is what guarantees the effectiveness of its consummation, the scene deserves quotation in its entirety:

13. The best description of how this concept of truth effects Proust's understanding of the symbol and its relation to a "material" rather than an ideal beauty, remains the following passage on Giotto's frescos, cited and read by Paul de Man: "But later on I came to understand that the overwhelming strangeness [*l'étrangeté saisissante*], the peculiar beauty of these frescos consisted in the important place taken up in them by the symbol, and that the fact that it was represented not as a symbol, since the thought symbolized was not expressed, but as real, as actually endured or materially handled [*effectivement subi ou matériellement manié*], lent to the significance of the work something more literal and more precise, and to its teaching something more concrete and striking" (1:82). Proust is not here denying the existence of logical truths or "immaterial symbols" in which the symbol would itself coincide and with the thought symbolized in it. Like the distinction between voluntary and involuntary memory, this one involves the question of the material effect or effectiveness when something occurs as an actual "event" rather than a mere "idea."

After a moment I would go in to kiss her; Françoise would infuse her tea; or, if my aunt were feeling agitated, she would ask for her tisane instead, and I would be in charge of measuring out onto a plate the amount of linden needed to put into the boiling water. The drying out of the stems had turned them into a capricious trellis in whose interlacings pale flowers opened up, as though a painter had arranged and placed them as ornamentally as possible. The leaves, having lost or changed their appearance, resembled the most disparate things—the transparent wing of a fly, the blank side of a paper label, the petal of a rose—but as though they had been stacked on top of one another, ground together, or interwoven as in the construction of a bird's nest [*mais qui eussent été empilées, concassées ou tressées comme dans la confection d'un nid*]. A thousand useless details, a charming prodigality on the part of the druggist, and which would have been left out of an artificial concoction [*qu'on eût supprimés dans une préparation factice*], gave me, like a book in which one is astonished to find the name of a personal acquaintance [*comme un livre où on s'émerveille de rencontrer le nom d'une personne de connaissance*], the satisfaction of realizing [*le plaisir de comprendre*] that these were actually the stems of real lindens, like those I had seen on the Avenue de la Gare, modified, precisely because they were not replacements, but themselves, except that they had aged [*modifiés, justement parce que c'étaient non des doubles, mais elles-mêmes et qu'elles avaient vieilli*]. And each new character being nothing but the metamorphosis of a previous character, in the little gray bulbs I would recognize the green buds that had not come to term; but especially the rosy gleam [*mais surtout l'éclat rose*], soft and lunar, that made the flowers stand out amid the delicate forest of stems in which they were suspended like little roses of gold—the sign, like the glow that still reveals on a wall the place of an effaced fresco [*comme la lueur qui révèle encore sur une muraille la place d'une fresque effacée*], of the difference between those parts of the tree that had been "in color" and those that had not—showed me that these petals were the very ones which before adorning the druggist's package had lent their fragrance to springtime evenings [*ces pétales étaient bien ceux qui avant de fleurir le sac de pharmacie avaient embaumé les soirs de printemps*]. That rosy candlelight was still their color, but half-extinguished and drowsy in this diminished life that now belonged to them [*à demi éteinte et assoupie dans cette vie diminuée qu'était la leur maintenant*], and that is like the twilight of flowers. Soon my aunt, who relished the taste of dead leaves or wilted flowers in the boiling infusion, was able to steep in it a petite madeleine [*Bientôt ma tante pouvait tremper dans l'infusion bouillante dont elle savourait le goût de feuille morte ou de fleur fanée une petite madeleine*], from which she would hold out to me a small piece when it had become soft enough. [1:51–52]

What becomes immediately evident to even the most cursory glance at this passage is the disproportionately small place allotted in it to the madeleine. Stranger still perhaps is the fact that the passage itself, a passage to which all the other passages in the *Recherche* can be said to point as to their origin and key, is not marked out by the narrator in any particular way. Rather, it is merely retold as just another of the links in a long chain of associated memories. But this chain, it should be remembered, was itself set off several pages earlier by the recognition of the capital importance of precisely *this* madeleine and *this* cup of linden tea: "And as soon as I had recognized the taste of the piece of madeleine steeped in linden tea and given me by my aunt . . . all of Combray and its surroundings . . . came out, town and gardens, of my cup of tea" (1:47–48). A scene in which the formalized sacrament of transubstantiation is itself transubstantiated into a material symbol that leaves its indelible mark on the subject of narration is of obvious exegetic interest: not only will it be paradigmatic for the functioning of all material symbols contained in the text, it should also help to reveal whatever aspects, if any, of its own marking operation must remain unremarked or inaccessible to the subject undergoing it.

The madeleine, it turns out, is itself just a cover-up for a deeper layer of symbolic functioning at work here. The identity of the two madeleines— and therefore of the narrator-personage as well—is not only a metaphorical structure that is tied to the metonymical links radiating outward from the center of Combray; it is also, and more importantly, an identity that is linked to and conditioned by a more fundamental metaphorical structure put into play by the linden tea. Genette's characterization of the Proustian "miracle" as a symmetrical and reciprocal alliance of metaphor and metonymy can now be completed by remarking that such alliances must themselves be grounded metaphorically. What is truly miraculous is that a metonymy could ever be said to relate to a metaphor by a "symmetry" and "reciprocity" that would itself be governed by an a priori metaphorical structure. Thus, the madeleine is not just the symbol that prefigures the narrator's future identity by a mere juxtaposition of the sensual and the spiritual—"the little scallop-shell of pastry, so richly sensual beneath its severe and devout folds" (1:47)—it is also a figure that recalls the underlying symbolic mechanism that conditions such a reciprocal relationship between inside and outside as a metaphorical relationship of symmetry and adequation. This mechanism, which is fully developed in the description of the linden tea, is first signalled by the casual reference to the infusion of herbal tea, which establishes the entire procedure as one of internalization and fusion. The French term, "infusion," moreover, is an especially fortunate choice here, since its semantic range covers the chemical process of maceration as well as the theological concept of a divine imparting of grace, uniting in this one word for interpenetration both poles of matter and spirit. What the passage attempts is nothing less than the reconciliation by an act of the mind of the transience of organic nature and the permanence of artistic representation; a reconciliation, it should be recalled, on which the entire *Recherche* depends for its own intelligibility.

Such a reconciliation can only be the result of overcoming a natural process of loss and increasing entropy. By themselves, those qualities of nature associated here with summer, blossoming flowers and trees, youth and objectivity in general, seem unable to preserve their freshness, much less their own identity, as when it is stated that "the leaves, having *lost* or changed their appearance, now resembled the most *disparate* of things." The passage of time, from summer to winter and concomitantly from outside to inside, is first perceived as nothing but a degradation, a constant wearing away that reduces even the metonymical links of natural experience to a state of dissolution and isolation, a rather unappetizing collection of dismembered flies, empty labels, and dispersed flowers. The human counterpart that immediately comes to mind for this insuperable process of loss is of course tante Léonie herself, a shriveled and wilted version of natural life, reduced to a state of skeletal rigidity, and trapped inside the colorless and stale tomb of her two adjoining rooms. But this extreme limit of decay also turns out to be closest to the reversed image of its renewal, and shortly afterward, aided by her library of medical and spiritual manuals as well as by "a statue of the Virgin and a bottle of Vichy-Célestins," tante Léonie becomes the explicit figure for a possible resurrection into eternal life.[14] The intervening step that prepares and allows for this reversal to take place is the transposition of nature, whose dominant figure in this passage is the linden blossom, into a text, "a book in which one is astonished to find the name of a personal acquaintance." It would be impossible to overestimate the importance here of recognizing this familiar name, since it is the possibility of maintaining some kind of identity throughout each of its stages that ensures that the process that leads from what can only be described retrospectively as natural perception to the now of textual representation can be effected without radical loss to the subject who has staked his entire future on it.

The strength of this claim to an unbreakable tie between nature and the book, between a natural process of organic decay and its recuperation in a

---

14. It is in the second paragraph immediately following the one quoted above that tante Léonie is described in the terms that made Gide, one of the readers of Proust's manuscript when it was submitted to (and rejected by) the NRF, doubt Proust's ability to use figurative language: "She held out to my lips her sad brow, colorless and tasteless, on which, at this hour of the morning, she had not yet arranged her artificial hair, and from underneath which the vertebrae stood out like a crown of thorns or the beads of a rosary . . ." (1:52).

textual act of understanding, is made to rest solely on the possibility of the blooming linden flowers being able to find their way essentially unaltered into tante Léonie's cup of tea. Such a claim is made explicit when the narrator speaks of reading and understanding the dried blossoms as though they were the written characters of a book: "And each new character being nothing but the metamorphosis of a previous character, in the little gray bulbs I recognized the green buds. . . ." The relay is helped to some extent by the fact that this one word, *caractère,* can be made to function simultaneously as an index of both natural "properties" and written "ciphers," exemplifying in an economical way the very "metamorphosis" that is being attempted here. At any rate, the persuasive value of the passage is beyond question when the narrator speaks of his satisfaction at realizing [*le plaisir de comprendre*] that what he has before his eyes are not mere substitutes or replacements [*non des doubles*], but rather the very same linden blossoms, though in a different, more permanent and useful form. Thus, and in spite of an occasional note of dissonance, introduced for example in the odd reference to an "effaced" fresco, there is a one-to-one correspondence established between nature and its transformation into a recognizable and intelligible text. This correspondence, it is important to notice, is itself modeled on a natural process, of what is called "aging" [*elles avaient vieilli*] in the passage in question. If frescos, books, names, and characters can redeem trees, streets, flowers, and petals, this is because, in essence, they can all be made to depend on the same, ultimately organic, laws of growth and aging. Effects of repetition or simulacrum are therefore downplayed to the advantage of natural cycles of change and progression, and if reference is made at one point to the ornamental technique of a painter, it is quickly reassimilated to the natural scheme of things when the narrator then assures us that this can be no "artificial concoction" (*préparation factice*).[15]

The consequences of this self-enclosed system of correspondences between the living blossoms and the dried blossoms is far-reaching, moreover, since it is capable of infinite expansion in time and space. Thus, and always according to a balanced economy of figural exchanges and reversals, it would finally be able to include even the "present" act of writing the text as well as its own reading, which is projected on to some hypothetical "future." It is

15. The genetic model that ensures the link between the growing plant and the writing of the text, which Proust inherits from Nerval, moreover, becomes even clearer at the end of the novel: "In this way my whole life . . . would and would not have been able to be summed up under this title: A vocation. It would not have been able to inasmuch as literature had played no role in my life. It would have been able to inasmuch as this life . . . formed an inner reservoir identical to the albumen that is stored in the ovule of plants and from which the ovule extracts the nourishment required to transform itself into a seed. . . . So too was my life in contact with that which would be accomplished through its maturation" (3:899).

also possible at this point to confirm Poulet's observation that the role of memory in the *Recherche*, which is present here in the figure of the "drying" or "preserving" of the objects of nature for future use by the mind, is proleptic as well as retrospective. The narrator is presently remembering an act of recognition that took place in his own past—the identity between the living blossoms and the dried ones—which act of memory simultaneously prefigures the future recognition—the identity between the experience of the boy and the writing of the man—that is only to take place after the novel will have been written and read. The writer who is "now" telling his story thematizes a remembered scene of preservation and assimilation that both looks back toward a "past" boyhood experience *as well as* forward to a "future" preservation and assimilation of the man by the writer who will be able to read this meaning out of his own text. It is as if the linden blossoms— insofar as they are both a past experience (already swallowed by the boy and remembered by the man) and a future figure (yet to be employed by the writer)—were themselves saying: "As often as you do these things, in memory of me shall you do them." The "me" in question, of course, is the identity of the boy, the man, and the writer, and it always remains to be confirmed yet once again in the "now" of reading by reassimilating their proximity in the textual memory. The proof of the system's efficacity is that each element can be substituted for any one of the others without entailing a loss of intelligibility for its overall functioning. Thus, the past can become present and future as easily and reversibly as the green bud and gray bulb become specular figures for the green boy and gray writer as well as for the green (naive) reader he once was, and the mature (gray) reader he will one day be.

The figural law of this system of transformations is the analogy of interiorization that is established between the textual layers comprising the blossoms, the boy, and the writer. Just as the blooming linden can be dried and brought inside the house without loss, so too can the dried linden be recognized by the boy as the past summer evenings he now consumes as an actual beverage. Finally, the novel would be the making available in linguistic "characters" of the whole internalizing process that leads to the ultimate identity of the self, which occurs as an act of reading its own writing. In this way, the text becomes the manifestation, on the outside as it were, of an inner experience of the writer remembering himself as a boy; a boy, moreover, who had brought the outside of nature inside his body by swallowing the tea that contained the preserved linden blossoms. Such spatial reversals of inside and outside that are then temporalized into a sequence are familiar to any reader of Proust. By not taking sufficient notice of the full extension of their symmetrical crossings, however, one runs the risk of mistaking what is in principle a dialectical and genetic structure, whose end point is already implicitly contained in its starting point, for a series of arbitrarily related fragments. Thus, for instance, Deleuze, whose principal concern is to isolate the realm of art from all the other activities described in the novel, is able to attribute to it a spontaneous freedom only by positing an "opposition" and a "break" between a "philosophical" and historical past and an autonomously "artistic" future toward which the *Recherche* is underway.[16] In order to do so, of course, he also has to establish a linear hierarchy of discrete moments between what he calls the signs of memory (the madeleine), of imagination (the steeples of Martinville), and of art (the *Recherche* itself). But for Proust, there would be no more opposition between such "material symbols" as there is between the linden blossoms and the residue of the textual leaves Marcel learns to read in the cup, and out of which he eventually writes his novel.

At any rate, the system of analogies set up between the change of seasons in nature and the transformation of the boy into the writer has become so resilient by the end of the passage that the narrator is able to cross back and forth between the antithetical regions of life and death, nature and art, outside and inside, without the least hesitation or obstruction. The long climactic sentence, which begins with the recognition that each new character of the linden is simply a natural metamorphosis of an earlier one, winds its way through the intricate comparison of the flowers' rosy hue with an old fresco and finally ends in the demonstration that these dead leaves were indeed the very linden petals that had once participated in the rites of spring. Now it is noteworthy that this proof is itself given in the form of an additional figure when it is further said that these were the same petals that, before *adorning* the druggist's package with a shape, had *graced* the springtime trees with a perfume. For by insisting that, whether dead or alive, these are lindens that share at least one essential property, this extra figure reinforces yet again the metaphorical link and possible substitutions between the blossoms and the dried petals. In this case, the property shared by blossoms and tea is that of a "flower" that, independently of its empirical status, is able to "bloom" as a rhetorical figure of embellishment.

This flower, which therefore graces Proust's text as well as both the druggist's package and the linden tree, is almost impossible to detect in translation. It is dependent for its full flowering on the idiomatic use of the French verbs *fleurir* and *embaumer* to mean "to enhance" or "to grace" by

---

16. See, especially, 131–34 of *Proust et les signes*. Deleuze's claim that in the art work an essence is so far "dematerialized" that it no longer "depends on the material conditions of incarnation [and] . . . no longer refers to anything outside its own formal structure" (200–01), contrasts sharply with Proust's insistence on a "material trace" that always retains a reference to what necessarily "precedes" its re-discovery in an actual work of art (3:879–81).

means of a shape or a scent. What this passage claims to demonstrate in French, then, is that, "ces pétales étaient bien ceux qui avant de *fleurir* le sac de pharmacie avaient *embaumé* les soirs de printemps." The loss of grace entailed in a more literal translation of the phrase is already a first indication of what is ultimately at stake in such figural crossings: "these petals were the very ones that before *flowering* the druggist's package had *embalmed* the evenings of spring," where the meaning aimed at in both cases is clearly "to embellish," thanks either to a beautiful appearance or fragrance. What is so effortlessly achieved in reading the French—the figural meaning of a visible or odoriferous "grace" that allows the dead and the living flowers to function in an analogous way and thus to be said to be "the same"—becomes much more difficult to swallow in the English translation. The meaning of the transitive verbs "to flower" and "to embalm" is anything but gracefully assimilated in our language, where it conjures up the antiseptic atmosphere of formaldehyde and mortuary preparations as much as the balmy freshness of spring promenades and aesthetic invention. This can be no mere accident in a passage that claims to reconcile the outside with the inside and the foreign with the domestic by means of an act of interiorization. That the restorative linden tea should produce a case of indigestion just by being translated into English may itself be a symptom of a further-reaching disorder.

For the English transposition of the linden blossoms merely brings out, in the same way that the delicate forest of stems highlights the suspension of rosy flowers, a figural play between foreground and background that was already, though more subtly, operative in the original. If the flowery glow of the original's figural meaning has a difficult time making it across to the English, it is equally true that what is underscored in its place by the translation is the literal spine of meaning that remains judiciously covered over by the idiomatic French. To some extent, then, it is the very coarseness of the translation's insistence on a literal process of "flowering" and "embalming" that serves to remind us that, beneath and beyond the shared attribute of the living and dried flowers' figural "gracefulness," what is essentially at issue here is precisely the possibility of substituting those living blossoms that literally "flowered" with these dead leaves that have been literally "embalmed." And it is only after we have been reminded of this that it becomes possible to notice that the passage has indeed already *switched* the literal attributes so that the preserved leaves are now said to be "flowering" inside the package while the "embalming" of the living blossoms has already occurred outside in nature. Such a switch, of course, is just one more example of the kind of chiasmic exchanges from nature to mind and to text out of which the entire passage is constructed. But in addition, this particular reversal from organic growth to artificial preservation is what is to be explained and demonstrated by the passage, rather than merely taken for granted in it. What is the status of a demonstration that uses what is to be proven as evidence for the truth of its argument?

In order to suggest an answer to this question it is necessary to look more closely at what happens in the passage when the attributes of nature and art are exchanged in the figure of the linden's flowering and embalming. First of all, the dried, dead flowers come back to life, they are resuscitated in a more permanent and accessible form than the fleeting blossoms. And unlike the natural flowers, the preserved blossoms can be articulated into a fixed pattern; constructed or "woven" (*tressé*) like a text, moreover, they can be measured according to fixed conventions and finally consumed by the hero. As such, the reflowering of the linden tea becomes the prefiguration of the narrator's own resurrection, which is prescribed at the end of the novel as the production of just such a textual work of art.[17] But as is also noted at the end, and in conformity with the symmetry required by the chiasmic exchange of properties, it is only possible for the dried leaves of the text to resuscitate when the living blossoms of nature are made to die, are sacrificed in their place. Quoting the scriptural text, "unless it die . . . ," the narrator will finally recognize the necessary connotations of death and burial that were all along implicit here in the verb "embaumer" (3:1044). Clearly, "embalming" is a metonymy for death, since it names a process or a ceremony that presupposes a death and a corpse upon which to operate. In the terms of the Christian allegory that is mimed throughout, the "madeleine" is also a proper name, Magdalene, and it has a specific role to perform in this sacrificial structure: "At that time, Mary Magdalene, Mary the mother of James, and Salome, brought spices, that they might go and *anoint* Jesus" (Mark, 16:1–2, emphasis added). The madeleine, then, names the faculty and the agent of the anointing or embalming it performs on the narrator's boyhood; through its homonymy with Mary Magdalene it smears the natural corpse of Combray with the perfumed oils of linden in order to preserve it ritually. The ceremony of the eucharist, which for the hero is the partaking of the linden-soaked madeleine, works as a prefiguration of the writer's resurrection as well as a commemoration of the boy's death and burial.

The coherence of this system of death and resurrection is guaranteed by the privileged status accorded in it to memory, conceived as the intermediate space between organic nature and subjective thought. This is the faculty by which nature's death is anointed and preserved while it awaits a resurrection in a future knowledge thanks first to its transfiguration into a work of

17. In the drafts, the trellis-work of the linden blossoms is compared to an antique lace, or "dentelle": "most of them . . . had turned the golden, almost russet color of an antique lace that is a bit worn [*fripée*] . . ." (*Etudes proustiennes*, 242). In the symbolist genealogy at work here, Nerval's lace metaphor must be torn by Mallarmé before it can find its afterlife in Proust.

art. Proust could not be clearer on this point when he has the narrator ask: "So then, wasn't the recreation by the memory of impressions that would later have to be elaborated, illuminated, and transformed into intellectual equivalents [*approfondir, éclairer, transformer en équivalents d'intelligence*], one of the conditions, in fact, the very essence of the work of art as I had just conceived it?" (3:1044). As the condition and essence of what Proust describes here as an "art of thought," this kind of memory belongs primordially and exclusively to the kind of subject it allows to come into being. That is why, not only in Proust but in the entire tradition to which his text constantly makes reference, the preservation effected by memory is always figured as a ceremony or a ritual, a participation by the human subject in the death (of natural experience) that is thereby preserved in a material impression. This, of course, will account for the crucial distinction made in the faculty of memory, which Proust complicates by attaching the paradoxical and potentially misleading epithets, between *mémoire involontaire*, which presupposes the full engagement of the subject in the sacrificial ritual of preservation, and *mémoire volontaire*, which is disengaged, disinterested, and formalistic memory.[18]

Like the readability of the proper name that guarantees the truth of a book, moreover, the ritual of *mémoire involontaire* must affix the material trace of what, in the linden tea episode, is called the "thousand useless details" that mark a given event as actually being "real" for the subject who thereby registers it as his own. As such, the mark is also a kind of signature, and it belongs to a "me" in whose memory the dead past is promised its future resurrection through the work of writing it out: for instance, through the second coming, as text, of Christ, Madeleine, or Marcel. Near the end of the *Recherche*, the narrator will insist that it is only thanks to the "somewhat aberrant particularity" that shapes the author's own paraph or signature that the truth of an individual's thought can become universally valid and available. This is so because the reader of such a signature is nothing other than his very own author: "Actually, each reader, when he reads, is his very own reader. . . . The recognition that the reader makes, in himself, of what the book says is the proof of its truth, and vice versa" (3:910,

18. In this sense, for Proust there are two kinds of reality, of self, of memory, of experience; one that is substantial and remains to be uncovered, the other a superficial and false, one could say ideological, version of the first. Insofar as the *mémoire volontaire* does not take the implication of the self in the operations of memory seriously enough, it is like the merely "possible" truths of abstract intelligence, only that it is oriented toward some hypothetical past rather than a hypothetical present or future: "Of course, it is possible to extend the spectacles of the *mémoire volontaire*, which no more engage the fibers of our very selves than would leafing through a book of picture images . . ." (3:873). The richest, though by no means simplest, discussion of this wobbly distinction occurs, interestingly enough, in Benjamin's essay on Baudelaire, "On Some Motifs in Baudelaire," *Illuminations*, trans. Harry Zohn (New York, Schocken Books, 1969), 157–63.

911). Books always say the same thing, then, and this is the survival, beyond the death of all natural experience, of the proper name: "a book is an enormous cemetery," Proust has his narrator say at one point, and learning how to read amounts to recognizing in it the construction of a monument to one's own name (3:903, 904).[19]

We are led back by the logic of this conclusion to the passage involving the hero's infusion of the madeleine and linden tea, since that is where the mechanics of the preservative power of the *mémoire involontaire* are fully worked out. As the place where an initial recounting in *Combray 1* of the memory of a material impression made during the subject's childhood (1:47–48) is then recomposed in *Combray 2* into a much more elaborate scenario (1:51–52), this passage can legitimately be taken as a model for the work of art that is called for by the writer at the end of the text. As such, it is itself an "elaboration, illumination, and transformation in intellectual equivalents" of the way involuntary memory functions as the unconditional principle of any art of thinking. It is, in strict accordance with Proust's own description, then, an allegory of memory, and therefore it must contain within itself all the elements necessary for the passage from experience to thought as well as their possible recombinations in the ultimate construction of the *Recherche*. We have already examined how this allegory works as a process of continuous internalization that moves from the flowering and death of nature to the preservative embalming of memory upon which depends any further flowering of textual reproduction and recognition. The only element in this functioning of memory that remains to be located and accounted for is that of the human agent who must at every stage underwrite and sign his participation in the sacrifice of nature.

For in order to guarantee that the art of thought that resuscitates on the far side of natural experience can be understood as a thoroughly human work, rather than an unheard-of species of monster, the subject of memory that initiates it must indeed be recognizable as "une personne de connaissance," a *personal* acquaintance. Such accounting hardly seems necessary, moreover, since the overwhelming presence in the scene of ritual ingestion of the boy himself, as well as of tante Léonie and the helping hand of the druggist-artist, should more than suffice as the gage of human participation here. Nonetheless, the premature and unexplained figural crossing of the attributes of life and death that can be traced back to the chiasmic substitution of the lindens' "flowering" for their "embalming," which, in defiance of

19. "In fact, if it is often said that his loves and losses have benefitted the poet, have helped him to build his *oeuvre*, if strangers who would least of all have suspected it . . . have each contributed a stone toward the erection of the monument they will never see, then it remains to be considered just how the writer's life does not end with this *oeuvre* . . ." (904).

a logic of cause and effect, occurs just before the proof concerning the possible relation of identity in life and death is concluded, should alert us once again to a potential complication in completing the trajectory memory assigns itself. For what kind of (rhetorical) trick would it be to switch "life" for "death" *before* these terms have been allowed to acquire their full ontological significance for the human subject that is to be defined solely in relation to them? How would it then be possible to resuscitate what has never actually died? Or conversely, what could it mean to kill something that has never actually lived?

These are questions that remind us that what is at stake in reading Proust is the possibility of establishing and maintaining a genealogy, though they do so in such a way that it now becomes difficult to avoid the interference in the discussion of a palpably ethical tonality. At what point can it be said that this became inevitable and not just a mere importation from outside the text? Certainly the intertextual reference in the *Recherche* to the figural pattern of the eucharist can never be completely isolated from the context of violence that necessarily surrounds the sacrificial death commemorated in it. The crown of thorns to which tante Léonie's skull is compared thus makes her into a prefiguration not only of an eventual resurrection, but also of those other calvaries for which the narrator will later feel himself personally responsible, in particular the sufferings of his mother and grandmother. One even begins to suspect that the analogy he will make between a book and "an enormous cemetery" may possibly have been dictated by similar feelings of guilt at having failed himself to live up to ethical responsibilities involving the welfare of others. In themselves, however— and no matter what the extent of the individual's turpitude, which in this case, and for the purposes of the story, seems to have been somewhat exaggerated—such feelings of personal guilt would not be able to account for the more radical question that asks about establishing the difference between life and death in the first place. And this question becomes unavoidable from the moment Proust's text uses nature, the natural cycle of the seasons and the organic process of the seed's maturation, as an allegorical figure for the embalming and preserving operations of the *mémoire involontaire*. Which makes it, from the very beginning, an ethical question, or rather, *the* ethical question: what constitutes "life," and "who" (or what) can determine the circumstances under which this process may be (rightly) interrupted?

For the allegory of memory is also a story about how the natural development of life, the growth of a seed, is interrupted and brought to a halt before it can complete itself. As a consequence, it is an allegory of what can thus be called "abortion," and it also includes the ethical dimension contained by this term. In order to make the linden tea in this text, nature must be "preserved," but in order to be preserved, the natural process of maturation must be interrupted short of its end point: "in the little gray bulbs I recognized the green buds that had not come to term. . . ."[20] Now it is at this point that the status of the signature, of the assurance of a "personal acquaintance" or *human* agent who would be recognizable as such throughout the process—which is none other than the sacrificial taking of natural life in order to turn it into an allegorical language signifying something else, something higher because more "elaborated and illuminated . . . *true* life"—becomes absolutely crucial. This is because it is one thing for someone to use nature in this way, to "nip it in the bud" and nourish one's own subjectivity with it cognitively and aesthetically, (physiologically as well). The (ethical) problem begins only when a question arises with respect to the line that *must* be drawn between the life that is said to be merely "natural" and the one that is determined as being, more or less, "human." In the same way, to say that the allegory of memory is also an allegory of "abortion" is, at least in principle, a rather innocent figure: it becomes (ethically) problematic only when, as in Proust, a question arises with respect to an understanding of the status—human or nonhuman—of the "buds" and "flowers" referred to within the allegory and that are cut down before they are allowed to come to term. The question of what is human, the ethical question, has brought us back to the question of the figure, or of what is rhetorical, that first disclosed it as such. This is what Paul de Man means when he says that ethicity is the referential version of a linguistic predicament; that is, ethicity is the ineluctable pressure to decide between literal and figural meaning when the referent at stake is the line dividing "human" from "nonhuman" as well as the concomitant value system of "right" and "wrong."[21] In the passage in Proust we have been dealing with, the interference of the ethical values of right and wrong with the cognitive determination of the rhetorical status of "bud" and "flower" would become truly problematic—and simultaneously imperative—were the line between human and nonhuman (in this case, the budding flowers) somehow to be crossed. Is there in fact a point in this text

20. The insistance on an interruption of the organic process at every point short of "completion" is even clearer in the drafts of this passage, where the anthropomorphic reference is not elided: "With very little effort one could recognize in a little yellow shell a bud that was going to open when the plant had died, in an anemone-red capsule a fruit that had not come to maturity, this bouquet of little bulbs that dreamily lays its heads one against the other, *like the heads of tender children*, are the seeds that did not come to maturity . . ." *Etudes proustiennes*, 245, emphasis added.

21. See, "Allegory (Julie)," in 206. See, also, "The Epistemology of Metaphor," in *On Metaphor*, ed. Sheldon Sacks (Chicago, University of Chicago Press, 1978, 1979): "One now sees that the figure is not only ornemental and aesthetic but powerfully coercive since it generates, for example, the ethical pressure of such questions as 'to kill or not to kill.'" In this case, de Man's formulation of the problem is derived from Locke, where the specificity of the example is "the predicament (to kill or not to kill the monstrous birth)" that can appear either as a "logical argument" or an "ethical issue" (17–18). For a slightly

where it becomes impossible to distinguish the behavior of the (nonhuman) flowers from that of the human subjects?

There are indications outside the passage itself that this may indeed be the case. It becomes rather unsettling, for example, to place the linden blossom episode side by side with the final "illumination" of what constitutes, in Le Temps retrouvé, the narrator's "vocation" as writer: "Thus my whole life . . . the memories of its sorrows and its joys, formed an inner reservoir identical to the albumen that is stored in the ovule of plants and from which the ovule extracts the nourishment required to transform itself into a seed. And this at a time when no one knows that the plant's embryo is developing as the locus of chemical and respiratory phenomena that are no less active for their remaining secret. So too was my life in contact with that which would be accomplished through its maturation" (3:899). For one thing, reading the two passages together reconfirms the complex spatiotemporal structure of memory: it is an interiorizing process that evolves through the novel, absorbing along the way the physiological functions of nourishment, fertilization, and even reproduction. Memory, in this novel, is an internalization powerful enough to link the acts of ingestion and generation in an eroticized phantasm whose extreme form would be cannibalism; it swallows the entire world and then tries to reproduce itself from out of its own stomach. Yet even here, where the writer's interpersonal relations are seen retrospectively as so many opportunities to reproduce himself from the fecondating traces left on the imprinted surface of his memory, the critical distinction between human and botanical (or animal) forms of life does not appear to be seriously threatened. As long as the writer, *as* human, remains the unquestioned "ground" for the metaphor, the "vehicle" of the plant's (or animal's) functioning can itself be assimilated into a figural balance that is achieved between two fully constituted and separate entities. More troublesome, from this point of view, is the fact that the late passage on the writer's vocation must presuppose the accomplishment of its own future, as a written text, on the basis of, or by analogy to, a prior knowledge of how the "natural" maturation of the plant works. But it is precisely this natural process of maturation that is categorically denied to the (linden) blossoms in the earlier passage. This occurs by way of a disruption of organic development, a premature intervention into the natural process without which the preservative powers of memory would be inconceivable. We seem to end up with the same kind of circular reasoning operating between the beginning and end of the novel that we already found within the space of a single

---

different, more extended and original reading of this gesture toward ethicity in de Man, see Werner Hamacher's "LECTIO: de Man's Imperative," in *Reading de Man Reading*, ed. Lindsay Waters and Wlad Godzich (Minneapolis, University of Minnesota Press, 1989), especially 183–87.

sentence in the earlier switch between the "flowering" and the "embalming" of linden blossoms. The proof of the analogy between the genesis of a plant and that of a writer cannot be made by presupposing the analogy as its own evidence, no matter how far the "proof" is extended textually.

There is a slight difference to be remarked here, however, since between the two passages, and thus between the beginning and end of the novel, the orientation of the power of memory has shifted subtly from a perspective on what actually has occurred in the past to what, as a result, *can* happen in the future. Where the earlier passage insists that the preserved tea petals are the very same as the blossoms that *once* began to flower, the later passage claims that the transposition of the writer's "life" into his "text" thanks to memory *will be* like the "maturation" of the plant's seed. We cannot rule out the possibility that the later analogy, which makes explicit the relation between the budding plant and the writer, and which is only hinted at in the earlier episode, is saying something far more complicated and less easy to assimilate than a casual reading would suggest. For there is no a priori reason to suppose that the concluding passage on the writer's vocation is in any way blind (or deaf) to what has already been said in the earlier section on the writer's apprenticeship. By claiming that the role to be played by memory in the writer's future is to be understood by analogy to the seed's maturation, which the text itself has already structured as a radical disruption of the process of organic development, the later passage may simply be reminding us that, until we have allowed this "abortion" to redetermine whatever is meant by "nature," "seed," "maturation," and even the concept of "future" itself, we have not yet sufficiently read the earlier version, which could not even be said to be "earlier" until it will have been read. What if this text were writing about the possibility of a kind of future that could only take place once we moved beyond the interruption of the natural order it has itself already produced? As such, the future would be the least natural event imaginable, and it would remain before "us" only as a secret possibility, requiring a kind of time and a kind of embryo different from anything "we" now know: "a time when no one knows that the plant's embryo is developing as the site of secret respiratory and chemical phenomena that are no less active for their remaining secret." And since, only a few pages after describing his own vocation in these terms, the narrator also appeals to a genealogical line that would include Nerval and Baudelaire, this reminder about what remains to be read would apply equally well to their texts.[22] "What remains

---

22. "One of the chef-d'oeuvres of French literature, Gérard de Nerval's *Sylvie* . . . has about it the same kind of feel as the taste of madeleine. . . . And in Baudelaire, of course, these reminiscences, which are even more numerous, are obviously less fortuitous, and as a result, decisive in my opinion. . . . So I would try to remind myself of those pieces by Baudelaire whose basis was the transposition of such a feeling, in order finally to get myself back into a filiation as noble as that one . . ." (3:919–20).

to be read," such would be the formula for what, still in embryo, could only occur or be produced in this text beyond the interruption of the (natural) plant's embryo and all that it conditions, including the concept of "abortion" itself. If there is still to be a history that could contain this genealogy—comprised at the very least of Nerval, Baudelaire, Proust, and by implication Mallarmé—it would be one that could be given only as a *future:* history would be the as-yet-to-be-accomplished "maturation" of what has already taken place in these writers as a textual "abortion."[23]

The implications of this conclusion for a reading of the episode of the linden blossoms are considerable, both from a rhetorical and an ethical point of view. First of all, it has the effect of making us responsible for this textual abortion, though we should not assume too quickly that such responsibility can be adequately understood, measured, or prescribed in the subjective or intersubjective terms in which responsibility is by tradition assessed. For by far the most curious thing about the linden blossoms in Proust is that their organic development is not checked or aborted by the intervention of a human subject, who could then be expected, as a person, to accept or pass along the responsibility for the interruption of natural development, though this responsibility is nonetheless real. It is rather nature her or itself that functions as the instance of intervention in its own process of natural growth. Which is also to say that nature is not primarily natural in this text. The burden of the reading would be to determine with as much precision as possible just how it is that what seems like nature can be the source of unnatural acts, and first of all, the inhuman agent of its own death sentence. The petals that announce the flowering of spring, cut it off in the same breath and, through a ritualized abortion, preserve it for future use in a state of suspended animation. One can hardly believe it, but where the

23. "Abortion," of course, is a political issue of some urgency as well as a "mere" rhetorical structure deployed and interrogated in Proust's text, although it may be a naive (or strategic) gesture to pretend that urgent political issues can simply be considered, much less decided, without reference to or interference from rhetorical structures. Barbara Johnson has written a thoughtful and provocative essay on the complex relation between figurative language and the question of abortion. Her remarks on the necessity of considering the gender of the mother whenever the question of "abortion" is raised would have a wholly salutary influence with respect to a reading of Proust's text. Instead of asking if Albertine is really a male (Albert) portrayed as a female figur(ine,) it would be more to the point to ask how Proust's signature can be read as that of a feminine operation of writing. Obviously, this should not be taken to mean that there is no (empirical) difference between a male and a female (writer), nor that there is nothing absolutely irreducible in the significance an "abortion" can have for a "woman." Rather, the displacement of the mother in Proust's text suggests that a mere (paternal or patriarchal) reduction of the metaphorical and conceptual to the empirical (or vice versa) would still remain inadequate to account for the "truth" of history, that is to say, the mater(n)iality of what actually occurs in history as abortion. See "Apostrophe, Animation, and Abortion," as well as "Mallarmé as Mother," in *A World of Difference* (Baltimore, The Johns Hopkins University Press, 1987).

symmetry of the figural crossing between art and nature would require only that the springtime blossoms be embalmed by the druggist before they are allowed to flower inside his package, reinforcing in this way the presence of the human subject throughout the internalizing process of memory, the text actually demonstrates, beyond any doubt, that "these petals were the very ones that had embalmed the evenings of spring before they flourished in the druggist's package."[24]

And whether we like it or not, it is the logic of the text that is consistent here, since according to Proust, true "life" can only be *recognized* or *re*-discovered by the subject who must stumble across it as if by accident, much like the narrator who loses his balance in the courtyard of the Guermantes. What makes the recognition possible is memory, but memory, as the intersection of the two disproportionate surfaces that come together in a material trace, is itself nothing but this "moment" of stumbling preserved in Proust's text when nature is no longer natural and the subject is not yet human.[25] This means, of course, that *la mémoire involontaire* is not involuntary because, unlike *mémoire volontaire*, it is not controlled by the subject; it is involuntary because in it the subject in control is not itself human, or dependent for its power on human intentions or desires. As such, as the possibility, that is, of turning away (from a nature that is no longer there naturally) and of turning toward (a human subject that cannot yet be present to itself as such) *mémoire involontaire* can only be language considered as pure figuration: the possibility. Memory, as this power of turning in language, is thus the unnatural and inhuman album(en) where an abortion of

24. Proust's sentence, "ces pétales étaient bien ceux qui avant de fleurir le sac de pharmacie avaient embaumé les soirs de printemps," must have seemed so incomprehensibly unnatural to his English translator, C. K. Scott Moncrieff, that it was corrected, even at the cost of its grammar, to something like, "ces pétales étaient bien ceux qui, avant de fleurir, le sac de pharmacie avait embaumés les soirs de printemps," since his translation reads, "these were the petals which, before their flowering time, the chemist's package had embalmed on warm evenings of spring." *Swann's Way*, trans. C. K. Scott Moncrieff, (New York, The Modern Library, 1928), 63. Petals can "embalm" natural flowering with a scent only because they can "embalm" natural flowering as a preserved and unnatural material trace: the condition of possibility in both instances is a law of figural supplementarity. There is nothing natural in making the scent of flowers function as an embellishment that can be added to or subtracted from natural growth.

25. The episode in question involves the narrator's loss of equilibrium when his foot seesaws between two unequally positioned paving stones (3:866–67), itself a figure taken from empirical experience to illustrate Proust's definition of "reality": "What we call reality is a certain relation between those sensations and these memories [of vague hopes and projects]" (3:889). As the locus of the passage from a mere jumble of sense perceptions to a system of organized relations and intentions, the material traces of memory are like the arbitrary concatenation, in a semiosis, of the two heterogeneous "surfaces" of perception and signification. The gap between the two paving stones, because it is represented as the homogeneous space of empirical experience, is therefore an inadequate or hobbled symbol for Proust's concept of the hobbling symbol.

nature is written down and stored as the embryonic promise of a human subject that is not yet there.

To be responsible for memory's abortion, then, cannot be taken to mean a simple return to a concept of human or natural responsibility. This would be to refuse to be reminded of the necessarily rhetorical dimension in ethics, in the mistaken belief that we already understood fully the difference between nature and culture, and thus what it means to be human. Rather, as a responsibility oriented toward the future "maturation" of a textual abortion in which both nature and culture and all their distinctions founder, it would be one that allowed this unnatural and inhuman element in the memory to be written into history as what "survives" them.[26] It would mean to produce genuine history precisely by "elaborating, illuminating, and transforming" this inhuman and unnatural element in which the language of memory outlives the impossibility of getting back to nature and getting on with being human. And this would be the truly critical aspect of Proust's text as well. For by reminding us about the necessarily linguistic structure of history, by reminding us that the turn to history must no longer be conceived on a natural model but that it cannot yet be founded on a purely human one either, Proust's text also helps to neutralize the place of usurped authority that is occupied whenever the representatives of so-called natural and human or moral law do not take into account the inhuman and unnatural element of which they too partake. History, as the future of this memory, must be written, can only occur as writing, but such writing becomes illegitimate from the moment it is read as a simple prescription whose coherence could be given or retrieved by recourse to natural or human and therefore transcendental principles. In Proust, the coherence of the prescriptive rule is torn irremediably when the blossoms interrupt their own flowering. In doing so they abort their natural development by inscribing it within a system of notation whose rhetorical principles remain in part irreducible to either organic or human models. Ethics, or ethicity, can only begin to occur historically when, in addition to filling mere (human) prescriptions, it goes on to register the marks of this inhuman tear. It is by a prodigality in exceeding the measure, by remembering the "thousand useless details" left by the inscription of the deadly blossoms that are neither wholly natural nor yet artificial, that the pharmacist in Proust shows how to be a writer of history as well as a reader of prescriptions, and, beyond all the dismembered flies and flowers, how to make room in a text for the future of a blank album.

---

26. In the drafts for this passage, Proust had considered having his description of the legible "characters" left in the preserved blossoms culminate in, "that burst of flowers that detaches them from all the rest, painted in gold with the thread of their stamens as though on a chasuble, that is survival . . ." (*Etudes proustiennes*, 245). The kind of survival at issue in Proust would not be incompatible with what Jacques Derrida has written about "living on." See, "Survivre," in *Parages* (Paris, Editions Galilée, 1986).

IV.

CATHY CARUTH

Unclaimed Experience:
Trauma and the Possibility of History

> . . . it took the war to teach it, that you were as responsible for
> everything you saw as you were for everything you did. The problem
> was that you didn't always know what you were seeing until later,
> maybe years later, that a lot of it never made it in at all, it just stayed
> stored there in your eyes.
>
> —Michael Herr, *Dispatches*

Recent literary criticism has shown an increasing concern that the epistemological problems raised by poststructuralist criticism, in particular
deconstruction, necessarily lead to political and ethical paralysis. The possibility that reference is indirect, and that consequently we may not have
direct access to others', or even our own, histories, seems to imply the
impossibility of any access to other cultures, and hence of any means of
making political or ethical judgments.[1] To such an argument I would like to
contrast a phenomenon arising not only in the reading of literary or philosophical texts, but emerging most prominently within the wider historical
and political realms, that is, the peculiar and paradoxical experience of
trauma. In its most general definition, trauma describes an overwhelming
experience of sudden, or catastrophic events, in which the response to the
event occurs in the often delayed, and uncontrolled repetitive occurrence of
hallucinations and other intrusive phenomena.[2] The experience of the sol-
dier faced with sudden and massive death around him, for example, who
suffers this sight in a numbed state, only to relive it later on in repeated
nightmares, is a central and recurring image of trauma in our century. As a
consequence of the increasing occurrence of such perplexing war experiences and other catastrophic responses during the last twenty years, physi-

1. For a recent expression of this opinion, see S. P. Mohanty, "Us and Them," in *The
Yale Journal of Criticism* 2/2 (Spring 1989).
2. There is no firm definition for trauma, which has been given various descriptions at
various times and under different names. For a good discussion of the history of the notion
and for recent attempts to define it, see *Trauma and Its Wake*, Volumes 1 and 2, ed. Charles
R. Figley (New York: Brunner-Mazel, 1985 and 1986).

YFS 79, *Literature and the Ethical Question*, ed. Claire Nouvet, © 1991 by Yale
University.

cians and psychiatrists have begun to reshape their thinking about physical and mental experience, including most recently the responses to a wide variety of experiences (including rape, child abuse, auto and industrial accidents, and so on) which are now often understood in terms of the effects of "post-traumatic stress disorder." I would propose that it is here, in the equally widespread and bewildering encounter with trauma—both in its occurrence, and in the attempt to understand it—that we can begin to recognize the possibility of a history which is no longer straightforwardly referential (that is, no longer based on simple models of experience and reference). Through the notion of trauma, I will argue, we can understand that a rethinking of reference is not aimed at eliminating history, but at resituating it in our understanding, that is, of precisely permitting *history* to arise where *immediate understanding* may not.

The question of history is raised most urgently in one of the first works of trauma in this century, Sigmund Freud's history of the Jews entitled *Moses and Monotheism*. Because of its seeming fictionalization of the Jewish past, this work has raised ongoing questions about its historical and political status; yet its confrontation with trauma seems, nonetheless, to be deeply tied to our own historical realities. I have chosen this text as a focus of analysis, therefore, because I believe it can help us understand our own catastrophic era, as well as the difficulties of writing a history from within it. I will suggest that it is in the notion of history which Freud offers in this work, as well as in the way his writing itself confronts historical events, that we may need to rethink the possibility of history, as well as our ethical and political relation to it.

The entanglement of Freud's *Moses and Monotheism* with its own urgent historical context is evident in a letter written to Arnold Zweig in 1934, while Freud is working on the book, and while Nazi persecutions of the Jews are progressing at rapid speed. Freud says:

> Faced with the new persecutions, one asks oneself again how the Jews have come to be what they are and why they have attracted this undying hatred. I soon discovered the formula: Moses created the Jews.[3]

The project of *Moses and Monotheism* is clearly linked, in these lines, to the attempt to explain the Nazi persecution of the Jews. But this can apparently be done, according to Freud, only through reference to a past, and in particular to the past represented by Moses. By placing the weight of his history on the naming of Moses, moreover, the liberator of the Hebrews who led them

3. Letter of 30 May 1934. Quoted from *The Letters of Sigmund Freud and Arnold Zweig*, ed. Ernst L. Freud (New York: Harcourt Brace Jovanovich, 1970).

out of Egypt, Freud implicitly and paradoxically connects the explanation of the Jews' persecution to their very liberation, the return from captivity to freedom. In the centrality of Moses thus lies the centrality of a return: the return of the Hebrews to Canaan, where they had lived prior to their settlement, and bondage, in Egypt. *Moses and Monotheism*'s most direct reference to, and explanation of, its present historical context will consist in Freud's new understanding of the story of captivity, or exile, and return.[4]

The notion of Jewish history, as a history of return, might seem unsurprising in the perspective of a psychoanalyst, whose works repeatedly focus on the necessity of various kinds of return—on the return to origins in memory, and on the "return of the repressed." But in the description of his discovery, in the concise little formula jotted down for Zweig, "Moses created the Jews," Freud suggests that the history of the Jews surpasses any simple notion of return. For if Moses indeed "created" the Jews,[5] in his act of liberation—if the exodus from Egypt, that is, transforms the history of the *Hebrews*, who had previously lived in Canaan, into the history of the *Jews*, who become a true nation only in their act of leaving captivity—then the moment of beginning, the exodus from Egypt, is no longer simply a return, but is rather, more truly, a departure. The question with which Freud frames his text, and which will explain both the Jews' historical situation and his own participation, as a Jewish writer, within it, is thus: in what way is the history of a culture, and its relation to a politics, inextricably bound up with the notion of departure?[6]

Freud's surprising account of Jewish history can be understood, indeed, as a reinterpretation of the nature, as well as the significance, of the Hebrews' return from captivity. In the biblical account, Moses was one of the captive Hebrews who eventually arose as their leader and led them out of Egypt back to Canaan. Freud, on the other hand, announces at the beginning of his account that Moses, though liberator of the Hebrew people, was not in fact himself a Hebrew, but an Egyptian, a fervent follower of an Egyptian

4. While the term "exile," used in the context of Jewish history, refers, strictly speaking, to the exile in Babylon, the Egyptian captivity was considered paradigmatic of this later event. Thus *The Encyclopedia of Judaism* says, under the heading "exile," that "it is this 'prenatal' Egyptian servitude which becomes the paradigm of *Galut* [exile] in the rabbinic mind." See Geoffrey Wigoder, *The Encyclopedia of Judaism* (New York: Macmillan, 1989).

5. "Created" is an accurate translation of the German text, which says "hat . . . geschaffen."

6. Among the more interesting attempts to grapple with the political dimension of *Moses and Monotheism* are Jean-Joseph Goux, "Freud et la structure religieuse du nazisme," in his *Les Iconoclastes* (Paris: Seuil, 1978); and Philippe Lacoue-Labarthe et Jean-Luc Nancy, "Le Peuple juif ne rêve pas," and Jean-Pierre Winter, "Psychanalyse de l'antisémitisme," both in *La Psychanalyse est-elle une histoire juive?*, ed. by Adelie et Jean-Jacques Rassiel (Paris: Seuil, 1981).

pharaoh and his sun-centered monotheism. After the pharaoh's murder, according to Freud, Moses became a leader of the Hebrews and brought them out of Egypt in order to preserve the waning monotheistic religion. Freud thus begins his story by changing the very reason for the return: it is no longer primarily the preservation of Hebrew freedom, but of the mono- theistic god; that is, it is not so much the return to a freedom of the past, as a departure into a newly established future—the future of monotheism.[7] In this rethinking of Jewish beginnings, then, the future is no longer continu- ous with the past, but is united with it through a profound discontinuity. The exodus from Egypt, which shapes the meaning of the Jewish past, is a departure that is both a radical break and the establishment of a history.

The second part of Freud's account extends, and redoubles, this rethink- ing of the return. For after the Egyptian Moses led the Hebrews from Egypt, Freud claims, they murdered him in a rebellion; repressed the deed; and in the passing of two generations, assimilated his god to a volcano god named Yahweh, and assimilated the liberating acts of Moses to the acts of another man, the priest of Yahweh (also named Moses), who was separated from the first in time and place. The most significant moment in Jewish history is thus, according to Freud, not the literal return to freedom, but the repression of a murder and its effects:

> The god Jahve attained undeserved honour when . . . Moses' deed of lib- eration was put down to his account; but he had to pay for this usurpation. The shadow of the god whose place he had taken became stronger than himself; at the end of the historical development there arose beyond his being that of the forgotten Mosaic god. None can doubt that it was only the idea of this other god that enabled the people of Israel to surmount all their hardships and to survive until our time. [62; 50–51][8]

If the return to freedom is the literal starting point of the history of the Jews, what constitutes the essence of their history is the repression, and return, of the deeds of Moses. The nature of literal return is thus displaced by the nature of another kind of reappearance:

> To the well-known duality of [Jewish] history . . . we add two new ones: the founding of two new religions, the first one ousted by the second and

7. It is interesting to note that this future can also be thought of in terms of the divine offer of a "promised land," and thus can be understood in terms of the future-oriented temporality of the promise.

8. All quotations of Freud are taken from Sigmund Freud, *Moses and Monotheism*, translated by Katherine Jones (New York: Vintage Books, 1939). The first set of page numbers following quotations refer to this text. The second set of numbers refers to James Strachey's translation of *Moses and Monotheism* in the Standard Edition of the *Complete Psychological Works of Sigmund Freud*, edited by James Strachey, Volume 23 (London: The Hogarth Press, 1964).

yet reappearing victorious, two founders of religion, who are both called by the same name, Moses, and whose personalities we have to separate from each other. And these dualities are necessary consequences of the first: one section of the people passed through what may properly be termed a traumatic experience which the other was spared. [64–65; 52]

The captivity and return, while the beginning of the history of the Jews, is precisely available to them only through the experience of a trauma. It is the trauma, the forgetting (and return) of the deeds of Moses, that constitutes the link uniting the old with the new god, the people that leave Egypt, with the people that ultimately make up the nation of the Jews. Centering his story in the nature of the leaving, and returning, constituted by trauma, Freud resituates the very possibility of history in the nature of a traumatic departure. We might say, then, that the central question, by which Freud finally inquires into the relation between history and its political outcome, is: what does it mean, precisely, for history to be the history of a trauma?

For many readers, the significance of Freud's questioning of history—his displacement of the story of a liberating return, by the story of a trauma— has seemed to be a tacit denial of history. By replacing factual history with the curious dynamics of trauma, Freud would seem to have doubly denied the possibility of historical reference: first, by himself actually replacing historical fact with his own speculations; and secondly, by suggesting that historical memory, or Jewish historical memory at least, is always a matter of distortion, a filtering of the original event through the fictions of traumatic repression, which makes the event available at best indirectly. Indeed, when Freud goes on, later in his work, to compare the Hebrews' traumatic experience to the traumas of the Oedipal boy, repressing his desire for the mother through the threat of castration, this leads many readers to assume that the only possible referential truth contained in Freud's text can be its reference to his own unconscious life, a kind of self-referential history which many have read as the story of Freud's "unresolved father complex."[9] And this analysis has itself reinterpreted the figure of departure and return in a very straightforward fashion, as Freud's departure from his father, or his departure from Judaism. For many critics the cost of Freud's apparently

9. See Edwin R. Wallace, "The Psychodynamic Determinants of Moses and Monotheism, Psychiatry 40:(1977). There is a long history of psychoanalytic interpretations of Freud's writings on Moses. Among the more interesting include Marthe Robert, d'Oedipe à Moïse: Freud et la conscience juive (Paris: Calmann-Levy, 1974), appearing in English as From Oedipus to Moses: Freud's Jewish Identity, trans. Ralph Manheim (London: Routledge and Kegan Paul, 1977); Marie Balmary, Psychoanalyzing Psychoanalysis, trans. Ned Luckacher (Baltimore: The Johns Hopkins Press, 1982). A review and critique of the applied psychoanalytic tradition in this context is to be found in Yerushalmi, Psychoanalysis Terminable and Interminable: An Exploration of Moses and Monotheism, Lectures given at Yale University (Fall 1989), forthcoming.

making history unconscious, or of depriving history of its referential literality, is finally the fact that the text remains at best a predictable drama of Freud's unconscious, and moreover a drama which tells the story of political and cultural disengagement.[10]

When we attend closely however to Freud's own attempt to explain the trauma, we find a somewhat different understanding of what it means to leave and to return. While the analogy with the Oedipal individual constitutes much of his explanation, Freud opens this discussion with another example that is strangely unlikely as a comparison for a human history and yet resonates curiously with the particular history he has told. It is the example of an accident:

> It may happen that someone gets away, apparently unharmed, from the spot where he has suffered a shocking accident, for instance a train collision. In the course of the following weeks, however, he develops a series of grave psychical and motor symptoms, which can be ascribed only to his shock or whatever else happened at the time of the accident. He has developed a "traumatic neurosis." This appears quite incomprehensible and is therefore a novel fact. The time that elapsed between the accident and the first appearance of the symptoms is called the "incubation period," a transparent allusion to the pathology of infectious disease. As an afterthought, it must strike us that, in spite of the fundamental difference in the two cases, the problem of the traumatic neurosis and that of Jewish monotheism, there is a correspondence in one point. It is the feature which one might term *latency*. There are the best grounds for thinking that in the history of the Jewish religion there is a long period, after the breaking away from the Moses religion, during which no trace is to be found of the monotheistic idea . . . thus the solution of our problem is to be sought in a special psychological situation. [84; 67–68]

In the term "latency," the period during which the effects of the experience are not apparent, Freud seems to compare the accident to the successive movement in Jewish history from the event to its repression to its return. Yet what is truly striking about the accident victim's experience of the event, and what in fact constitutes the central enigma revealed by Freud's example,

10. There are of course a number of exceptions to this standard interpretation. Among them are the works by Goux, Lacoue-Labarthe and Nancy, Winter, and Yerushalmi, cited above, as well as Ritchie Robertson, "Freud's Testament: *Moses and Monotheism*," in *Freud in Exile*, edited by Edward Timms and Naomi Segal (New Haven: Yale University Press, 1988). Useful treatments of Freud and Judaism include Philip Rieff, *The Mind of the Moralist* (New York: Anchor, 1961), and Martin S. Bergmann, "Moses and the Evolution of Freud's Jewish Identity," *Israel Annals of Psychiatry and Related Disciplines*, 14 (March 1976). A useful bibliography can be found in Peter Gay, *Freud: A Life for Our Time* (New York: Doubleday, 1988). Gay's own discussion in this work of Freud's Jewish identity and generally of the writing of *Moses and Monotheism* is highly illuminating.

is not so much the period of forgetting that occurs after the accident, but rather the fact that the victim of the crash was never fully conscious during the accident itself: the person gets away, Freud says, "apparently un-harmed." The experience of trauma, the fact of latency, would thus seem to consist, not in the forgetting of a reality that can hence never be fully known; but in an inherent latency within the experience itself.[11] The historical power of the trauma is not just that the experience is repeated after its forgetting, but that it is only in and through its inherent forgetting that it is first experienced at all. And it is this inherent latency of the event that paradoxically explains the peculiar, temporal structure, the belatedness, of the Jews' historical experience: since the murder is not experienced as it occurs, it is fully evident only in connection with another place, and in another time. If return is displaced by trauma, then, this is significant in so far as its leaving—the space of unconsciousness—is paradoxically what precisely preserves the event in its literality. For history to be a history of trauma means that it is referential precisely to the extent that it is not fully perceived as it occurs; or to put it somewhat differently, that a history can be grasped only in the very inaccessibility of its occurrence.

The indirect referentiality of history is also, I would argue, at the core of Freud's understanding of the political shape of Jewish culture, in its repeated confrontation with antisemitism. For the murder of Moses, as Freud argues, is in fact a repetition of an earlier murder in the history of mankind, the murder of the primal father by his rebellious sons, which occurred in primeval history; and it is the unconscious repetition and acknowledgment of this fact that explains both Judaism and its Christian antagonists. Indeed, Freud says, when Paul interprets the death of Christ as the atonement for an original sin, he is belatedly and unconsciously remembering the murder of Moses which still, in the history of the Jews, remains buried in uncon-sciousness. In belatedly atoning, as sons, for the father's murder, Christians feel Oedipal rivalry with their Jewish older brothers, a lingering castration anxiety, brought out by Jewish circumcision, and finally a complaint that the Jews will not admit the guilt which the Christians, in their recognition of Christ's death, have admitted. By appearing only belatedly, then, the historical effect of trauma, in Freud's text, is ultimately its inscription of the Jews in a history always bound to the history of the Christians. The

11. It is also interesting that the two vehicles, coming together, seem to resemble the two men named "Moses" and the two peoples coming together, in a missing meeting, at Qades. Freud describes this event also as a kind of gap: "I think we are justified in separat-ing the two persons from each other and in assuming that the Egyptian Moses never was in Qades and had never heard the name of Jahve, whereas the Midianite Moses never set foot in Egypt and knew nothing of Aton. In order to make the two people into one, tradition or legend had to bring the Egyptian Moses to Midian; and we have seen that more than one explanation was given for it" (49; 41).

Hebrews' departure, that is, or their arrival as a Jewish nation, is also an arrival within a history no longer simply their own. It is therefore, I would like to suggest, precisely in the very constitutive function of latency, in history, that Freud discovers the indissoluble, political bond to other histories. To put it somewhat differently, we could say that the traumatic nature of history means that events are only historical to the extent that they implicate others. And it is thus that Jewish history has also been the suffering of others' trauma.[12]

The full impact of this notion of history can only be grasped, however, when we turn to the question of what it would mean, in this context, to consider Freud's own writing as a historical act. In the various prefaces which he appends to his work, Freud himself imposes this question upon us by drawing our attention to the history of the text's own writing and publication. The process of the actual writing of the book took place between 1934 and 1938, during the period of Freud's last years in Vienna, and his first year in London, to which he moved in June of 1938 because of Nazi persecution of his family and of psychoanalysis. The first two parts of the book, containing the history of Moses, were published before he left Austria, in 1937, while the third part, containing the more extensive analysis of religion in general, was withheld from publication until 1938, after Freud had moved to London. In the middle of this third part, Freud inserts what he calls a "Summary and Recapitulation" (or *Wiederholung*, literally "repetition"), in which he tells the story of his book in his own way:

> The following part of this essay [the second section of Part Three] cannot be sent forth into the world without lengthy explanations and apologies. For it is no other than a faithful, often literal repetition of the first part. . . . Why have I not avoided it? The answer to this question

12. It is important to note that Freud does not imply the necessity for any particular kind of persecution; that is, while he insists on what appears to be a kind of universality of trauma, he does not suggest that the response to trauma must necessarily be the mistreatment of the other. In fact, he distinguishes Christian hatred of the Jews from Nazi persecution, describing the former as determined by an Oedipal structure, while of the latter he says: "We must not forget that all the peoples who now excel in the practice of anti-Semitism became Christians only in relatively recent times, sometimes forced to it by bloody compulsion. One might say that they all are "badly christened"; under the thin veneer of Christianity they have remained what their ancestors were, barbarically polytheistic. They have not yet overcome their grudge against the new religion which was forced on them, and they have projected it on to the source from which Christianity came to them. . . . The hatred for Judaism is at bottom hatred for Christianity, and it is not surprising that in the German National Socialist revolution this close connection of the two monotheistic religions finds such clear expression in the hostile treatment of both" (117; 91–92). A brilliant exploration of the relation between Judaism and Christianity in five authors, which takes off from the question of return in the story of Abraham, can be found in Jill Robbins, *Prodigal Son and Elder Brother: Augustine, Petrarch, Kierkegaard, Kafka, Levinas* (University of Chicago Press, 1991).

is . . . rather hard to admit. I have not been able to efface the traces of the unusual way in which this book came to be written. In truth it has been written twice over. The first time was a few years ago in Vienna where I did not believe the possibility of publishing it. I decided to put it away, but it haunted me like an unlaid ghost, and I compromised by publishing two parts of the book. . . . Then in March 1938 came the unexpected German Invasion. It forced me to leave my home, but also freed me of the fear lest my publishing the book might cause psychoanalysis to be forbidden in a country where its practice was still allowed. No sooner had I arrived in England than I found the temptation of making my withheld knowledge accessible to the world irresistible. . . . I could not make up my mind to relinquish the two former contributions altogether, and that is how the compromise came about of adding unaltered a whole piece of the first version to the second, a device which has the disadvantage of extensive repetition. . . . [131–32; 103–04]

Reading this story Freud tells of his own work—of a history whose traces cannot be effaced, which haunts Freud like a ghost, and finally emerges in several publications involving extensive repetition—it is difficult not to recognize the story of the Hebrews—of Moses' murder, its effacement, and its unconscious repetition. The book itself, Freud seems to be telling us, is the site of a trauma; a trauma which in this case moreover appears to be historically marked by the events which, Freud says, divide the book into two halves: first, the infiltration of Nazism into Austria, causing Freud to withhold or repress the third part, and then the invasion of Austria by Germany, causing Freud to leave, and ultimately to bring the third part to light. The structure and history of the book, in its traumatic form of repression and repetitive reappearance, thus mark it as the very bearer of a historical truth that is itself involved in the political entanglement of Jews and their persecutors.

But significantly, in spite of the temptation to lend an immediate referential meaning to Freud's trauma in the German invasion and Nazi persecution, it is not, in fact, precisely the *direct reference* to the German invasion that can be said to locate the actual trauma in Freud's passage. For the invasion is characterized, not in terms of its attendant persecutions and threats, of which the Freud family did in fact have their share, but in terms of the somewhat different emphasis of a simple phrase: "it forced me to leave my home, but it also freed me . . ." [(sie) zwang mich, die Heimat zu verlassen, befreite mich aber . . .].[13] The trauma in Freud's text, is first of all a trauma of leaving, the trauma of *verlassen*. Indeed, it is this word which actually ties this "Summary and Recapitulation" itself to the traumatic

13. German quotations of *Moses and Monotheism* are taken from Sigmund Freud, *Studienausgabe* Band 9, Frankfort on Main: (1982).

structuring of the book, in its implicit referral to two earlier prefaces, appended to the beginning of Part III. These two prefaces, subtitled "Before March 1938" (while Freud was still in Vienna), and "In June 1938" (after Freud had resettled in London), describe, respectively, his reasons for not publishing the book, and his decision finally to let it come to light, announced as following in the second preface:

> The exceptionally great difficulties which have weighed on me during the composition of this essay dealing with Moses . . . are the reason why this third and final part comes to have two different prefaces which contradict—even cancel—each other. For in the short interval between the two prefaces the outer conditions of the author have radically changed. Formerly I lived under the protection of the Catholic church and feared that by publishing the essay I should lose that protection. . . . Then, suddenly, the German invasion. . . . In the certainty of persecution . . . I left [verliess ich], with many friends, the city which from early childhood, through seventy-eight years, had been a home to me. [69–70; 57]

The "interval between the prefaces" which Freud explicitly notes, and which is also the literal space between "Before March 1938" and "In June 1938," also marks, implicitly, the space of a trauma, a trauma not simply *denoted* by the words "German Invasion," but rather *borne* by the words "verliess Ich," "I left." Freud's writing preserves history precisely within this gap in his text; and within the words of his leaving, words which do not simply refer, but which, through their repetition in the later "Summary and Recapitulation," convey the impact of a history precisely as what *cannot be grasped* about leaving.

Indeed, in Freud's own theoretical explanation of trauma, in the example of the accident, it is, finally, *the act of leaving* which constitutes its central and enigmatic core:

> It may happen that someone gets away [literally, "leaves the site," "die Städte verlässt], apparently unharmed, from the spot where he has suffered a shocking accident, for instance a train collision.

The trauma of the accident, its very unconsciousness, is borne by an act of departure. It is a departure which, in the full force of its historicity, remains at the same time in some sense absolutely opaque, both to the one who leaves, and also to the theoretician, linked to the sufferer in his attempt to bring the experience to light. Yet at the same time, this very opacity generates the surprising force of a knowledge, for it is the accident, in German, *Unfall*, which reverberates in Freud's own theoretical insight drawn from the example, which is laced in the German with other forms of *fallen*, "to fall":

As an afterthought, it must strike us [es muss uns auffallen], that in spite of the fundamental difference between the two cases [Fälle], between the problem of traumatic neurosis and that of Judaic monotheism, there is a correspondence in one point, namely, in the character one might describe as *latency*. There are the best grounds for thinking that in the history of the Jewish religion there is a long period, after the breaking away [*Abfall*] from the Moses religion, during which no trace is to be found of the monotheistic idea. . . . [14]

Between the *Unfall*, the accident, and the "striking" of the insight, its *auffallen*, is the force of a fall, a falling which is transmitted precisely in the unconscious act of leaving. It is this *unconsciousness of leaving* which bears the impact of history. And it is likewise first of all in the unconsciousness of Freud's reference to his departure in his own text that, I would suggest, we first have access to its historical truth.

The full impact of this history occurs for *us*, however, in yet another aspect of the act of leaving, in what Freud calls "freedom." In the "Summary and Recapitulation" Freud says:

It forced me to leave my home, but it also freed me of the fear lest my publishing the book might cause psychoanalysis to be forbidden in a country where its practice is still allowed.

Leaving home, for Freud, is also a kind of freedom, the freedom to bring forth his book in England, the freedom, that is, to bring his voice to another place. The meaning of this act is suggested in a letter which resonates with these lines from the "Summary," a letter written by Freud to his son Ernst in May 1938, while Freud was waiting for final arrangements to leave Vienna:

Two prospects keep me going in these grim times: to rejoin you all and— to die in freedom.

Freud's freedom to leave is paradoxically the freedom, not to live, but to die: to bring forth his voice to others in dying. Freud's voice emerges, that is, as a departure.[15] And it is this departure which, moreover, addresses us. In the

---

14. It is also worth noting that what is translated here as "As an afterthought" is *nachträglich* in German, the word Freud uses elsewhere to describe the "deferred action" or retroactive meaning of traumatic events in psychic life; here what is *nachträglich* is Freud's theoretical insight, which thus also participates in the traumatic structure. An excellent discussion of the structure and temporality of trauma in early Freud can be found in Cynthia Chase, "Oedipal Textuality," in *Decomposing Figures: Rhetorical Readings in the Romantic Tradition* (Baltimore: The Johns Hopkins Press, 1986), and Jean Laplanche, "Sexuality and the Vital Order, in *Life and Death in Psychoanalysis*, trans. Jeffrey Mehlman (Baltimore: The Johns Hopkins Press, 1976).

15. The resonance of the letter to Ernst with *Moses and Monotheism* is also apparent in the lines which follow those quoted above: "I sometimes compare myself with the old

line he writes to his son, the last four words—"to die in freedom"—are not, like the rest of the sentence, written in German, but rather in English. The announcement of his freedom, and of his dying, is given in a language that can be heard by those in the new place to which he brings his voice, to us, upon whom the legacy of psychoanalysis is bestowed. It is significant moreover that this message is conveyed not merely in the new language, English, but precisely in the movement between German and English, between the languages of the readers of his homeland and of his departure. I would like to suggest that it is here, in the movement from German to English, in the rewriting of the departure within the languages of Freud's text, that we participate most fully in Freud's central insight, in *Moses and Monotheism*, that history, like the trauma, is never simply one's own, that history is precisely the way we are implicated in each other's traumas. For we—whether as German- or as English-speaking readers—cannot read this sentence without, ourselves, departing. In this departure, in the leave-taking of our hearing, we are first fully addressed by Freud's text, in ways we perhaps cannot yet fully understand. And, I would propose today, as we consider the possibilities of cultural and political analysis, that the impact of this, not fully conscious address, may be not only a valid, but indeed a necessary point of departure.[16]

Jacob who, when a very old man, was taken by his children to Egypt, as Thomas Mann is to describe in his next novel. Let us hope that it won't also be followed by an exodus from Egypt. It is high time that Ahasuerus came to rest somewhere."

16. Robert Jay Lifton's marvelous treatment of trauma in Freud, in "Survivor Experience and Traumatic Syndrome," points to the relation between the later development of the notion of trauma and the occurrence of World War I. It would be interesting to explore the way in which the notion of trauma inscribes the impact of war in Freud's theoretical work.

NATHANIEL LAOR

The Moral Import of Madness to Literature*

I. PREFACE

In the attempt to establish an objective and autonomous literary reality, deconstructionists exclude the author of the text as context necessarily relevant to literary reading. Ought there to be any literary checks on the pleasure one could draw out of reading a text? No, is the answer given by some deconstructionists: a text has its own autonomous reality, and where it resists the reader's attempt to interpret it freely, precisely there it promises greater pleasure: the reader's pleasure in deconstructing the resistance of the text. For this resistance may be overcome by the reader's new choice of a new context. Nevertheless, deconstructionists add as a new afterthought, as a mere implication: some reading is vulgar and some sophisticated—as otherwise there could be no use for literary criticism. Which kind of pleasure is vulgar, however, and which kind is sophisticated? This question assumes there are some constraints on pleasure, including pleasure from hermeneutic readings.

Deconstructionist writing in itself constitutes a body of literature, which like any other offers resistance to the limitation put on it by some particular reading. Resistance, we remember, is the salt of reading, according to Deconstruction. What resistance do deconstructionist texts offer? This depends on the reader: according to Deconstruction, it is strictly a private matter between the reader and the text. How, then, do we distinguish between vulgar and sophisticated readings of deconstructionist texts?

*This essay is based on my homage to Stephen Fleck, M.D., Professor Emeritus and former Deputy Chairman of Yale Department of Psychiatry: "Why is Socrates Hard to Stomach? or The Role of Aggression in Psychiatric Education," *Psychiatric Quarterly* 11 (1989): 10–13.

YFS 79, *Literature and the Ethical Question*, ed. Claire Nouvet, © 1991 by Yale University.

Quite generally, any move meant to help discriminate the vulgar from the sophisticated reading will add a third party to the reader-text diad: the authority. Who decides which authority? The reader. The reader is at liberty to be and remain vulgar. Alternatively the reader is free to become sophisticated, or enjoy texts in a more sublime manner. Hence the reader is responsible for the aesthetics of the text. This outcome brings morals to literature. The autonomy of the reader intertwines with the autonomy of the text. Aesthetics thereby assumes an extraliterary context. What could meaningfully remain of Deconstruction once it is turned on itself?

It will be rash to conclude that if Deconstruction resists itself and, thereby, leads to the collapse of some of its renowned claims, this also amounts to its final demise. Such a verdict can only be the pitiful outcome of a mistrial, perhaps due to the misrepresentation of the spirit of Deconstruction. This essay may be viewed as an apology on behalf of this spirit for its aesthetic irony, moral force, epistemological skepticism and, above all, ontological commitment to texts.

II. WHO WAS SOCRATES?

Socrates was brought to trial twice; once in a mock court of friends and once in the law court of Athens, twice accused; once by a friend and once by a foe. A demon he surely was. Alcibiades, his admirer, accused him of arrogance[1]; Meletus, his detractor, charged him with corrupting the youth.[2] They both were stung by the gadfly who could not submit—he yielded neither to instinct nor to authority; he obeyed his own daimon only, he explained. ("Daimon, from the Greek, divine Power . . . applied to the 'genius of Socrates'".)[3]

How ridiculous he must have appeared in his renowned fits of abstraction. How ridiculous they must have felt, caught in the game, serving as butts of a joke; Alcibiades was burning with love for Socrates who was "playing his little game of irony, and laughing up his sleeve at the whole world" ("Symposium," 568); Meletus was consumed by a desire for revenge against Socrates who claimed his "advantage over the rest of mankind" in "not possessing any real knowledge of what comes after death," and since he knew so clearly that "to do wrong and disobey" his superior, "whether God or man, is wicked and dishonorable," he would willingly submit to death

1. Plato, "Symposium," trans. M. Joyce, in E. Hamilton and H. Cairns, *The Collected Dialogues of Plato* (Princeton: Princeton University Press, 1961), 526–74. Henceforth cited in the text.

2. Plato, "Apology," trans. H. Tredennick, op.cit., 3–26. Henceforth cited in the text.

3. H. G. Liddel and R. Scott, *Greek-English Lexicon* (Oxford: Clarendon Press, 1968, [1843]), 365.

rather than transgress the law ("Apology," 15). Was this a comedy or a tragedy? Neither. Or both.

What makes one look ridiculous? What makes one see another as ridiculous? One appears as ridiculous, Socrates taught, when one exhibits "a certain kind of badness," acting in opposition to the inscription at the temple of Apollo at Delphi: Know thyself.[4]

"Apollo," as Robert Graves explained,[5] "was Zeus's son by Leto. . . . Apollo earned Zeus's anger . . . when his [Apollo's] son Asclepius, the physician, had the temerity to resurrect a dead man, and thus rob Hades of a subject. . . . Zeus killed Asclepius . . . and Apollo in revenge killed the Cyclopes. Zeus was enraged" and Apollo had to serve a humbling sentence. "Having learned his lesson, he thereafter preached moderation in all things: the phrases 'Know thyself!' and 'Nothing in excess!' were always on his lips. He brought the Muses down from their home in Mount Helicon to Delphi, tamed their wild frenzy, and led them in formal and decorous dances." Now, Apollo's well-mannered Muses are not ridiculous when they act reasonably. For, the irrational Muses are now enlightened. The ridiculous is the symptom of the lack of self-knowledge, and one who knows oneself to be ridiculous is ridiculous as a clown, not as the one laughed at.

The rule of Apollo, however, was forcefully resisted by orgiastic Dionysus, son of Zeus and Semel: "He was born in Winter as serpent . . . became a lion in the Spring, and was killed and devoured as a bull . . . at midsummer" (Graves, 108). But Dionysus was subsumed by victorious Apollo, and came to dwell at Delphi (Graves, 109). Consequently, the later priests who oversaw the Orphic Mysteries were serving Apollo and Dionysus as one deity. Nevertheless, they could not maintain this divine union: "they called the demigod whose raw bull's flesh they ate 'Dionysus' and reserved the name Apollo for the immortal Sun, distinguishing Dionysus, the god of the senses, from Apollo, the god of the intellect" (Graves, 115).

Dionysus thus has two faces, one before He submits to Apollo, and another after. The face of a contemptible ridiculous demon is that of the totally uninhibited and so, seemingly, of one not afraid of self-knowledge. Yet this is an error. After Dionysus acquires self-knowledge He is transformed. The transformation is effected by the command, Apollo's command, to go beyond one's self.

Implicate thyself! Apollo has demanded of the demon. How could Dionysus have responded except by putting Himself to ridicule—there is no more to Dionysus than Himself. At this divine moment of excess—of in-

4. Plato, "Philebus," trans. R. Hackforth, op.cit., 1129.
5. R. Graves, *The Greek Myths* (New York: George Braziller, Inc., 1955) vol. 1, 76. Henceforth cited in the text.

sight into Himself, that is—in a spasm of putting Himself to ridicule, Dionysus is transformed and gives birth to comedy. He is then not ludicrous anymore; rather he is humorous. Always on display, he now has a part in a play. The conduct inviting censure is thus over and ridicule gives way to self-ridicule.

It is thus self-knowledge which transforms the ridiculous into the humorous, the censurable into the comic. Yet comedy is not unconditional self-knowledge. Perhaps, on the contrary, it undermines self-knowledge by the search for relief: perhaps it soothes rather than prompts. Some comedies offer mere relief, others prompt self-searching. Which is which? Comedies usually offer a final relief in their final act where all the play characters are invited to partake in a celebration under the patronage of Eros—a feast, a wedding, or a birth of a child. For the true comedian such a celebration, too, is thoroughly comic.

As Robert Graves tells the story, "some argue that Eros was Aphrodite's son by Hermes . . . or by her own father Zeus. . . . He was a wild boy, who showed no respect for age or station but flew about on golden wings, shooting barbed arrows . . . or . . . setting hearts on fire with his dreadful torches" (Graves, 58). Eros is thus a rascal and the quest for Him is unending. This, perhaps, is why prompting self-knowledge requires one step beyond humor: irony. But irony is hard to stomach.

How remarkably similar are the fates of Socrates and of Jesus at the hands of their fellow humans. But only Socrates, not Jesus, seemed somewhat of a buffoon to his people: when they mocked Jesus he was not ridiculed but tormented; Jesus is the lamb, not Socrates; perhaps he is the satyr. Why, then, did the Athenians sit in judgment on a mere billy-goat?

This, I think, was Socrates' horrible act. He assumed vis-à-vis his fellow human a position which is beyond comedy. This position was traditionally ascribed to the divine, yet Socrates was a mere human. He set himself up as an example and demanded that all Athenians follow him: each one should pursue his own destination; to that end one must, first and foremost, meet one's own self offstage. Most of those who contemplated this option got lost; they had no self-knowledge and no knowledge of where to turn next. Little wonder that they became aggressive. And naturally they turned their aggression against Socrates. They saw him, and him alone, at the center stage, but no longer as a figure of fun, only as a clown mocking their own bewilderment.

Human, all too human, Socrates, the author of his own moral drama, also ended up as an actor in a morality play. Having supplied Aristophanes with enough material for a comic character, that was his own character's tragic fate: caught in the act, at times—a clown or a hero—he could not but ridicule or pity his fellow Athenians. At times, then, Socrates stepped out of

his self-appointed role; he ridiculed others and then drew on their ambivalence and aggression. It is only natural that the Athenians wished to
know to which of their feelings they should rightfully submit, which to
direct at Socrates. Was Socrates a player in tragedy or comedy? They wanted
to know. To this end a trial was called. In the trial Socrates was forced to
choose between staying true to himself and saving his neck; choosing between his heroic and comic roles. He chose to stay true to himself; he told
his fellow Athenians the choice was theirs, not his. They did not believe him
and demanded that he prove his sincerity by drinking the hemlock. He
remained committed to his quest for Eros to the last moment. He proved his
sincerity, playing it by their rules to the last, forcing them to resolve their
ambivalence themselves.

An apology, perhaps, was due. As Socrates was the paragon of propriety,
he tendered one. He suggested that he be fined and promised that his friends
would pay the fine. This only left the ambivalence floating and so worsened
matters. Why? He risked a misunderstanding of his message, yet he remained adamant. Why? Was he simply caught in his own web as an actor
reading the prescribed lines of a play? Or was he in control? If he was, what
exactly was his self-appointed role? Why did he refuse to apologize in a
manner acceptable to his prosecutors? Such an apology would solve the
ambiguity and establish him finally as either a hero or a clown, but not both;
and it would also deprive him of his shield of irony. Giving up his irony
would amount to the yielding of his sword as well. He thus presented
Meletus with the dilemma: to win the court trial or to support the morality
of the Athenian law, to remain corrupt or to care for souls—his own as much
as those of his fellow citizens of Athens.

This was Socrates' own self-appointed role: a soul doctor, he said as often
as he could. This is how he wished to be known. He guaranteed his fellow
human nothing substantial, however, nothing but irony. Unlike his great
disciples, he thought he had nothing substantive to offer and could serve
solely as midwife—to deliver a moral reminder on the incessant pursuit of
self-delivery. Everyone, he taught, should experience a true rebirth of the
soul.

The court-trial ended tragically. The mock trial, if it took place at all, was
written up later, and in order to replace the court-trial—in order to serve as a
challenge; and so it did—for the whole tradition of Western moral philosophy to date.

III. WHO WAS NIETZSCHE?

Socrates traded a peaceful old age for immortality. Immortal, he is always
available for a fresh public trial. His late accuser is his admirer Friedrich

Nietzsche. What may Socrates as a cultural phenomenon indicate? This is Nietzsche's question. Why are we fascinated by Socrates? Nietzsche's very attempt to answer this question reflects his own fascination: his fascination with his own idealized and ambivalent self, projected onto Socrates' life-story. Hence, in Nietzsche's hands, Socrates could not help but turn both totem and taboo, the unattainable and the untouchable at once. As such, Socrates is indeed a cultural phenomenon, worthy of further investigation in the quest of self-knowledge.

What, then, may Socrates as a cultural phenomenon indicate? What cultural function does his teaching and his life-story serve? Does our interest in his teaching go beyond the interest in sheer ratiocination and argumentation as a cover-up for the suppression of instinct? Is our fascination with Socrates' life-story more than a mere moral perversion, i.e., a morbid fascination with human suffering? Can we learn from Socrates and expect not to pay with our own lives as he did with his?

No, was Nietzsche's answer. Socrates' teaching is decadence; as such it constitutes a serious threat to both culture and life. Socrates could herald the absolute reign of Apollo only after having taken the life of Dionysus. It was the spirit of Tragedy, the spirit of Art, that Socrates murdered, said Nietzsche. His act vanquished both the noble and the sublime. Rightfully did the Athenians execute the despised! To pity him is to recoil from genuine feeling. The proper response is nausea.

What evokes pity? What makes one seem pathetic? The judgment of one as pitiful, taught Nietzsche,[6] is nothing but the noble expression of the craving, which goes beyond reason, without any recoil vis-à-vis horror, for transcendence, for beauty, for the sublime. It is differentiated by its opposite, the pathetic, which leads neither to a cathartic experience nor to self-knowledge, but to the vulgar suffering of life as a mere incurable disease. *Pathei Mathos* (suffering educates), says Dionysus before he meets Apollo; nonetheless, we are now told, the pathetic Socrates responded with defiance. But one who observes himself from the outside and finds himself to be pathetic is pathetic no more. Yet according to Nietzsche, the simultaneous experiences of suffering and of self-knowledge detract from each other: the insistence on having them both at once precludes nobility, which is the reflection of courage in the face of both unconditional insight and torment. Tormented Dionysus thus has two faces, one before He submits to Apollo and another after. Before He has an awesome face of a genuinely horrible yet pure hero and so He evokes our unconditional pity; and after He

---

6. F. Nietzsche, *The Birth of Tragedy Or: Hellenism and Paganism, New Edition With an Attempt at a Self-Criticism*, trans. W. Kaufmann (New York: Random House, 1967 [1886]), 89–98. Henceforth cited in the text.

is a mask-face of a perverse character feigning suffering, and thereby, avoiding unconditional self-knowledge.

Implicating Himself, Dionysus did submit to Apollo. But the self-ridiculing demon still a demon is, and even in excess. Dionysus thus accepted self-flagellation as a penalty for defiance. He thereby gave birth to a pathetic farce, the subversive morality of slaves: a comedy, a tragedy—the demon is laughing. Dionysus awaits His revenge since the Socratic demon was set free.

This is why Nietzsche said that Socrates was teaching Christian slave morality. It is not Dionysus but we who should be set free, said Nietzsche. As Dionysus is bound to return eternally, we are bound to imagine His murder. Acquit Socrates and the illusion of the death of Dionysus disappears. Dionysus the Phoenix, Apollo the Sphinx. Choose between Prometheus or Oedipus and pay with your liver or your eyes. Such is the price for the magical relief of the swelling of ignorance.

This, then, according to Nietzsche, is the ironic lesson of Socrates: Oedipus the Logician will be banished and Prometheus the Hero will go mad. Any dialogue concerning the limit of knowledge must succumb—not to reason but to magic. Hence where one is driven to the limit of everyday discourse, where one goes mad with Dionysus, whereof one can no longer speak, thereof one must not remain silent—one can thereof only scream. This, perhaps, is what Socrates, according to Nietzsche, meant, when he said he was ignorant of that which lies beyond any human experience. From this perspective Socrates' last act was not a rational effort to care for souls— his own and his fellow Athenians'—but a mere self-consumed scream in his fusion with Dionysus. Having responded to Socrates' scream with pity, we evoke magic in the service of repeating his struggle. Shall we now repeat Nietzsche's *cri du coeur*, or shall we join him in his more critical moments when he was relentlessly searching for Eros? We should rather answer Nietzsche's final questions: 'what, then, is the significance, physiologically speaking, of that medium out of which tragic and comic art developed—the Dionysian madness? Is madness perhaps not necessarily the symptom of degeneration, decline, and the final stage of culture? Are there, perhaps—a question for psychiatrists—neuroses of *health*? Of the youth and youthfulness of people? Where does that synthesis of God and billy-goat in the satyr point?" (Nietzsche, 21)

IV. WHO WAS LACAN?

"In itself," said Jacques Lacan, "dialogue seems to involve a renunciation of aggressiveness; from Socrates onwards, philosophy has always placed its hope in the triumph of reason. And yet ever since Trasymachus made his stormy exit at the beginning of the Republic, verbal dialectic has all too often proved a failure"[7]. Since Freud emphasized the capacity to cure madness through some form of verbal dialectic, asked Lacan, how did he improve upon Socrates? He did so by illuminating the instinctive aspect of human life, was Lacan's answer; Humans are not reasonable enough to be trusted to carry on a dialogue and follow reason alone because their reason is damaged by their demon, their aggressiveness. Yet it is their demon that guides them on to self-betterment, claimed Lacan, in disagreement with all those who see in Eros the primary force of growth; it is the demon's task to resist seduction and maintain a person's own path. It is, however, the demon's inability to ignore seduction which, according to Lacan, turns dialogue into fight for either life or love. Reason, taught Lacan, is thereby inevitably subverted.

It takes two to tangle, said Freud, and suggested to the analyst the practice of abstinence. Lacan thereby viewed the silent analyst as a sphynx, the receptacle of both the aggression of the analysand as well as the prohibition of the dead Master. Lacan thus refused to communicate with anyone except the demon. Such communication, taught Lacan (who followed Freud's "Analysis Terminable and Interminable" in this regard), has its limits, for one cannot go beyond one's earthly self. Whenever one recognizes this, said Melanie Klein, one is depressed. Lacan, however, had set out to respond forcefully to Trasymachus and therefore was looking for more. He settled[8] on an erotic ideal: though life itself is inherently the perversion of autonomy, it is not incompatible with the hope to be delivered and attain freedom; this hope is justified, he thought, but, for the common person, it is bound to be frustrated, since it goes beyond psychoanalysis: it is due to the life-story of the anathematized great philosopher of Amsterdam; the beloved Spinoza—the lamb and the satyr at one.

Trasymachus, the buffoon of the *Republic*, said might is right. If so, then Meletus proved himself right when he prosecuted Socrates in a court of law and led him to his execution. Nietzsche had proclaimed Socrates a failure for having sought the rule of reason; therefore he, Nietzsche, executed his imaginary Socrates in his own literary court. But Socrates never boasted of the power of reason to settle matters, rather he demonstrated its power to unsettle. Socratic reason is weak—inviting commitment to argument, it discourages trust in its results. In the last analysis, truth, like Eros, is a rascal and rests beyond anything imaginable; nonetheless, it is the only friend worthy of a search—limited only by morality.

---

7. Jacques Lacan, *Ecrit*, trans. A Sheridan (New York: Norton, 1977), 12.

8. Jacques Lacan, *The Four Fundamental Concepts of Psychoanalysis*, trans., A Sheridan (New York: Norton, 1978), 275.

V. WHY IS SOCRATES HARD TO STOMACH?

Socrates must have been aware of the effects of his psychotherapeutic practice. Those who were freed of their idols but not from the need for them, were surely provoked by his unwillingness to serve as one; they either fell in love with him or hated him. Socrates' response to his suitors' frustration was with irony and this constituted his own beauty. His response to his enemies' frustration was exactly the same. What difference does irony make to a psychotherapeutic practice?

The dramatic puppets *Eiron* and *Alazon*, the persecutor and the persecuted, the self-deprecator and the impostor, these were Socrates' mythic forebears, and Nietzsche wanted to reduce him to these figures of fun. He thus reduced his genius to sheer madness, confirming thereby the judgment of the Athenian court. But Socratic irony cannot be understood when separated from its aesthetic and moral structure of aggression. It engages the muse without banishing the demon. Indeed, it invites one's own demon to set itself free as an artistic daimon, seduced only by reality—the reality of the human person. Perhaps the proper name for such a drama is *eironeia*. Since it goes beyond comedy and tragedy *eironeia* threatens all characters involved in these traditional forms as well as their audience (provided these take the play seriously enough, and are ready to follow Eros beyond their socially determined roles).

This, then, is why Socrates is hard to stomach. Socratic *eironeia* demands the unconditional surrender of the demon, yet sets it free immediately, without giving it any new terms. No wonder it often met great resistance within the breasts of the citizens of Athens. Tradition and internal demons united on keeping the Athenians locked in their roles as play-characters, thickly armored so as to protect their madness. Beset by Socrates' demands, they reacted. By law, the Athenians said to their daimon, your freedom or your life! They wished Socrates to be polite and even more, that he betray his belief in the morality of the insensible soul and proclaim his belief in the sacredness of the heavenly bodies. But freedom has it own logic which the human demon itself cannot avoid with impunity. Wrongdoing damages the soul, taught Socrates. Insofar as pure desire is oblivious to earthly limits, it is free to transcend any given human predicament; unguided, however, it is demonic and mutilating. Nonetheless, the possibility of having an image of the free demon is the precondition for human autonomy—the freedom to keep the animal checked and alive and sizzling, to transcend its given bounds. Out of this spasm of freedom humanity is born.

Your desire or your beauty, says Apollo to Dionysus. Vainly looking at the mirror, unable to give up either, the abhorring satyr is caught in the swelling of irony; He can only opt for a third pole—autonomy—which of necessity confers upon Him the image of humans. This very image, however, is vulnerable, since it blends with empathy, which for so many, makes the demand of unconditional surrender hard to stomach. Dionysus thus lurks behind and one is thereby always free to go mad. Consequently many scholars—psychiatrists as well as literary critics—retreat to mere abstract texts—"scientific," "literary," and others. All too reasonable, some of these scholars devotedly recite chants before Apollo's image, whereas others, in their fits of abstraction, feel free to go beyond reason. The clinician committed to living texts does not. Reining the demon, he keeps searching for Eros.

VI. AFTERTHOUGHT

The question remains: Can one remain autonomous after unconditional surrender? The logic of madness proper is that of unconditional surrender and loss of autonomy. Or is it? We do not know unless we know all kinds of unconditional surrender which spare autonomy and are consistent with it. Only then can we understand the subtle tension between madness and autonomy.

Incidentally, we can say that the unconditional surrender to the principles of deconstruction still spares autonomy. The autonomy of the reader intertwines with the autonomy of the text. We now can also say that the unconditional surrender to the principle of autonomy spares autonomy. What else?

VINCENT P. PECORA

Ethics, Politics, and the Middle Voice

Increasingly these days, "ethics" seems to be a matter of public concern. In the academic arena of literary criticism and theory, which will be my main focus here, ethics-talk has been revived for a number of reasons, many of them related to the nature of "poststructuralist" thought or a "postmodern" society.[1] J. Hillis Miller's recent lectures, published as *The Ethics of Reading*, make an intervention in such debates: these essays attempt both to defend new theory against the charge of nihilism, and to resituate literary criticism itself in an Arnoldian realm of "sweetness and light," where the play of the critical intelligence can take place free from the pressure of political engagement with the issues of the day. In Miller's view, this play of the mind freed from constraints (as in Schiller's aesthetics) is the *only* truly ethical approach to the literary text, though one which at the same time reveals the true nature of all ethical judgment as itself a species of linguistic difference. At the same time, it is only fair to say that the politics-talk which for Miller is too pervasive in criticism today has in no sense reached some felicitous distance from more bourgeois notions of ethics, though structuralist and poststructuralist revisions of the Marxian canon, no less than the tradition of Western Marxism they revise, tend to mystify this relationship. Ernesto Laclau and Chantal Mouffe's *Hegemony and Socialist Strategy* is perhaps the most sophisticated attempt so far to synthesize a poststructuralist critique of Western metaphysics with a neo-Marxian pol-

1. In addition to the small number of examples I will address in this essay, one could also cite Wayne Booth, *The Company We Keep: An Ethics of Fiction* (Berkeley: University of California, 1988); Tobin Siebers, *The Ethics of Criticism* (Ithaca: Cornell University, 1988); Jean-François Lyotard and Jean-Loup Thébaud, *Just Gaming*, trans. Wlad Godzich (Minneapolis: University of Minnesota, 1985); Luce Irigaray, *Ethique de la différence*

YFS 79, *Literature and the Ethical Question*, ed. Claire Nouvet, © 1991 by Yale University.

itics. But as I will try to show, ethics is hardly a "deconstructed" term here, and so the Laclau/Mouffe intervention also requires that the relationship between ethics and politics be reexamined.

It is perhaps no accident that at a time when the possibility of viable adversary politics in Western Democracies (that is, more or less collective and coherent opposition to existing structures of power) has been once again reduced to mere neurotic fantasy, ethics should return to critical discourse. I take politics to mean collective relations to existing, and in many cases traditional, exercises of power, whether such relations are openly conflictual or open to negotiation. In this sense, "adversarial" politics aims not simply at what Marx called "political emancipation"—that is, a just distribution of political rights guaranteed by the state—but also at emancipation from economic and cultural domination. I take ethics to mean relations between an autonomous, self-determining subjectivity and a set of potentially, but never actually universalizable values—a "normative" discourse always to some extent in flux, dependent both on the inertia of tradition (an "ethos") and the appearance (at the least) of potential justification by universalizable reason. Politics—the arena of the contestation of human interests—may or may not conceive of itself as ethically based, but it inevitably has recourse to the language of ethics in order to secure and maintain hegemony. Ethics will by definition claim political transcendence and will thus disavow any relation to the existing (political) exercise of power.

Politics-talk then is simultaneously "ethical" and "unethical"—that is, it will either use existing rules (in an unauthorized way) against those who already control their application, or it will juxtapose an excluded or repressed rule against those rules already in place. Ethics-talk is, in its own self-conception, apolitical, but in any society structured and driven by domination, all specific and public invocations of ethics will be thoroughly political. It would be tempting to claim either that ethics-talk is always the mere ideological supplement to contingent political interest, or that politics-talk is nothing more than an ideological imposition on necessary eth-

---

sexuelle (Paris: Editions de Minuit, 1984); Jacques Lacan, *Ethique de la psychanalyse: 1959–1960* (Paris: Seuil, 1986); Jürgen Habermas, *The Theory of Communicative Action,* trans. Thomas McCarthy (Boston: Beacon, 1984), especially vol. 2, and *Moralbewusstsein und kommunikatives Handeln* (Frankfurt: Suhrkamp, 1983), especially chap. 3. Martin Jay, in "The Morals of Genealogy: Or is there a Post-Structuralist Ethics?" *The Cambridge Review* (June 1989): 70–74, takes more or less seriously the poststructuralist claims of "ethical anarchism" and "ecstatic community" (in texts ranging from Georges Bataille to Jean-Luc Nancy), claims which he then finds disturbingly subversive. In opposition, my argument will emphasize the always self-cancelling, if blustering, rhetoric of such claims, rhetoric which when directed at the question of "ethics" generally reveals itself to be deeply conservative of existing relations.

ical values. But the need to resolve social conflict makes either of these claims difficult to maintain publicly. Politics is always permeated by the recognition that ethical belief, however strong or complete, is necessarily insufficient to promote the fulfillment of human interests, though politics-talk cannot consolidate and extend particular interests—cannot achieve hegemony—without the rhetorical invocation of ethics. The only ethics-talk that was completely apolitical would be that which did not have to be expressed. And the only politics-talk that could avoid implicit ethical invocations would be the purely technical discussion which arose from a society already devoid of domination, and hence in no need of hegemonic articulations.

In the Western industrialized nations, the reduction of adversary politics to neurosis obviously takes place on many fronts, and has gone on for some time—neoconservative nostalgia should be understood as the political norm of big, state-supported capitalism. The withering of Soviet-style communism has for many in the West simultaneously served to prove the inadvisability of adversary politics of whatever stripe. Any "politics" that cannot be contained within the format of legislative debate (and even this form of opposition is increasingly decried as "partisan" and "polarizing") has once again begun to seem ungrateful. What the news industry often implies with its "Marxism is dead" slogans is that "politics" is dead, at least the kind of nasty politics where individuals and groups treated unjustly (or completely forgotten) by business-as-usual legislative and judicial processes get angry enough to demand structural change, and not just token "compensation." Indeed, facing the imminent collapse of the Warsaw Pact and the consolidation of American power, the jingoist wing of the bureaucracy (in deliberate emulation of Hegel) has even proclaimed "the end of history"—all except for the fine tuning.[2] If I am correct, the jingoist bureaucrat's "end of history" thesis is not as far from the new "ethics of reading" and "socialist strategy" as one might at first imagine.

Now, the return of ethics as a theoretical problem is by no means simply a bad thing, any more than is legislative debate or judicial due process. But it is important to remember that personal "ethics" and public "politics" (now in the reduced sense of legal rights), though obviously with long and complex philosophical genealogies, form a paradoxical, mutually supporting dyad in Western liberal capitalism that is itself an effect of opposition, emphasized by Marx, between civil society and the state. Kantian practical reason, with its explicit recognition of what can be called two contingent necessities derivable from the categorical imperative—the treatment of

2. For this new-jingoist version of the imperial bureaucracy's older "triumph of the West" thesis, see Francis Fukuyama, "The End of History?" *The National Interest* 16 (1989): 3–18.

subjects as ends rather than means, and the self-legislation of the autonomous will—can be considered the theoretical exposition of the civil soci-
ety/state dyad.[3] In many ways, of course, criticism and theory have come a
long way from Kantian imperatives. Indeed, after the social and intellectual
upheavals of the 1960s, one might claim that it is no longer possible to
pretend that "ethics" and "politics" represent distinct discourses or practices—the personal *is* the political. My sense, however, is that despite much
rhetoric and reform, not only has such a synthesis not occurred, but critique
is as dependent as it ever was on a distinction still implicit in late capitalist
social relations. What the new ethics-talk might mean, then, and how we
got here, deserves hard critical reflection, no matter how "sincere" the
motives behind such talk are.

The most obvious point to make about the difference between more
conventional ethics-talk (for example, Kantian definitions of morality as
"the relation of actions to the autonomy of the will, i.e., to possible universal lawgiving by maxims of the will" [*Metaphysics of Morals*, 58]) and the
contemporary version is that the shift is due, precisely, to "difference"—to
the structuralist/poststructuralist rethinking of subjectivity in terms of
discursive structures. This still fairly recent remapping of ego cogito and
transcendental loci onto a languagelike field—of multiple positions, unstable relations, infinite possibilities of combination and articulation, and always deferred essences—is simultaneously the ground and the motivation
of contemporary debate.[4] At the same time, however, it must be acknowledged that this remapping of subjectivity has yielded far more than a new
perspective on ethics. For it has had an equally profound effect on the way
adversary politics is conceived. Indeed, one could claim that it was primarily
the political impasse of the Cold War that initially gave relevance to the
attempts to rethink subjectivity along discursive lines. If Kantian liberal
individualism was dead, so was the Marxian alternative which identified
subjectivity with social collectivities essentialized (if only "in the final
determination") by class origins, antagonisms, and teleologies. Another way

3. See, for example, Immanuel Kant, *Foundations of the Metaphysics of Morals*, trans.
Lewis White Beck (Indianapolis: Bobbs-Merrill, 1959), 39, 47, and 57. See also, of course,
Kant, *Critique of Practical Reasons*, trans. Lewis White Beck (New York: Macmillan,
1956), especially 30–42. Henceforth cited in text.
4. The overwhelming agreement within criticism and theory on the terms of this
debate since the poststructuralist intervention should not, however, obscure the fact that
other epistemological grounds for an adversarial politics can be articulated. Noam
Chomsky, for example, has maintained that something like a Cartesian/Kantian subjectivity is a necessary assumption if constructive resistance and positive change—"creative
acts of self-perfection"—are to be expected (see "Language and Freedom," in *The
Chomsky Reader*, ed. James Peck [New York: Pantheon, 1987], 146). See also, S. P. Mohanty, "Us and Them: On the Philosophical Bases of Political Criticism," *Yale Journal of
Criticism* 2: 2(1989): 1–31.

of saying all this, as I have already implied, is that if the rupture in theoretical discourse over the last thirty years has finally produced J. Hillis Miller's *The Ethics of Reading*, it has also produced Ernesto Laclau and Chantal Mouffe's *Hegemony and Socialist Strategy*. How should the relations between such diverse texts be understood? What is their difference, and is it worth preserving? I shall return to Miller, and to Laclau and Mouffe. But first, I would like to descend for a moment into the land of the middle voice.

I

Although there are at this point numerous ways of opening a discussion of the contemporary remapping of subjectivity, I want to begin with the term "middle voice" (rather than with "sign" or "discourse," for example) because it will implicate a variety of complex theoretical issues all at once. I take the term from Jacques Derrida's 1968 essay "La Différance," where *"la voix moyenne"* is used to illustrate a crucial claim. For of course Derrida's well-known neologistic gerund, with its vocally buried *a*, suggests both the active, causal properties of the present participle (*différant*) and hence the verb, as well as the passive, already effected or constituted properties of the noun (*différence*). I would like to concentrate here on the grammatical trope that, in my view, is the vehicle—and purpose—of Derrida's argument, a grammar that for Derrida first appears as a virtual metaphor, and ends as actual history and repression.

> We must consider that in the usage of our language the ending -*ance* remains undecided *between* the active and the passive. And we will see why that which lets itself be designated [*se laisse désigner par*] *différance* is neither simply active nor simply passive, announcing or rather recalling something like the middle voice, saying an operation that is not an operation, an operation that cannot be conceived [*ne se laisse penser*] either as passion or as the action of a subject on an object, or on the basis of the categories of agent or patient, neither on the basis of nor moving toward any of these *terms*. For the middle voice, a certain nontransitivity, may be what philosophy, at its outset, distributed into an active and a passive voice, thereby constituting itself [*se constituant*] by means of this repression.[5]

Like many passages in Derrida's work, this one formally imitates its philosophical claims in the rhetoric of late Heideggerian phenomenology. An

5. Jacques Derrida, *Marges de la philosophie* (Paris: Editions de Minuit, 1972), 9; *Margins of Philosophy*, trans. Alan Bass (Chicago: University of Chicago, 1982), 9; hereafter, *MP* (Bass translation) in the text.

operation/nonoperation, which "lets itself be designated," is either "announcing or recalling something like the middle voice." Even here, language allows itself to do things with itself: "Differences, thus, are 'produced'—deferred—by *différance*" (*MP*, 14). The question of agency—what or who defers?—thus prompts an elaboration, after Saussure, of the notion that linguistic differences "play"—as both causes and effects, and not as a function of an originary speaking subject. Such play is itself constitutive of "all the pairs of opposites on which philosophy is constructed," each pair—such as concept/intuition, culture/nature, *tekhnē/physis*—being a further "unfolding of the same as *différance*" (*MP*, 17). The differential relation forbids the assignation of active and passive roles, and works commutatively: culture is that which differentiates itself from nature, as well as that which designates and defers the closure of its own meaning by means of the notion of nature; and nature, besides constituting itself as culture's other, also defers its final significance (or its own fulfillment) with the notion of culture. Such terminological commutativity reproduces itself ubiquitously, appearing even in Heidegger's destructive reinscription of metaphysics as ontico-ontological difference, an "ontology of beings and beingness" (*MP*, 21).

What Derrida produces here is an *economy*, "an energetics or economics of forces," but an economy of a particular kind. There is on the one hand circulation and exchange which is unwittingly a totalized "unfolding of the same" (as in Nietzsche's critique of Kantian "faculties"), where the aim is always to return, and often by elaborate detour, to a deferred fulfillment (or presence), as if reaping the *profit* from a homecoming calculated to occur in advance. This is the *restricted economy*.[6] On the other hand, Derrida also wishes to announce or recall circulation and exchange that has forsaken profit, yielding an "expenditure without reserve" that takes into account nonmeaning, the "nonreserve," and death. This is the *general economy* (*MP*, 19). Derrida thus links the restricted economy to the "Hegelian" interpretation of the economy of *différance:* the philosopher as the ultimate speculator, as the one who can always turn a profit by means of a negating/conserving sleight of hand called *Aufhebung.* (Freud's "pleasure principle" also serves as a model here.) This restricted economy, one might say, is "capitalist" (in the most ahistorical sense), or at least is coextensive with what Bataille calls "political economy."[7] The general economy, on the other hand, as derived from Bataille and Levinas, "exceeds the alternative

6. For Nietzsche's critique of Kantian faculties, see *Beyond Good and Evil*, trans. Walter Kaufmann (New York: Vintage, 1966), 18.

7. See Derrida, "From Restricted to General Economy," *Writing and Difference*, trans. Alan Bass (Chicago: University of Chicago, 1978), 270–73. Hereafter cited in the text. For Bataille's views, see *La Part maudite* (Paris: Editions de Minuit, 1967).

of presence and absence"; it is explicitly described as the "Other"—the "enigma of absolute alterity"—delimiting the "ontology of presence" (*MP*, 21). The general economy, then, is . . . what? In a note, Derrida insists that it is "revolutionary," and that "one would commit a gross error in interpreting these propositions [of Bataille] in a 'reactionary' sense" (*Writing and Difference*, 337 n33). I would suggest that things are hardly as straightforward as Derrida would like them to be. Grounded in the "otherness" of *dépense*, Bataille's "general economy" is in the main a radicalized version of Western anthropology's notion of symbolic exchange, or total prestation: those festivals of the distribution and destruction of wealth in Northwest America, first described by Franz Boas, and designated as "potlatch," those rituals described by Branislaw Malinowski, for example, of gift-giving and circulation in Melanesia, those constellations of practices Marcel Mauss summed up under the heading of *The Gift*.[8] Indeed, Derrida would seem to "recall" just such a genealogy: "we must conceive of a play in which whoever loses wins, and in which one loses and wins on every turn" (*MP*, 20). One must remind oneself here, since Derrida provides no citations, that Boas and Malinowski and Mauss conceived (or described) such "play" early in this century—much of the antidialectical work had already been done.

The larger relationship between Derrida's notion of general economy and Western anthropology must be addressed separately. What I wish to focus on at present is the implicit (anthropological) relationship between three sets of oppositions: of restricted to general economies, of Being to a *différance* that is "'Older' than Being itself" (*MP*, 26), and of Western metaphysics to the "middle voice" that it has repressed. What has been masked for Derrida by Western philosophy (and, in the present context, by Western ethics, at least from Aristotle to Kant) is a "certain nontransitivity" (what I have been calling a commutativity) that has been redistributed by philosophy into active and passive moments. Like Nietzsche before him, Derrida chides philosophers for putting too much faith in "grammar." But Derrida himself imagines (and asks his readers to "try" to imagine) another, more primitive, "grammar"—or rather, in quite specific terms for a Western speaker of Indo-European languages, the grammar of the Other—that is, the grammar of the middle voice. But on what basis can such a claim be made?

The short answer would seem to be Emile Benveniste. (The longer answer—which I can only hint at here—would obviously also refer to Martin

8. See, for example, Franz Boas, *Kwakiutl Ethnography*, ed. Helen Codere (Chicago: University of Chicago, 1966), 77–104; Branislaw Malinowski, *Argonauts of the Western Pacific* (Prospect Heights, Illinois: Waveland, 1984), especially 81–104; and Marcel Mauss, *The Gift*, trans. Ian Cunnison (New York: Norton, 1967). See also Michele Richman, *Reading Georges Bataille: Beyond the Gift* (Baltimore: Johns Hopkins University Press, 1982).

Heidegger's reflections on the idiom *"Es gibt* [there is, it gives], and more specifically to his attempt to go beyond both phenomenology and the "grammatisch-logischen Auslegung" of *"Es gibt"* in a long parenthesis of "Time and Being."[9] It should be clear, however, that Heidegger's maneuver itself depends on a curious faith in an alternative [to] grammar.) Derrida quotes Benveniste extensively in "The Supplement of the Copula: Philosophy Before Linguistics," among other essays. For the passage from "La Différance," the crucial precursor is Benveniste's "Active and Middle Voice in the Verb," from 1950.[10] But Benveniste's essay can at best be a problematic basis for Derrida's trope. Benveniste's general claim is not that the opposition between active and passive voice in the Indo-European verb has been generated out of a single, unstable "middle voice." Rather, he presents the modern, seemingly fundamental active/passive distinction as a contradictory development of earlier oppositions. Greek grammarians had established a triple division, with the middle voice intermediate between active and passive. Benveniste's thesis is that this Greek doctrine was itself imposed on an earlier stage, where the passive was only a modality of the middle voice. "The Indo-European stage of the verb is thus characterized by an opposition of only two diatheses, active and middle" (*PGL*, 145). Benveniste then effectively transforms the issue of grammatical voice from a question of a subject acting or being acted upon to "a relationship between subject and process. In the active, the verbs denote a process that is accomplished outside the subject. In the middle, which is the diathesis to be defined by the opposition, the verb indicates a process centering in the subject, the subject being inside the process" (*PGL*, 148). To illustrate his point, Benveniste begins by supposing that "a typically middle verb, such as Gr. κοιμᾶται 'he sleeps'" were to be "endowed secondarily with an active form" (*PGL*, 149). In such a case, the middle is converted into a transitive in the production of an active form. "'He sleeps' produces κοιμᾶ 'he puts [someone] to sleep.'"

It is in Benveniste's description of this "conversion" in a select number of verbs that one perhaps finds the sources of Derrida's metaphor of repression. "Thus," Benveniste writes of such verbs, "starting from the middle, actives are formed that are called transitives, or causatives, or factitives, and which are always characterized by the fact that the subject, placed outside the process, governs it thenceforth as agent, and that the process, instead of

9. See Martin Heidegger, "Zeit und Sein" (1962) in *Zur Sache des Denkens* (Tübingen: Max Niemeyer, 1969), 18–20; "Time and Being" in *On Time and Being*, trans. Joan Stambaugh (New York: Harper and Row, 1972), 17–19.

10. Emile Benveniste, "Active and Middle Voice in the Verb," *Problems in General Linguistics*, trans. Mary Elizabeth Meek (Coral Gables, Florida: University of Miami, 1971); hereafter, *PGL* in the text.

having the subject for its seat, must take an object as its goal" (*PGL*, 149). That is, again, "ὀρχέομαι 'I dance'>ὀρχέω 'I make (another) dance." It is easy to see how the middle voice could be assumed to possess logicotemporal priority. From this point, a short leap produces Nietzsche's central notion that philosophers invented the agent of an action in order to be able to enforce causal logic; the lightning strikes, and there is only a process, but our grammar in fact doubles the deed to provide a causal explanation (and thus some sense of power over the process).[11] In fact, however, Benveniste is making a rather different sort of observation. It is not the transitivity of the verb which is the distinguishing characteristic of the active; transitivity is only a "necessary product" of the conversion. Rather, it is the subject's exterior relationship to the process that marks the active. Thus, "δῶρα φέρει 'he bears gifts'" in the active; but "δῶρα φέρεται 'he bears gifts which involve himself' (=he carries away gifts which he has received)" in the middle voice. And, in the example that is perhaps most perplexing given the uses to which Derrida will put the middle voice, Benveniste opposes "θόμους τιθέκαι 'to establish laws'" in the active with "θόμους τιθέκαι ' to establish laws and include oneself therein' (=to give oneself laws)" in the middle. Benveniste's larger argument is that the crucial grammatical issue is *where* agency is located with reference to process. In Benveniste's version of the middle voice, "the subject is the center as well as the agent of the process; he achieves something which is being achieved in him" (*PGL*, 149). But this argument radically complicates Derrida's simpler inference that some more primordial linguistic form like the middle voice was repressed and distributed into calculable active and passive terms. In the end, Benveniste does not imply any Nietzschean a-subjectivity within the middle voice at all; his analysis actually expands the concept of agency. From Benveniste's perspective, one might be warranted in concluding that the Kantian categorical imperative is the very essence of the middle voice ("to establish laws and to include oneself therein").

My purpose here is not to suggest another, more "authentic" etiology for the middle voice, but rather to call into question the reified, nondifferential form it takes in Derrida's essay. Even as he recalls the importance of the middle/active diathesis for societies based on the "reciprocity" of services, Benveniste insists (as does Derrida, of course) that "it is in the nature of linguistic phenomena, since they are signs, to realize themselves in oppositions and only thereby to convey meaning" (*PGL*, 151). In this sense, the middle voice can only beg the question it would seem designed to sublate. There could no more be a middle voice without difference from its other(s)

11. See, for example, Friedrich Nietzsche, *Beyond Good and Evil*, 23–27; and *On the Genealogy of Morals*, trans. Walter Kaufmann and R. J. Hollingdale (New York: Vintage, 1969), 45.

than there could be any linguistic positivity without difference. The attempt to imagine a general economy beyond the confines of a restricted one—actually a footnote to Western ethnology—can be only as much a further example of a restricted economy as it can be a utopian gesture toward a general one (as much Hegel as Nietzsche). Unless, of course, the utopian gesture is suppressed and mystified ethnological nostalgia in the first place. My point is that, like the jargon of phenomenology, the middle voice only superficially "dissolves" older logical and ethical dilemmas of subject/object relations. Moreover, as Benveniste's essay implies, this prephilosophical "grammar" which would seem to declare the utter vitiation of ethics in the Kantian sense—since all moral agents would only be the necessary supplement posited as legitimating origin by ethics-talk—in fact quite easily becomes one more necessary *reproduction* of ethics, and precisely at that point where it would seem most impossible. The undifferentiated general economy of the middle voice signals, in this sense, the return of precisely that mystified "mana" of value that has been somehow purified of cruder "active" and "passive" codings.

Indeed, the mystification is extended whenever Derrida miraculously rediscovers a certain "active" component in the middle voice, not (ironically) unlike the seminarian's discovery of new "faculties" in Nietzsche's anecdote. His admonition to think this "moving discord" in Nietzschean terms (*MP*, 18)—that is, "without *nostalgia*," or from the vantage of "the other side of nostalgia, what I will call Heideggerian *hope*"—is itself only another form of nostalgia, precisely because it "recalls" nothing more than an existential formalism, an abstract commitment to the "law" governing the chain of *différance* which is its proper element. What always enables the continuity of Derridean analyses, in the face of the centrifugal discord they claim to be subject to, is the pre-determined (one might again say, existential) commitment that "reading" implicitly makes to "the law it gives itself." While the project as a whole may claim to shake (or "solicit") complacent illusions that self-given laws can somehow "practically" ground themselves—*the* Kantian illusion, as it were—the law of solicitation is itself no less foundational than the Kantian imperative, in that its primary effect is only to remind us, precisely, that our laws are neither more nor less self-given. Indeed, I will go so far as to claim that it is just the empty (Kantian) formalism of the law and liberal ethics that all this "solicitation" cannot help but fall back upon when it is called to defend itself against the charge of nihilism. In Kant, the formal requirements of "lawfulness" were seen to be sufficient guarantee of the particular substance of the law. Once again, it would seem, with the formal requirements of rhetorical "solicitation," we are asked to rely on the good will of the philosopher who "solicits" our assent by being true to his own methods.

II

That the formality of this solicitation in fact depends on the basic acceptability of Enlightenment notions of ethics and politics—the notion that autonomously willed self-legislation is the only rational form of ethics and politics—is apparent when Paul de Man reads Rousseau's "social contract." De Man's argument concludes with the following claims. One, Rousseau shows us "that the political destiny of man is structured like and derived from a linguistic model that exists independently of nature and independently of the subject." Two, this observation in turn for de Man enforces the inevitable "'politicality' . . . of all forms of human language, and especially of rhetorically self-conscious or literary language," implying for the moment that language is a subgenre of politics. Three, since this is so (and here the commutativity of the middle voice appears), all politics can in turn only be a subgenre of rhetoric, derived "from a tension between man and his language," and hence having nothing to do with relations between man and things, man and other men, or man and God. And finally, this then means that, "far from being a repression of the political, as Althusser would have it, literature is condemned to being the truly political mode of discourse."[12] De Man's point is one that has also been central to figures like Jean Baudrillard: that the invocation of a "reality" (for example, the economic category of "need") to which discourse, whether political or literary, refers is always in fact a metaphorical construction. Since politics-talk is always a contingent discourse constructed around such fictional invocations, and since literary language is most aware of its fictionality, literature is the only "truly political mode of discourse." Ignoring the misreading of Althusser here, one would then also find de Man implying that the only truly "political" form of activity is the writing, reading, and discussion of literature (now defined as a special, self-conscious use of language)—a position taken up explicitly by J. Hillis Miller, who merely substitutes "ethics" for "politics."

But what enables such conclusions on de Man's part is a fundamental Enlightenment/Romantic belief in the nature and power of a *poiesis*—though de Man will insist on the rigorously antiaesthetic, epistemological character of all specifically literary (or textual) poiesis. Since the "fictionality" of the civil order destabilizes it, because it depends on a verbal ruse that will destroy it once the ruse is demystified, the only true politics (and hence, the only truth about politics) is to be found, ironically, where Schiller himself thought he had discovered it: in an aesthetic—or rather, for de Man, a nonaesthetic, "literary"—realm which nevertheless, and not at all unlike Schiller's aesthetic, still claims to produce a "truly political mode of dis-

12. Paul de Man, *Allegories of Reading* (New Haven: Yale University, 1979), 156–57.

course." This is a realm where the true questions of politics—freedom and necessity—are to be found in their true (rhetorical) relation.[13] The only difference, though an illusory one, is that for de Man this realm (the literary) is not actually "aesthetic" in any traditional Romantic sense; it is not the place where the opposition of freedom and necessity is *sublated*, but rather where the continual *"différance"* of one term into the other (like "culture" and "nature" in Derrida) is given its most self-conscious expression. Curiously, what this means, I think, is that de Man does not believe Rousseau and Kant when they claim to recognize the "contingency" of "law." It also implies that, for de Man, those who engage in politics-talk neither admit nor recognize the merely contingent nature of their claims. Yet from one perspective, the only adequate reading of Marx (as even de Man implies) would surely be one that recognized not only the contingent status of the "state," but of "economic determination" too, since the latter only serves as a critical tool as long as the former's power remains to be contested. Why, one might ask, does de Man feel so certain that politics-talk is only engaged in by those who do not recognize the contingent nature of their discourse, and that all who engage rigorously with literature do? Somehow, in spite of his focus on rhetoric, de Man actually believes in Enlightenment, perhaps even more than Rousseau or Kant did—but he thinks it only takes place in literature.

It is this same disavowed faith that runs through J. Hillis Miller's attempt to define an "ethics of reading." When Miller turns to de Man's work, it is precisely the utter "fictionality" of our judgments that supposedly threatens all moral and political orders. Yet Miller sounds like nothing so much as a new Voltaire: "An ethical judgment is always a baseless positing, always unjust and unjustified. . . . And yet the imposition of a system of ethics is absolutely necessary . . . in the double sense that it *has* to be made and that there can be no civil society without it."[14] Nietzsche, it would seem, was never so reasonable. In fact, Miller simply makes explicit the necessary dependence of all "deconstructive" poetics on the empty formality of "law." Miller's notion of an "ethics of reading" is a phenomenological reduction of Kantian lawfulness to its existential essence: the ethical "moment" is simultaneously a "response to something," an "I *must* do this", and a stimulus which "leads to an act. It enters the social, institutional, political realms, for example in what the teacher says to the class or in what the critic

13. For Schiller's aesthetics and their ambiguous relation to politics—simultaneously preparation for, and sublation of, true politics—see *On the Aesthetic Education of Man*, trans. Reginald Snell (New York: Ungar, 1983).

14. J. Hillis Miller, *The Ethics of Reading* (New York: Columbia University, 1987), 55; hereafter, *ER* in the text.

writes" (*ER*, 4).[15] Moreover, because this ethical abstraction is an existential datum, it must not be subordinated to cruder impositions of political interpretation, and here Miller invokes the clear distinction between "ethics" and "politics" I tried to question at the beginning of this essay. The ethical moment in reading "must be sui generis, something individual and particular, itself a source of political or cognitive acts, not subordinated to them" (*ER*, 5). Like Kant's ethics, Miller's tells us only to obey the law—in this case, the law of (or more specifically, behind) the text—and nothing more.

At first, it may seem that Miller is building a defense, albeit a strangely pleasureless one, of old-fashioned literary formalism—"It is so hard, too hard," he warns in his schoolmaster's voice, "to keep one's attention on the text." But he also claims that "political, social, and historical" explanations are prompted perhaps by a "fear of literature, an aversion of the eyes from some anarchic power that is felt in it and that one would like to tame, control, or repress" (*ER*, 5). As in Derrida's nostalgia for "absolute alterity," Miller feels that the "anarchic power" of literature is repressed by the (metaphysical) grammar of traditional hermeneutics. Treating contexts as "causes," for example, is only due to the lure of "intellectual mastery." Why, one wonders, does Miller not consider his brave commitment to "anarchic power" to be a political statement? Of course, Miller is no anarchist, and his ethics is in fact the far safer commitment to Nietzsche's tragic contest between Dionysus and Apollo, an anarchy which is at the same time a law. In reading, something "unique and unforeseen has occurred," though always "as something which is bound to happen" (*ER*, 53). Actually, Miller's readings allow very little that is unforeseen to occur, almost by definition, for each text can only be the return of the same. The supposedly unpredictable forces of the literary text always reveal only the law of their own operation,

15. In one sense, then, Miller's "ethics of reading" is derived directly from Derrida's comments early in *Dissemination* (trans. Barbara Johnson [Chicago: University of Chicago, 1981]), which proscribe both the complete freedom of the reader/commentator "to add any old thing," as well as a static, normative "'methodological prudence'": "One must then, in a single gesture, but doubled, read and write. . . . The reading or writing supplement must be rigorously prescribed, but by the necessities of a *game*, by the logic of *play*, signs to which the system of all textual powers must be accorded and attuned" (64). It is this "gesture" that Miller rewrites as the authentically "ethical" performance. On the other hand, however, one should recognize that both Derrida's and Miller's strategies here could be underwritten, ironically enough, by the "ethical" phenomenology of Sartre in "Qu'est-ce que la littérature?": "For freedom is experienced [e.g., in reading] not in the enjoyment of free subjective functioning, but in a creative act required by an imperative" (*"What is Literature?" and Other Essays* [Cambridge: Harvard University, 1988], 56). Miller of course would resist those moments where Sartre tries to go beyond Kantian aesthetics toward a political notion of "freedom"; but the difficulties raised by a phenomenological "ethics" of reading surely plague Sartre's text right from the start.

which is precisely that all laws are fictions built on the sand of anarchic powers. As in de Man, this is all we know about literature, and all we need to know. Anything else would imply the coercive force of "politics."

On the surface, then, Miller's claims are unabashedly Romantic. Indeed, as Miller notes toward the end of his book, reading is precisely that sublime realm where Schiller declared that "freedom and necessity come together, become indistinguishable" (*ER*, 116). From this perspective, Miller's "ethics of reading" is merely an Arnoldian application of Schiller's playful sublime. But of course, Schiller's play of the imagination is also in turn reduced to the "call" and "response" of language itself, as in Heidegger's late formulations: "language speaks. If we let ourselves fall into the abyss denoted by this sentence, we do not go tumbling into emptiness. We fall upward, to a height."[16] Embedded in Miller's Romantic existentialism are various Heideggerian notions of language, time, even "historicity." "Language promises, but what it promises is itself. This promise it can never keep. It is this fact of language, a necessity beyond the control of any user of language, which makes things happen as they do happen in the material world of history" (*ER*, 35). Miller can thus explain that reading is not really subject simply to the law of the text, but "to the law to which the text is subject." Such a law is of course the law of "*différance*," that anarchic force in language which, if faced with courage, calls us to a "responsibility" we "must" follow, and bids us "do" something by producing one more text which reminds us that all responsibility is nothing more than an irresistible response to anarchic forces.

Lost here in the jargon of the new "authenticity" of reading, the performative value of such an exercise can only repeat, *ad nauseam*, the antifoundational foundations of ethics already required by Kant's practical reason. In spite of the heroic gestures, Miller's "ethics of reading" quite conventionally implies that "ethics" is a category ontologically prior to politics. Further, as I tried to show above, such a claim itself assumes a certain essential plenitude in ethics, one simply unattainable in practice: "I would even dare to promise that the millenium would come if all men and women became good readers in de Man's sense, though that promise is exceedingly unlikely to have a chance to be tested in practice" (*ER*, 58). If everyone behaved "ethically," no matter what the ethics, there would be no need for politics—one more paraphrase of the Kantian law. But such a perspective betrays a fundamental misunderstanding of the relation between "ethics" and "politics," one which Miller's attention to the structure of

16. See Martin Heidegger, "Die Sprache," in *Unterwegs zur Sprache* (Pfullingen: Neske, 1959); "Language," in *Poetry, Language, Thought*, trans. Albert Hofstadter (New York: Harper and Row, 1975), 191.

linguistic deferral should have uncovered. "Ethics" is never adequate because all "universal" imperatives are doomed to be partial and contingent, and "politics" is what we call the attempt to supplement that inadequacy; but "politics" in turn cannot be engaged without the inevitable invocation of "ethics." In his attempt to preserve an open space of freedom within a literary text from the deterministic (for Miller, "political") codings of sociological criticism (a familiar refrain of the old New Critics, it will be remembered), Miller's middle voiced-grammar—"ethical judgment and command is a necessary feature of human language"—instead collapses that space through an "ethics" even more empty and formal than the Kantian variety, though one equally efficient at guaranteeing cosmically clean hands. In the process of totalizing "ethics" once again (the millenium would occur if we could all be ethical, though we can't), Miller has of course produced one of the most political statements of all: things can't help being the way they are.

III

It would be an error, however, to pretend that the history of Marxian (political) critique had actually escaped from the contradictions of the middle voice. One can of course begin with Marx's assumption in *The German Ideology* that the "proletariat" names a class which is outside of class, simultaneously the productive base of the entire society and the one group systematically excluded from existing social structure, at once defined by particular and adversarial interests and defining itself in terms of universal interests at the revolutionary moment of its formation. Throughout Marxian theory, the working class has borne the weight of a struggle to elaborate its practices in terms of a political middle voice. If praxis is characterized by invocation of will, self-determination, and decision, the contingent nature of this activity appears out of step with historical necessity, and thus as no more than the expression of limited, partial interests. If praxis is on the other hand characterized by the structural determinations and requirements of the evolution of capitalist political economy, then the necessity of locating interests within that evolutionary process suddenly appears to breed passive acquiescence. The larger debates within Western Marxism almost always take shape within a field defined by two axes: the question of the potential universality (and hence of the "essential" nature) of the working class; and the question of the location (in Benveniste's sense) of this historical subject in relation to the "process" of which it is the "agent." The search for a method that would unite theory and practice is then the search for a historical grammar of the middle voice (in Derrida's sense) that has itself been repressed and distributed into active and passive moments by capitalist reification. All the other contradictions which have haunted traditional Marxian thought, such as that between a guiding (active) party elite and a loyal (passive) following, would thus evaporate when such a grammar was "recalled" or "announced."

The development of Marxian theory after Merleau-Ponty can be explained in part as the attempt to resolve such contradictions philosophically by borrowing heavily from the phenomenology of Husserl and Heidegger. Althusser's abandonment of any notion of the subject other than that which has been always already interpellated by ideological apparatuses, and his insistence on the overdetermination of historical processes, represents a crucial shift.[17] On the one hand, the ground for Althusser's move is a phenomenological attempt (following Heidegger and Merleau-Ponty) to overcome all hypostatized oppositions between subject and object, to allow language to speak the opposition and its subversion all at once: both subject and object are constructed only in and through language. On the other hand, however, Althusser is simply carrying dialectical materialism to its logical extreme, to that point where ideological (superstructural) processes are themselves reconceived in material terms: if for Marx language is nothing other than "practical consciousness," then ideology can only be understood as the concrete activity of social apparatuses, from institutions to family life, which enable material reproduction.[18] In the first case, a potentially infinite field of "discourse" begins to open up, in which the conditions of discursive unity as well as the possibilities for contestation are both radically contingent; this is the line of thought followed by Michel Foucault. In the second, ideological representation itself becomes a form of material circulation—a kind of symbolic exchange—which is always tied, "in the final instance," to economic determination; here, Pierre Bourdieu's work is the most accomplished example. In both cases, however, the problems of a political middle voice are reinscribed. Foucault's work will lead to the "radical contingency" of hegemony in Laclau and Mouffe, an attempt to rethink the middle-voiced impasses of orthodox Marxism and poststructuralism in a synthesis which, I will claim, only escapes from such impasses through uncriticized ethical claims. Bourdieu's work will tend toward the dead end that all structural-functionalist work produces when it adheres rigorously to a middle-voiced methodology.

Thus, for Michel Foucault, the positivity of a discursive practice con-

17. See especially Louis Althusser, "Ideology and Ideological State Apparatuses," *Lenin and Philosophy and Other Essays*, trans. Ben Brewster (New York: Monthly Review Press, 1971), 127–86; and "Contradiction and Overdetermination," *For Marx*, trans. Ben Brewster (London: Verso, 1982), 89–128.

18. See Karl Marx and Friedrich Engels, *The German Ideology*, Part One, trans. W. Lough, ed. C. J. Arthur (New York: International, 1977), 47.

stitutes a *historical* a priori which is not simply a synchronic "structure" or "mentality." "It is defined as the group of rules that characterize a discursive practice: but these rules are not imposed from the outside on the elements that they relate together; they are caught up in the very things that they connect."[19] The relation between the "elements" of a discourse and its "rules" is thus presented as one between a process and a pure "exteriority" that can only be conceived as the defining field of unification for the process, a field which is itself somehow "transformable." At the conclusion of *The Archaeology of Knowledge*, Foucault explicitly embraces the grammar of the middle voice in attempting to characterize the positivities of discursive practices in relation to their enunciating subjectivities. "These positivities are not so much limitations imposed on the initiative of subjects as the field in which that initiative is articulated (without, however, constituting its center), rules that it puts into operation (without it having invented or formulated them), relations that provide it with a support (without it being either their final result or their point of convergence)" (*AK*, 209). Thus, Foucault claims not to have denied "the possibility of changing discourse," but only to have "deprived the sovereignty of the subject of the exclusive and instantaneous right to it."

And yet, just as clearly, Foucault has no wish "to exclude the problem of the subject, but to define the positions and functions that the subject could occupy in the diversity of discourse" (*AK*, 200). Moreover, those "positions and functions" are not simply to be determined by the discontinuities that erupt spontaneously within history. Rather, they are embedded in and constituted by "power/knowledge" relations against which Foucault's work is explicitly directed. That is, Foucault would seem to show great concern not only for mapping a constituted subject's *given* position and function, but for the degree to which "emerging" subjectivities' ability to "occupy" in turn other positions and functions—to speak and be heard, to gain power over the rules "and redirect them against those who had initially imposed them"—is itself facilitated or denied by particular social configurations of discourses and "extra-discursive" practices.[20] In the last decade of his life especially, Foucault began to reevaluate the Nietzschean idea of a genealogy of morality, of rights and duties, as well as to propose an ethic of "care for the self" that tried to redefine "ethics"—in nonnormative, non-Christian and non-psychoanalytic terms—as a relation of the self to itself, as a question of self-management or an "aesthetics of existence," rather than as a relation of the

19. Michel Foucault, *The Archaeology of Knowledge*, trans. A. M. Sheridan Smith (New York: Harper, 1972), 127; hereafter, *AK* in the text.

20. See, for example, Michel Foucault, "Nietzsche, Genealogy, History" and "Intellectuals and Power," in *Language, Counter-Memory, Practice*, trans. Donald F. Bouchard and Sherry Simon (Ithaca: Cornell University, 1977), especially 150–51, 208, 213, and 216.

self to some externally adopted or internally legislated "code." Foucault's "ethics" must be seen as an attempt to explore a notion of the self beyond simple recognition of its discursively constituted position and function—one that, for all its rigor in avoiding cruder normative codes, did return his critique to Kantian questions of autonomous will, maturity, and enlightenment.[21]

The specific relation of this new "ethics" to what I have been calling "politics" remains contradictory in Foucault's work, a discrepancy due no doubt to Foucault's deep suspicions about the power of modern discourse to turn ethics itself, like psychiatry or sex, into one more field for institutionalized control.[22] In late discussions of such issues, for example, Foucault appears to imply both the need for an articulation of ethics and politics within adversarial movements (though a need that could not be met by any simple "return" to earlier codes or perspectives), and the contrary need for a clear separation of the two domains. Thus: "Recent liberation movements suffer from the fact that they cannot find any principle on which to base the elaboration of a new ethics. They need an ethics, but they cannot find any other ethics than an ethics founded on so-called scientific knowledge of what the self is, what desire is, what the unconscious is, and so on." But later: "For centuries we have been convinced that between our ethics, our personal ethics, our everyday life and the great political and social and economic structures there were analytic relations, and that we couldn't change anything, for instance, in our sex life or our family life, without ruining our economy, our democracy. I think we have to get rid of this idea of an analytic or necessary link between ethics and other social or economic or political structures."[23] Foucault's struggle with an ethics/politics articulation reiterates, I think, both the necessity and the difficulty the relation has posed for contemporary criticism—one which has not only been further obscured by approaches like Hillis Miller's, but remains unaddressed in the work of Laclau and Mouffe.

For Bourdieu, on the other hand, the primary means of satisfying the

21. See, for example, Michel Foucault, *The History of Sexuality: An Introduction,* trans. Robert Hurley (New York: Pantheon, 1978); "What is Enlightenment?" and "Politics and Ethics: An Interview," trans. Catherine Porter, in *The Foucault Reader,* ed. Paul Rabinow (New York: Pantheon, 1984), vol. 1, 31–50 and 373–80; and "The Ethic of Care for the Self as a Practice of Freedom: An Interview," trans. J. D. Gauthier, S. J., in *The Final Foucault,* ed. James Bernauer and David Rasmussen (Cambridge: MIT, 1988), 1–20.

22. In this sense, Foucault's difficulties recall Jürgen Habermas's own attempts to retrieve some notion of a life-world autonomous from, yet linked to, a rationalized public sphere.

23. Michel Foucault, "On the Genealogy of Ethics: An Overview of Work in Progress," in Hubert L. Dreyfus and Paul Rabinow, *Michel Foucault: Beyond Structuralism and Hermeneutics,* second ed. (Chicago: University of Chicago Press, 1983), 231 and 236.

requirements of a middle voice are to be found in the structural/ functionalist notion of the *habitus*. In Bourdieu's "science of practices," the *habitus* represents the interchange between two distinct forms of capital—cultural and material—which guarantees the reproduction over time of existing relations of domination and subordination, that is, the reproduction of all mechanisms of any distinction whatsoever.

> The structures constitutive of a particular type of environment (e.g., the material conditions of existence characteristic of a class condition) produce *habitus*, systems of durable, transposable *dispositions*, structured structures predisposed to function as structuring structures, that is, as principles of the generation and structuring of practices and representations which can be objectively "regulated" and "regular" without in any way being the product of obedience to rules, objectively adapted to their goals without presupposing a conscious aiming at ends or an express mastery of the operations necessary to attain them and, being all this, collectively orchestrated without being the product of the orchestrating action of a conductor.[24]

The *habitus*, itself the "product of history," at the same time produces practices, and thus history; it produces not only continuities and regularities, but—and here it goes well beyond Althusser's or Foucault's notion of discontinuous rupture—"it is at the same time the principle of transformations and regulated revolutions," which can be accounted for neither by "mechanistic sociologism" nor by "voluntarist or spontaneist subjectivism" (*OTP*, 82).

Indeed, Bourdieu elaborates the notion of a middle voice in some detail when he attempts to explain how merely coordinated practices are transformed into collective action. Such action can be constituted only in the dialectical relation between an already functioning *habitus*—"a matrix of perceptions, appreciations, and actions"—and an *"object event,"* a conditional stimulus which demands a determinate response, but only from those predisposed (due, for example, to the "awakening of class consciousness") to constitute such a response. Moreover, the relationship between *habitus* and event is itself neither wholly coordinated, since these are the products of different "causal series," nor wholly independent, since both are engendered, "in the last analysis, by the economic bases of the social formation in question" (*OTP*, 83). But since the economic bases are themselves what they are only because of the continuous systems maintenance performed by the habitus, we have once again reached the commutative stasis of middle-voiced grammars. In Bourdieu, of course, there is no hint of

24. Pierre Bourdieu, *Outline of a Theory of Practice*, trans. Richard Nice (Cambridge: Cambridge University Press, 1986), 72; hereafter *OTP* in the text.

a return to ethics as there is in Foucault—to his credit, Bourdieu revitalizes a more traditional Marxian focus on the material economy. And it must be admitted that Bourdieu's mapping of the circulation of value between material and symbolic economies usefully formalizes the more casual insights of older modes of cultural critique. But it must also be noted that the felicitous notion of an "objective event" which is simultaneously outside of and yet produced by the habitus would seem to forestall the hegemonic articulation of political positions even as it obviates any need for ethics. Unlike Foucault, who at least recognized the necessary discrepancies between a theoretical structure dependent on irrational discontinuities and the practical requirements of "political" and "ethical" choices, Bourdieu comes close at times to a rhetoric of pure magic.

IV

At this point, I would like to turn to Laclau and Mouffe. Having effectively jettisoned the latent economic determinism and structural functionalism in Althusser, they seem to put everything up for grabs: there is no necessary or essentializable subjectivity, objectivity, human nature, need, desire, class, power, autonomy, society, historical process, arche, logos, or telos. All such supposed identities are in fact always already constituted by and through a discursive articulation—"a *political construction* from dissimilar elements."[25] At the same time, such contingency does not at all imply endless fragmentation or simple dissolution. The impossibility of any totalizing "suture" of dissimilar elements prevents both the extension of a hegemonic formation into a closed organic whole, as well as the absolute, static dispersion of elements precluding any and all articulations; that prevents both the reification of subjectivity around some falsely naturalized identity, and the completely achieved and unchanging fragmentation of the subject into unarticulable elements. "The game of overdetermination" is what then "reintroduces the horizon of an impossible totality" (*HSS*, 122). It is within this horizon that politics takes place, a space always already inhabited by its own inability to suture itself closed. *Antagonism* is then the articulated relation produced by a "logic of equivalence" defined against that which it excludes, yet implicitly accepts, as its other. In a sense, Laclau and Mouffe produce what is perhaps the most elaborate version of a middle-voiced politics yet invented. By assuming the phenomenological collapse (following Merleau-Ponty) of subject-object essentialism, Laclau and Mouffe will be able to account both for the limits and the openness of all

---

25. Ernesto Laclau and Chantal Mouffe, *Hegemony and Socialist Strategy* (London: Verso, 1985), 85; hereafter *HSS* in the text.

social formations in terms of the discourses producing them.26 Thus, "social agents do not, as referents, constitute any formation"; rather, it is only through the hegemonic articulation constituting them as "social agents"— a middle-voiced grammar of self-articulation—that the social formation comes into being. Simultaneously permanently open and differentially sutured, "society" is a dynamic surface of possibilities that can never be fully achieved, or fully dispersed, of externalities that produce internal essences only as supplements.

If these were the only conclusions to be drawn from Laclau and Mouffe's poststructural notion of hegemony, one would be hard pressed to discern the specifically "socialist" dimensions of their project. But hegemonic formations are not merely constructed and transformed through antagonism and equivalence. The growing expansion and distension of hegemonic "limits," a displacement "proper to contemporary societies," spells the end of hegemonic politics itself (HSS, 144). The modern "precariousness" of the internal limits defining hegemonic articulations—having moved far beyond simple bipolar conflicts—threatens the very notion of a hegemonic formation. And here is where a phenomenological sublation and a historical one merge in their socialist vision. "If every frontier disappears, this does not simply mean that the formation is more difficult to *recognize*. As the totality is not a datum but a construction, when there is a breaking of its constitutive chains of equivalence, the totality does something more than conceal itself: *it dissolves*" (HSS, 144). On the other hand, their point is that once the *phenomena* of certain hegemonic formations are no longer recognized, the hegemonic formations themselves no longer exist, since such formations can be nothing more than the product of social relations articulated by discursive practices—a conclusion that, in more general terms, effectively means there is no operative difference between what social agents understand to be the case, and what is the case. Such notions alone carry troubling implications, especially given twentieth-century European history. But Laclau and Mouffe also reveal their own unerring faith in the progressive dissolution of internal hegemonic frontiers through the necessary practice of hegemonic politics—though the ground for such a faith, beyond a certain vague Hegelian logic, is nowhere indicated in their book. In fact, as their last chapter makes clear, this self-dissolution of hegemony by means of hegemony will entail an "ethical" supplement to their otherwise "political" descriptions.

26. See for example HSS, 146 n16: "The limits of the conception of meaning inherent in every phenomenology, insofar as it is based on the irreducibility of 'the lived', must not make us forget that in some of its formulations—and particularly in the work of Merleau-Ponty—we find some of the most radical attempts to break with the essentialism inherent in every form of dualism." See also Maurice Merleau-Ponty, *The Prose of the World*, trans. John O'Neill (Evanston, Illinois: Northwestern University Press, 1973), 85–86.

Why should this inner dialectic within hegemonic politics be called "ethical"? Precisely because, if it is to avoid the charge of logical determinism which Laclau and Mouffe quite effectively hurl at much earlier Marxian theory and is to move beyond a faith in middle-voiced political processes, the self-dissolution of hegemonic limits must open itself to active engagement, to the commitment which provides the meaning to the word "strategy" in their title. And this commitment is based on Kantian/Enlightenment notions so reminiscent of existing liberal ideology that Laclau and Mouffe must simultaneously embrace and disavow "ethics" itself. For Laclau and Mouffe, a fundamental historical rupture occurs with the French Revolution which results "in the establishment of a new legitimacy, in the invention of democratic culture" (*HSS*, 155). It is only through this "decisive mutation in the political imaginary of Western societies" two hundred years ago that "the logic of equivalence was transformed into the fundamental instrument of production of the social" (*HSS*, 155). This "democratic revolution" (a phrase they take from Tocqueville) is itself necessary if simple relations of *subordination* (for example of serf to master, of woman to man) are to be suddenly "articulated"—that is, are to be understood and constructed as if from some discursive "exterior"—as relations of *oppression* and *domination*. (For proof, Laclau and Mouffe point to the appearance of Mary Wollstonecraft's *Vindication of the Rights of Woman* in 1792 as determining the "birth of feminism through the use made in it of democratic discourse" (*HSS*, 154). Their entirely unexamined claim is that Wollstonecraft's feminist critique was only possible on the basis of the already announced Rights of Man.)

And how are relations of subordination, where there is no external or judgmental discourse or agent to appeal to, rearticulated as antagonistic relations of domination, "which are considered as illegitimate from the perspective, or in the judgment, of a social agent external to them" (*HSS*, 154)? The answer is fairly straightforward: "in order to be mobilized in this way, the democratic principle of liberty and equality first had to impose itself as the new matrix of the social imaginary" (*HSS*, 154–55). Thus, the Rights of Man—founded, as liberal democratic tradition has always put it, "on no other legitimacy than the people" (*HSS*, 155)—erupts into the life of Western Europe, and changes everything: a new discursive exterior, a new discursive "agent" as it were, becomes the ethical authority demanding an end to political (legal) inequality. (Laclau and Mouffe's understanding of the French Revolution would thus appear to be virtually indistinguishable from Kant's late view—it is a "moral cause inserting itself" into historical time, like a divine annunciation of human perfectibility.[27] The struggle against

27. See Kant "An Old Question Raised Again," trans. Robert E. Anchor, in Kant, *On History*, ed. Lewis White Beck (New York: Library of Liberal Arts, 1963), 143 and 146. In

economic inequality is then simply the extension of a legal demand into economics, thus recasting Marxian critique as a subcategory of an ongoing "democratic revolution." For all practical purposes, Laclau and Mouffe's argument actually ends with their annunciation of the "democratic principle."

How and why this "democratic revolution" came about are the more conventional sorts of historical questions curiously ignored in the book, though such questions were clearly on the minds of political theorists from Rousseau to Marx. In fact, it is hard to see how the "democratic principle" operates other than as a historical deus ex machina, a sort of Hegelian unfolding without the Hegel or the unfolding, although its timing here is predictably French. As Margaret Thatcher recently reminded the world, the English have always thought that the "democratic revolution" began with Magna Carta. Christopher Hill, among others, might take particular exception to Laclau and Mouffe's history of democracy.[28] It is also hard to see why this "democratic revolution"—if it is so sudden and decisive an event—came about in Western Europe. There is so little discussion of such issues that the purely contingent, historical, and discursive character of this democratic principle begins to acquire a dimension of "externality" to existing discursive articulations that is of another order from what one might call run-of-the-mill "externality." That is, it becomes the external discourse of discourses, the judicial agency beyond contingent agents. Laclau and Mouffe know that if "socialist strategy" is to be addressed, they must avoid the major problem of a purely middle-voiced method that the bulk of Foucault's work left behind: "the struggle against subordination cannot be the result of the situation of subordination itself" (HSS, 152). A "socialist strategy" cannot be content with Foucault's dictum that power simultaneously oppresses and enables. The question they wish to pose then is both crucial and truly "strategic": under what conditions do individual relations implicitly understood and resisted for some time as oppressive ones emerge as distinctly "political" relations—as relations articulated by means of a hegemonic discourse? But Laclau and Mouffe's response is finally quite indistinguishable

---

this essay, the last piece of writing he completed, Kant elaborates a perspective on the Revolution that does not at all appear to be incompatible with that of Laclau and Mouffe. "For such a phenomenon in human history *is not to be forgotten,* because it has revealed a tendency and faculty in human nature for improvement such that no politician, affecting wisdom, might have conjured out of the course of things hitherto existing, and one which nature and freedom alone, united in the human race in conformity with inner principles of right, could have promised. But so far as time is concerned, it can promise this only indefinitely and as a contingent event" (147).

28. See, for example, Christopher Hill's discussion of the seventeenth-century Levellers who "moved forward to a conception of natural rights, the rights of man," or his chapter on "The English Revolution and the Brotherhood of Man," in *Puritanism and Revolution* (New York: Schocken, 1964), 75–82 and 123–52.

from the ideological self-understanding of late eighteenth-century liberal thought. That is, their response is "ethical," and in the most Enlightened sense of the word.

Indeed, one could say that the ethics of the democratic principle—liberty and equality, now applied to the notion of hegemonic articulation—governs the entirety of Laclau and Mouffe's contribution to socialist strategy. What they require is "the autonomization of the spheres of struggle and the multiplication of political spaces," which means that more classical (Jacobin) concentrations of "power and knowledge" can be given no priority over racial or gendered ones, for example, (Of course, the radical equivalence posited here of all resistance to oppression yields perverse anomalies when it is combined with phenomenology's deconstruction of subject/object dualisms. Why, for example, such a principle—the equivalence and autonomy of all struggles against domination—would not implicitly extend to the German *Kampf* collectively and hegemonically "articulated" against "Jewish domination" in the 1920s and 1930s is an open question. In such cases, to call the obvious gap between objective reality and subjective discourse an error of naive essentialism would be moronic; to maintain on the other hand that the Nazi "articulation" itself erred simply by not recognizing the equal status of other hegemonically produced relations is somehow to miss the point entirely.) With the emergence of a "plurality of subjects," Laclau and Mouffe attempt to construct the project of a radical democracy on the basis of a new *social logics*. By completing the principle of democratic equivalence with the construction of a new "'common sense' which changes the identity of the different groups, in such a way that the demands of each group are articulated equivalentially with those of the others," Laclau and Mouffe claim to have found the strategic formulation of Marx's dictum "that the free development of each should be the condition for the free development of all" (*HSS*, 183). In more concrete terms, however, Laclau and Mouffe have taken traditional notions of liberal democratic ideology and translated them into the sphere of hegemonic politics: there are now hegemonic blocs that delimit, define, and alter one another the way autonomous agents did formerly. The difference, of course, is that Laclau and Mouffe do not accept the older liberal assumption of *"one* single space of equality"—a "plurality" of subject spaces is for them irreducible.

What then is the mechanism behind this tenuous balance between the necessary extension of a logic of equivalence (built into the "decisive mutation" which occurred two hundred years ago) and the necessary preservation of the always contingent plurality of subject positions? What mechanism, that is, "articulates" *equality* with *liberty?* It is, precisely, an "ethical principle" which is simultaneously "more valid" than ever before, yet founded on no essential, "natural" rights (*HSS*, 184), an ethics whose form recalls that of Kantian liberal thought yet which now insists on truly collective and democratic expression. "It is not liberalism as such which should be called into question, for as an ethical principle which defends the liberty of the individual to fulfill his or her human capacities, it is more valid today than ever." At the same time, however, this ethical principle must itself be given new meaning: "what is involved is the production of *another* individual, an individual who is no longer constructed out of the matrix of possessive individualism" (*HSS*, 184). Laclau and Mouffe's strategic project not only depends on this invocation of liberalism as an ethical principle, but takes that principle to its logical extreme. That is, they want not only "ethical" individuals in the traditional Kantian sense; they want to see the construction of "new individuals" altogether through the penetration of that ethic beyond its superficial (superstructural?) application. In spite of the benign reasonableness of their concluding remarks on the benefits of a moderate utopianism, Laclau and Mouffe's vision is startlingly grandiose: the constitution of new, more perfectly equal and liberated individuals by means of the completely contingent and nonteleological self-overcoming of hegemonic politics, a nonsublating sublation that depends upon a realization of liberal ethics so totalizing that it rivals any previous utopia. Marx of course projected the victory of already existing subject positions—the universalization of nonclass, proletarian interests. For a supposedly nonessentialist position, the problems proliferate at every turn. Whence this suddenly introduced notion of a fulfillment of "human capacities" in a text otherwise strenuously phrased to avoid such hypostatizations? What remains of the contingent nature of politics if a notion of personal fulfillment can be introduced whenever it is needed? Isn't this what politics-talk always does anyway? What are these abstract "human capacities" in a world where the human subject is itself always only a product of hegemonic articulation? And how can it be said that the decisive articulation of this new logic of liberty and equality for all was suddenly able "to impose itself" (*HSS*, 155)— albeit in the middle voice—in France, and in 1789?

V

My objective, however, is really not to discover something otherwise hidden from Laclau and Mouffe. As a footnote to their introductory chapter makes clear, they would appear already to have preempted the force of my critique.[29] "We do not question the need for ethical judgments in the founding

29. Norman Geras has written what might be called the definitive critique of *Hegemony and Socialist Strategy* from within the assumptions of traditional Western Marxism in "Post-Marxism?" *New Left Review* 163 (1987): 40–82. Geras's strongest point is simply the necessarily "arbitrary" character of Laclau and Mouffe's notions of oppression and liberation, of "exploitation and privilege," due to their rejection of any "normative" discourse. My claim here is that, buried within the text, Laclau and Mouffe have in fact inscribed the normative as an ethical intervention in historical time.

of a socialist politics. . . . Our argument is that from the presence of ethical judgments it does not follow that these should be attributed to a transcendental subject, constituted outside every discursive condition of emergence" (*HSS*, 46 n53). But I do want to point to the ambiguity at work both in the body of the text, and in this disavowing footnote. On the one hand, there is a "need" for ethical judgments in socialist politics; on the other, this need is immediately translated as a mere "presence" that is contingently constituted. What is this generalized, irreducible (an irreducibility on which their critique of Kautsky depends) "need" that suddenly appears, like "human capacities" later, which is simultaneously defined as nothing more than one contingent discourse among others? At issue, I would claim, is precisely its priority as *the* external discourse of discourses handed down in 1789—a priority that, even in Laclau and Mouffe's language, seems to suggest an "agent" outside of, yet constituted by an existing agency, a nontranscendent transcendental subject. Laclau and Mouffe have hardly escaped the Kantian subjectivity they disown if they are forced to recall a Kantian "ethical principle" that seems to drag such subjectivity along with it wherever it goes.

What is of course at stake is Laclau and Mouffe's ambivalent commitment to the grammar of the middle voice. They relinquish all notions of actual, material *interest*, hypostatized along class lines and universalizable in struggle and revolution—a path with its own obvious aporias. But they are then left with a vague, though equally objectionable, Hegelian machinery: the (necessary) fulfillment of implicit capacities by means of (contingent) historical circumstances. The "discourse of democracy," it seems, is the contingent product of a certain "Western" social logic, and of the (presumably still contingent) self-overcoming of previous hegemonic articulations, but because it also has something to do with the mediation of the fulfillment of human capacities, it acquires a "decisive" force, and grounds ethical judgment. What this also means is that Laclau and Mouffe, perhaps even more than Marxian theorists before them, are left with a contradictory expression of the link between "discourse" and "strategy," between theory and practice. Because the new "discourse of democracy" already signals the self-dissolution of hegemonic politics—the revolution has occurred, as it were, though not everyone knows it—"socialist strategy" must not only refrain from laying exclusive claim to the democratic discourse, but must in fact allow itself to be subsumed as only a contingent moment within the pluralistic multiplication of social spaces. (One could discern here the trace of *perestroika* within their project.) Yet somehow, effective "strategy" needs to make ethical judgments (judgments which also implicitly privilege its perspective), since continued opposition to domination depends on the active articulation of a new socialist hegemony. It is as if the term "socialist strategy" had supplanted, and taken on the problems of, older proletarian praxis: it must work toward hegemony, even as it withers away. But if this is the case, it is difficult to see how Laclau and Mouffe's rigorous deconstruction of essentialist political categories actually avoids a return to the earlier mystifications of theory and practice carefully exposed in the first two chapters of their book.

Laclau and Mouffe must hide their ethics even as they recall and deploy ethics as a rhetorical category. They know that their argument depends on an ethical invocation which somehow has accreted to itself the character of greater necessity and priority than the always contingent articulations of hegemonic formations. But they also know that any overt statement of how those ethical principles came to be privileged would ring with the same unwarranted, essentialist, and foundationalist tones heard in traditional liberal democratic discourse. Laclau and Mouffe *need* Kantian, universalizable ethics. They would just rather not draw our attention to this crucial "supplement" on which the political strategy of pluralist and libertarian articulation will inevitably depend. Not unlike de Man and Miller, though with decidedly more promising political aims, Laclau and Mouffe often seem most interested in insisting on the illusoriness of all naturalized articulations, even as they remind their readers of the necessity of hegemonic strategies—that is, in reiterating precisely that quality of ethical judgment which Kant presupposed, now as the new basis of radical political discourse.

Still, there are crucial distinctions to be maintained, and more than rhetoric at stake. By embracing the new jargon of authenticity, Miller reproduces a conventional notion of ethical responsibility made all the more acquiescent toward existing forms of political domination for being elaborated in turn as only one more effect of a middle-voiced grammar. On the other side of the fence, as it were, Laclau and Mouffe implicitly acknowledge that the ethical gesture is inescapable and insufficient at the same time. And yet, they are dedicated enough to Althusserian methods to be more than uncomfortable with this complicity. Their ambivalence, I would claim, amounts to an elaborate disavowal, one which ironically serves to reinforce the credibility of precisely that blinding poststructuralist faith in *différance* and "absolute alterity" which Laclau and Mouffe implicitly challenge throughout their book. What began as a critique of existing adversarial politics winds up affirming the automatic nature of "progressive" politics itself in Western-style democracies. Once again, it begins to appear that things just cannot help being the way they are.

While there would seem to be no way of redeeming Miller's views for anything but trite, existential platitudes, Laclau and Mouffe's project was not bound to conclude in what could easily be taken as nothing more than an apologia for an existing public sphere differentiated by "interest group" legislative lobbying. Their faith in the liberating significance of increasing social rationalization is not the only conclusion possible in a work that rightly reminds adversarial politics of the contingent character of social relations and historical change, of the conditional character of human identity. But when the phenomenological reduction of a political grammar is allowed to superimpose itself on a historical one, the synthesis of a contingent historical process with the evolution of human identity begins to look suspiciously like the cunning of reason *redivivus*. The fundamental questions that *Hegemony and Socialist Strategy* declines to address—How is it that the invention of a "new legitimacy," the "democratic revolution," occurred? What is the specific relationship between the development of capitalism and the invention of a new legitimacy (the big Marxian question, after all)? How can it be said that this new legitimacy, though just as contingent as every other, comes to represent an ethical principle, a discourse superseding all others?—are, I would suggest, not merely details to be filled in later. They are questions basic to what I have been calling the inevitable complicity between politics-talk and ethics-talk all along in this essay. There is indeed a crucial difference between Miller's "ethics" and Laclau and Mouffe's "strategy." The real task ahead is preventing the mysterious grammar of *Hegemony and Socialist Strategy* from justifying in its own way the ambivalent detachment of Gramsci's "traditional" intellectual, to which role Miller bravely hails his readers. Of course, most of them will have heard the call before.

THOMAS KEENAN

Freedom, the Law of another Fable

> It is popular to talk about freedom, but how many of us in the world
> are sure we are talking about the same thing when we use the word?
> *Uhuru* in Africa is different from liberty in Philadelphia. Freedom in
> Hollywood is not quite what *liberté* is in Paris. Nor is freedom in
> Washington exactly what's meant by the word *svoboda* in Moscow, or
> *tszuyu* in Peiping. . . . This peculiar word "freedom"—with hundreds
> of definitions—has been debased in the coinage of communications. It
> might be helpful to go back to the original derivation of word—. . . the
> word "liberty" traced back to its roots means "growing up" or
> "maturing" or "taking responsibility."
>
> —Ronald Reagan[1]

I. READING SADE?

What happens (to us)—if anything, which cannot of course be taken for
granted before the fact—when we *read?* Is reading possible, and are we free
to do it? Since we only ever read *something*, no matter how ill-defined or
trembling its status as an object for a subject might be when reading is the
verb, a response calls for an example.

With Sade, for example, Michel Foucault has lyrically suggested just the
opposite:

> The precise object of "sadism" is not the other, nor its body, nor its
> sovereignty: it is all that could be said [*c'est tout ce qui a pu être dit*]. Even
> farther and still in retreat [*encore en retrait*], it is the mute circle where
> language deploys itself: to this whole world of captive readers, Sade, the
> captive, withdraws the possibility of reading [*à tout ce monde des lec-
> teurs captifs, Sade, le captif, retire la possibilité de lire*].[2]

Are we—captive, captivated, obsessive, everyday and everynight readers
that we unavoidably are—*free* to read Sade? What are we captives of if not

1. Ronald Reagan, with Richard C. Hubler, *Where's the Rest of Me?* (New York: Dell, 1981 [1965]), 339–40.

2. Michel Foucault, "Le Language à l'infini," *Tel Quel* 15 (Autumn 1963):44–53, 50; "Language to Infinity," in Donald F. Bouchard, ed., *Language, Counter-Memory, Practice* (Ithaca: Cornell University Press, 1977), 53–67, 62.

YFS 79, *Literature and the Ethical Question*, ed. Claire Nouvet, © 1991 by Yale University.

the very language in which those texts are written and which they take as their object, and hence are we not somehow *bound* to read Sade? With the possibility of reading withdrawn from those who can still nevertheless be called (and be called readers), does the opposition of freedom and necessity retain any pertinence? In this impossibility, who responds? More exactly, who is addressed? After all, as Foucault rightly continues, this possibility of reading has been withdrawn so effectively, "so well, that to the question of knowing to whom the work of Sade was addressed (and addresses itself today), there is only one answer: no one [*si bien, qu'à la question de savoir à qui s'adressait (et s'adresse de nos jours) l'oeuvre de Sade, il n'y a qu'une réponse: personne]*" (50;62). Who reads, and how, a text addressed to no one, and what status does it have? Something happens. This text "withdraws from itself—but by confiscating it in a gesture of repetitive appropriation—the space of its language; . . . it can, and in the strict sense, must [*devrait*] continue without stopping [*sans arrêt*], in a murmur that has no other ontological status than that of a . . .contestation" (50;62–63). We, and others,[3] encounter this *murmure sans arrêt* every time we let ourselves be called by a text not destined for us, and it goes without saying that no text is ever (structurally speaking) addressed particularly to one or more of us; it could not be a text, something written or said in a language, if it were able to specify its reader.[4] A text is an open apostrophic structure, a call incapable of encoding in advance or predetermining the response it might receive or who might give it. Addressed, to no one. Evidently, that is reading's only chance, its terrible freedom and its exhilarating captivity.

It is this possibility—reading Sade—that Maurice Blanchot has put into question more rigorously than any other reader of Sade.[5] "Whoever has read in Sade only what is readable there, has read nothing [*Qui n'a lu dans Sade que ce que Sade a de lisible, n'a rien lu*],"[6] concludes the opening paragraph of Blanchot's reading of Sade's "Français, encore un effort si vous voulez être républicains," the revolutionary political tract inscribed (and read aloud)

---

3. Thanks here to Jeffrey Nunokawa.

4. See Jacques Derrida, "Signature Event Context," trans. Jeffrey Mehlman and Samuel Weber, in *Limited Inc* (Evanston: Northwestern University Press, 1988), 1–23, 7, on the necessary disappearance of the receiver implied by the iterative (alternative) structure of writing.

5. In addition to the passages to be discussed, see for instance Blanchot's remark in "La Raison de Sade," in *Lautréamont et Sade* (Paris: Minuit, 1949 [1963]), 15–49; translated as "Sade," in Marquis de Sade, *The Complete Justine, Philosophy in the Bedroom, and other writings*, trans. Richard Seaver and Austryn Wainhouse (New York: Grove Press, 1965), 37–72: "it is almost not possible to read it, . . . a perfectly unreadable work" (18;38). Future citations from this essay will be noted as *LS* and *CJ*.

6. "L'Inconvenance majeure," introduction to Sade, "Français, encore un effort . . . " (Paris: Jean-Jacques Pauvert, 1965), 7–51, 10; partially translated by June Guicharnaud as "The Main Impropriety (excerpts)," *Yale French Studies* 39 (1967): 50–63. Most of the citations from Blanchot are to these texts, noted as *IM* and *MI*.

within *La Philosophie dans le boudoir*.[7] How could we read something other than what is readable, and why would reading only this readable turn out to be reading nothing at all? What else is there in the text of Sade, if the activity of reading exceeds merely what can be read? In other words, if what is simply readable is nothing, as far as reading goes, then reading what can already be read is not enough, is not even reading. How? What can be read has already been read, and reading it amounts to nothing more than applying a ready-made interpretive code to a set of signs, in order to (re)interiorize their essentially accidental exteriority. What is to be read here is something else, neither something already read, nor even something readable, but some excess of inscription of language that remains when the work of reassimilating or incorporating the readable is done, a textual element not susceptible of being reduced to something codable.

There is much in Sade ready to be decoded and understood—the text calls out for this rationalization: what Blanchot has called "la raison de Sade" can never be underestimated. But Sade's interpreters pay the price of erasing what cannot be read in his text, which is to say his text insofar as it is a text, language, and not merely meaning or saying something. Granted that what Sade has to say, what is readable there, is difficult enough. But overcoming the interferences posed by his text and its language for the sake of what it has to say—no matter how enlightening, outrageous, dangerous, even evil—is not reading. Nothing could be more deluded than to expect that we could avoid that work, and simply be done once and for all with interpreting, making sense. Except perhaps thinking that it is all there is to do.[8]

Which means that (1) we never *read* just once, and (2) what Blanchot calls reading demands the risk of a terrible insusceptibility, a resistance to affect or pathos, the radical in-difference Sade calls *apathie*, without pathos.[9] "Too bad for those whom these great ideas corrupt, too bad for those who fasten only upon the evil in philosophical opinions, susceptible of being corrupted by everything. . . . It is not to them, not at all, that I speak; I address myself

---

7. Quotations are from the new edition of Sade's complete works: *Oeuvres complètes du Marquis de Sade 3: Justine, Opuscules politiques, La Philosophie dans le boudoir . . .* (Paris: Pauvert, 1986), in which *La Philosophie dans le boudoir* = 374–561, "Français, encore un effort" = 490–536. (Thanks to Elissa Marder for making me read this text.) We have used, with modifications when necessary, the English version in: Marquis de Sade, *The Complete Justine* (see note 5). Citations in the text refer first to the French edition and then the English.

8. See Werner Hamacher, "LECTIO: de Man's Imperative," trans. Susan Bernstein, ed. Wlad Godzich and Lindsay Waters, *Reading de Man Reading* (Minneapolis: University of Minnesota Press, 1989), 171–201 especially, 188.

9. Blanchot defined "what Dolmancé calls *apathie* [as] a state of high tension and clear insensibility" (*IM*, 28; *MI*, 54). In this regard, recall that Paul de Man approached a definition of the ethical as precisely this resistance to pathos. See the discussion of "pathos" and "ethos" in "Allegory (*Julie*), in *AR*, 198 and 206–07.

only to those people capable of understanding me [*capables de m'entendre*], and they will read me without danger" (506;311). Who? *Personne.*

II. WHAT DO YOU CALL WHAT WE'RE DOING?

What enables—which would be also to say, what disables—reading? Blanchot's answer is difficult enough: language, and its ease. "Sade is difficult reading. He is clear, his style is easy, his language without detour? (*IM*, 10). Everything is called by its name(s): "He aspires to logic; he reasons," and the reason is that of the *logos*, the word that names and relates, properly. Sade's ease, the clarity and distinction in representation, by which the "great truths" (525;329) he has to tell are brought into the light of day and discourse, finds its privileged example in those opening moments of *La Philosophie* during which Eugénie learns the correct and proper names, *sans détour*, for a bewildering variety of organs and activities (especially the "lesson" in the third dialogue, 396–404;199–208). For example:

> **Eugénie.**— . . . But a word, dear friend, a word has just escaped you again and I don't understand it. What do you mean by this expression *whore?* Pardon me, but you know, I'm here to learn. [*Mais un mot, chère amie, un mot vient de t'échapper encore, et je ne l'entends pas. Qu'entends-tu par cette expression de putain? Pardon, mais tu sais? je suis ici pour m'instruire.*] [404;208]

> **Eugénie.**—Oh, dearest, what pleasures you give me! . . . What do you call what we're doing there? [*Ah! ma bonne, que tu me fais de plaisir! . . . Comment appelle-t-on ce que nous faisons là?*] [400;204]

In more ways than one, "j'appelle un chat un chat" is the strategy of the Sade of the *Philosophie*.[10] But the will to clarity pushes beyond the striving for precision in descriptive vocabulary and grammatical linkages to the modality of their rhetorical deployment. If there are many questions about the articulation of names with things and activities here, and just as many answers, the emphasis is nevertheless on the naming as such, the activity of calling or giving names itself—"j'aime qu'on me nomme ainsi," says Saint-Ange (404;208). For Eugénie, here to learn, the learning is (in) naming, the lesson is a lesson in names, not simply about names, in general or in particular, but an event in naming. The text underlines the constitutive duplicity of naming and calling: both the inaugural gift of an insignia, the bestowal of a name, and the interpellation or identification of the bearer of a name by

10. See Blanchot, "La Littérature et le droit à la mort," in *La Part du feu* (Paris: Gallimard, 1949), 291–331, 302; "Literature and the Right to Death," trans. Lydia Davis, in *The Gaze of Orpheus* (Barrytown, NY: Station Hill Press, 1981), 21–62. Hereafter noted when necessary as *LDM* and *LRD*.

means of it. Reading as understanding takes this latter articulative, relational moment as its focus, determining the name as the coded, significant, meaningful marker (whether literal or figurative, it matters not, as Eugénie and her teachers demonstrate) or the thing. But the success of this effort depends on an *active* moment that cannot be incorporated into this cognitive economy—the name as affirmation, as call.

"Something," Blanchot writes, "is sought in Sade. The search, which is that of a new lucidity, is not pursued in an interrogatory mode by rather by clear, assured, and always decisive *affirmations*" (*IM*, 13). What is affirmed in Sade? The search proceeds through the postulates and demonstrations of "analytic reason," but one which for Blanchot is attracted by something else it can in no way account for. Reason and its names, the sunshine of enlightenment, find themselves exceeded by themselves, propelled or interpellated, drawn out from themselves, by their very articulation, by their capacity to reason or to name, called to affirm (in the name of reason) something else, something other than reason or the proper name, that remains hidden in the nocturnal darkness of language and thus exercises a certain magnetism. For Blanchot, Sade is difficult not because something is left unsaid or unreasoned in an irrational obscurantism, but because "reason is excessive" (*IM*, 15), and because of the "alliance, the mixture of a clarity and an obscurity, which troubles and complicate our reading, renders it internally violent" (*IM*, 14). The difficulty is that the obscurity can thus not simply be cleared up by more reasoning or better names; it is in fact just that attraction to say or do *more*, that *exigence d'excès*, in which naming and reading are not halted or negated but disturbed, complicated, suspended, temporalized, repeated—which is to say—affirmed, demanded, called for. There is no one name or thing to read here, but a mixture, more than a name. More than any name as a coded unit(y) in a signifying system, more than meaning(s). Reading is in trouble because names affirm, call to others beyond anything they or any reason can possibly account for—the force, the interruptive intervention of this elsewhere opened by the call, complicates reading by refusing to let it stop, tears it apart by attracting it beyond itself without going anywhere else. "This *exigence d'excès* does not affirm simply his right to reason . . . but knows itself more reasonable than it [reason]" (*IM*, 14–15). The affirmation of the name, more than an answer to a question, resists understanding even as it demands it and as it frustrates any attempt to stop, to treat it as simply impossible (no despair or nihilism here).

Sade, perhaps, is crazy, as we all must be in our best nocturnal hours, but what he writes does not succumb to such a judgment. The sign [of this] is that we always leave off [*sortons*] reading him less troubled in sensibility than belied [crazed] [*démentis*] in thought, not convinced, but somehow incited [*proposés*] to a way of understanding which escapes us and still attracts us. From there, in spite of ourselves and regardless of our desire for a simple logic, we take up reading again, carried away by a movement which will no longer stop. [*IM*, 13]

It is this movement away, on and on, this self-exceeding reading in spite of our selves, which must be read here, in Sade and in Blanchot. "Français, encore un effort" is structured by this repetitive movement, the movement of *encore un effort* itself, and it calls on a twisted or divided temporal 'logic' to teach a difficult lesson in reading its affirmations—all those names. "I'm here to learn," says Eugénie, and the lesson we learn with her is not about something else, not even about itself as some object called language. The lesson is nothing other than (the) reading, insofar as it depends on and cannot fail to encounter language or a text (in its possible unreadability) again and again, without pathos [*a-pathie*] but simply as what happens. And it is taught by example.

III. THE FABLE OF FREEDOM

In fact, all of *La Philosophie dans le boudoir* is nothing if not a pedagogical text, and more precisely a text which teaches about (the ethics and politics of) teaching, even if the famous altered letter in its epigraph suggests a kind of oscillating hesitation over the proper relation that reading might take up with regard to that teaching. Where the *Philosophie*'s first edition bore the epigraph "the mother will *pre*scribe its reading to her daughter," the next version found the mother giving contrary orders: "the mother will *pro*scribe its reading to her daughter." The text, though, argues that the most effective instruction is given not by command—whether prescription or proscription—but by example. If it teaches most effectively, as it often suggests, by "joining a little practice to the theory [*joignant la pratique à la théorie*]" (398;202), its theory and its practice share the trait of progressing *by example* (as the preface "Aux Libertins" spells out in recommending that its addressees follow its "models" and "examples" [309;185]). Recall the advice of "Français, encore un effort": that to make good citizens one should "give them . . . many more examples than lessons [*donnez-leur sur ce grand sujet [Dieu] plus d'exemples que de leçons*]" (499;305). The lessons given by the "instituteurs immoraux" rely again and again on the enumeration of examples, not only the tableaux vivants acted out or practiced by the teachers and their eager student (as well as her considerably less willing mother), but also a multitude of more abstract models from Socrates to the Romans to the Tahitians, from the animal kingdom to the world of plants and minerals. We will borrow a word from Sade and call these examples *fables*, taking seriously their tendency to draw didactic lessons from the so-called natural world in the manner of La Fontaine or the authors of *Aesop's*. The fables are generally deployed to provide models of ethical action, to instruct their readers in what must (prescription) or must not (proscription) be done. (The classical fable teaches the one who is free how to exercise that liberty, how to enjoy it responsibly. It takes freedom [to know, to act, and to speak] as its presupposition, and teaches it as a practice. It defines freedom as self-knowledge, as knowing one's name and living up to or within it.) That Sade's ethical tales conclude in immorals rather than morals in no way changes their structure, and only confirms their (perhaps disturbing) pedagogical force.

For example—but it is not just one example among other, concerning as it does freedom—consider the problem raised by "la belle et dépravée Saint-Ange" (*IM*, 9) midway through the third dialogue.[11]

> **Mme De Saint-Ange.**—Listen to me, Eugénie. It is absurd to say that as soon as a girl is weaned from her mother's breast she must from that moment become the victim of her parents' will, and remain that way to her last breath. It is not in a century when the extent of the *droits de l'homme* has come to be widened with so much care that girls ought to continue to believe themselves their families' slaves, when it is clearly established that these families' powers over them are absolutely chimeric. [414;218]

Faced with this illusion or fiction of dependence, an example from what is called "nature" is provided in order to demystify or delegitimate the belief—this is the basic gesture of *La Philosophie*, a relentless hammering away at the idols as merely fictional constructs: chimera, fantasms, phantoms, ghosts, . . . fables. And more often than not—this is the excessive movement marking this text—this antifable is itself structured as a fable. Here is what Mme. de Saint-Ange says:

> Let us listen to nature on such an interesting question, and let the laws of animals, so much closer to her [nature], provide us for a moment with examples. Do paternal duties among [animals] extend beyond primary physical needs? Do not the fruits of the pleasure of male and female possess all their freedom, all their rights? As soon as they are able to walk and feed themselves, from that instant, do the authors of their days recognize them? And do they [the young, in their turn] believe they owe something to those who gave them life? Doubtless not.

11. For another, even more explicitly fabulous, example, see the tale of the wolf and the lamb in *Justine*, 176–77; 608.

Fabula docet:

> By what right thus are the children of men compelled to other duties? . . .
> Is it not prejudice alone that prolongs these chains? . . . Let us hope that
> eyes will be opened and that in assuring the freedom of every individual
> the fate of unhappy girls will not be forgotten; but, if they are so unfortu-
> nate as to be forgotten, then of their own accord rising above usage and
> prejudice let them boldly trample the shameful irons with which we
> presume to subjugate them. [414;219].[12]

The standard elements of the classical fable are present here: the turn to
animals for examples of human behavior (one paragraph later Saint-Ange
suggests to Eugénie that "the destiny of the woman is to be like the female
dog or wolf [*comme la chienne, comme la louve*]"), the claim that such
examples constitute laws (*"les lois des animaux . . . nous servent un moment d'exemples"*), and the narrative structure of a movement in time from
one condition (dependence) to another (freedom) turning on a decisive moment (*"dès cet instant"*), here, an instant of self-recognition and self-suffi-
ciency (*"sitôt qu'ils peuvent marcher et se nourrir seuls"*).

Sade's fable warps this third element, though, in making the instant of
emancipation, the break into the condition of freedom, itself break with the
conditions of possibility for the first condition (namely, recognition of the
other). It makes a difference, because this fable is an argument about freedom, a declaration of Eugénie's independence—a radical break which cuts
off any relations of recognition and indebtedness, in either direction, between the animal and its offspring. The narrative tells the story of the movement from a narrative (I authored you, I come from you, I depend on you) to
the oddly *a*narrative (I owe you nothing, I do not recognize you, you?). It
relates relation and irrelation, narrates the break into something that makes
narrative impossible.[13] This implies that the movement is irreversible, in
the sense Paul de Man gives to that word.[14] The outcome—since it is not
based on a dialectic of master and slave or of *ressentiment*—rather than
reaffirming them ruins the conditions that gave rise to it. No recognition, no
authority, no duty. No mirror. Independence does not depend, here, even
negatively, on that from which it has separated. The fable (*mythos*) spells
trouble for the *logos*, the relation, that it seems to serve, in that freedom or

---

12. In "Français, encore un effort" this critique occurs at 517; 321.

13. It goes without saying that the possibility of a narrative articulation between
parent (more exactly, *mother*) and child (daughter) is put at stake by *La Philosophie dans le
boudoir*. See Angela Carter's exemplary reading in "The School of Love," in *The Sadeian
Woman* (London: Virago, 1979), 116–36.

14. See Paul de Man, "Anthropomorphism and Trope in the Lyric," in *The Rhetoric of
Romanticism* (New York: Columbia University Press, 1984), 241–42. Henceforth cited in
the text.

emancipation is exemplified as the absolute absence of relation or tie, as doing without.[15] Hence Saint-Ange can spell out the fable's immoral as a lesson in corporal singularity and natural autonomy, iterating and reiterating: "Your body is yours, yours, alone [*ton corps est à toi, à toi, seule*]; in all the world there is only you who has the right to enjoy it and to make it enjoy as seems good to you" (417;221). Blanchot recasts the *moralité* of the fable as follows:

> Each of us must do as he pleases, each of us has no other law than his own pleasure. . . . This morality is based on the primary fact of absolute solitude. Sade has said it and repeated it, in every conceivable form: nature has it that we are born alone, there is no sort of relation [*rapport*] between one person and another (*LS, 19/CJ*, 40).

Of course, just because it's impossible doesn't mean it doesn't happen. If there is a relation to others, we owe it to nothing other than this impossibility—because no subject masters the time and space of the encounter, deprived as we are of any ground of symmetry or reciprocity on the basis of which it might recognize itself or any other, we are instead opened by it. From the singularity of this event are derived what Sade calls freedom and rights ("all their freedom, all their rights"). We will return to this.

This fabulous declaration of independence[16] is structured by the logic of the *encore:* Sade insists that this fable (the animal law of liberty) takes a prior fable, precisely insofar as it is a fable, for its target. The next application of the lesson concerns the liberation from the purely fictional or conventional bonds of marriage (first the family, then marriage). "To chain them by the absurd link of a solitary marriage [*hymen*] is obviously to outrage the fate [*destination*] that nature imposes on women" (415;219), holds Mme. de Saint-Ange; later she urges "among all the bonds to be burst, those whose annihilation I'd recommend first would surely be those of marriage. . . . No, Eugénie, no, it is not for that end that we are born; those absurd laws are the work of men, and we must not submit to them" (418–19;222–23). Thanks to the example from the laws of animals, that man-made institution, and its pretensions to law, have already been dismantled. "We are rid of this chimera today" (420;224), she says. What a wife does is of concern to her only, and dishonor or outrage no longer matter; the only harm done is to

15. On "doing without," see Derrida, "Limited Inc a b c," trans. Samuel Weber, in *Limited Inc,* 49–50.

16. Is not every declaration of independence just as fabulous? Doesn't it have to be? See Jacques Derrida "Déclarations d'Indépendance," in *Otobiographies* (Paris: Galilée, 1984), 11–32; "Declarations of Independence," trans. Tom Keenan and Tom Pepper, *New Political Science* 15 (Summer 1986): 7–15, for an analysis of the abysmal superimposition of performative and constative, and the weird temporality thus required, in such affirmations.

pride, which is to say, to nothing: "this pretend wound is thus only a fable, whose existence is impossible" (420–21;224).

The fable of freedom, having recourse to a more originary order of existence, undoes the aberrant laws of human institutions with examples from what Hegel called "the animal kingdom of the spirit."[17] Blanchot: "*la première et la dernière instance, c'est la nature. Autrement dit, pas de morale, c'est le règne du fait*" [the first and last instance is nature. In other words, no morality; the fact reigns] (*LS,* 40;*JC,* 62). Français, encore une fable. It exposes human morality and ethics as fictive constructs, inventions substituted for nothing, mere phantoms entirely lacking in (any justified claim to) existence if not in effect. In a word, it reveals instituted law as fable, by telling a fable. It exposes it to its fabulous origin with a fable of origin.

A certain political tradition has made of this exposure the definition of liberty. Isaiah Berlin associates it with "Marx and his disciples," but it describes this moment in Sade's argument quite well. Freedom is understanding that social institutions are created by humans, unmasking the "myth" that "man-made arrangements [are] independent forces."[18]

> Not until we have reached a stage at which the spells of these illusions could be broken, that is, until enough men reached a social stage that alone enabled them to understand that these laws and institutions were themselves the work of human minds and hands, historically needed in their day, and later mistaken for inexorable, objective powers, could the old world be destroyed. . . . [143]

Freedom or liberation is the event of this understanding: knowing and acting are articulated in the free subject, define it as free. This "understanding is appropriate action." I am free if and when I understand this negative lesson, and a positive lesson as well: that laws are necessary. I am free then only if I in turn impose a law on myself "having understood [that . . .] it conforms to the necessities of things" (143–44). Berlin associates this "positive" concept of freedom (distinguished as "profoundly divergent and irreconcilable" [166] from the "negative" liberty of simply "not being interfered with by others" [123]) with "the thought and language of all the declarations of the rights of man in the eighteenth century, and of all those who look upon society as a design constructed according to the rational laws of [among other things . . .] nature" (148). The free subject of this law recites this creed:

> I wish, above all, to be conscious of myself as a thinking, willing, active being, bearing responsibility for my choices and able to explain them by

17. "Le Règne animal de l'Esprit" was the original title of Blanchot's "La Littérature et le droit à la mort," in *Critique* 18 (November 1947): 387–405; Blanchot quotes the phrase at *LDM,* 295.

18. Isiah Berlin, "Two Concepts of Liberty" (Oxford: Clarendon Press, 1958), 142–43.

references to my own ideas and purposes. . . . I am free because, and in so far as, I am autonomous. I obey laws, but I have imposed them on, or found them in, my own uncoerced self. [136]

The self-understanding of the transparently reasonable and readable subject depends on its definition as natural, and nature means possibility. Berlin paraphrases: "Knowledge liberates not by offering us more open possibilities amongst which we can make our choice, but by preserving us from the frustration of attempting the impossible" (144).

This attempt, of course, is what Sade's text does not seek to evade, in spite of its deep investment in nature and its laws, and the effort ultimately puts the possibility of this self-understanding into question. Here, though, knowledge does liberate, as it has before—after all, this is not even the first fable to be exposed (nor is it the last). This undoing gesture defines the movement of Sade's text, and especially in "Français, encore un effort," In fact, the particular critique of ethical norms (here, family and marriage) as fabulous inventions which we have just followed is itself based on a previous critique of fables. The first section of "Français, encore un effort," having taken for granted the practical revolutionary demystification of royal authority, is devoted to religion, before morals even get into the act, and the program is unambiguous: "let us not be content with breaking scepters, we will pulverize the idols forever" (494;300). What we might call Sade's first critique, in this relentlessly enlightening text ("j'aurai contribué en quelque chose au progrès des lumières, et j'en serai content" [490;296], concludes the tract's opening sentence), is of that particular rhetorical aberration by means of which organized human religions have claimed the right or the ability to speak on behalf of the divine, or rather, as Sade puts it, to make the gods speak. This ventriloquism of the *"dieu vain"* [empty god] (494;300) or more strictly speaking the prosopopeia by which the absent—whether dead, never alive, or simply in flight—are given a face and a voice and make to speak, has been for Sade the second and perhaps the most important victim of the Revolution he now seeks to "consolidate" or render permanent (497;303).

We sensed that this chimerical divinity, prudently invented by the first legislators, was in their hands only a way to chain us, and that, reserving to themselves alone the right to make this phantom speak, they knew very well to make it say only what would support the ridiculous laws by which they pretended to serve us. [494;300]

Hence the call to practice the critical gesture, yet again, and behead "a phantom more illusory still [*encore*] than a king could ever be" (498;303). Even if the priests have been dispatched along with the king, their human all-too-human artifact "that infamous and fabulous religion" (490; 296) survives, living on to haunt the already considerable effort of demystification with the threat of a relapse, in spite of its essential "incoherence with the system of liberty" (495;301). Freedom is freedom from fable, and this rhetorical survival, no matter how aberrant its animation was and continues to be, still plays its role in fable and requires, for the sake of freedom, "*encore un effort;* since you labor to destroy all prejudices, do not let any of them subsist, because it only takes one to bring them all back" (495;301).

Where fable had taught—and chained—before, a resolutely human and freely chosen (that is to say, freely read) institution and its laws will now take its place: "Let us take the greatest care to avoid mixing any religious fable into our national education. Never lose sight of the fact that it is free men we want to shape [*former*]: (498;304). For the free, namely those "without religious fables," the responsibility that keeps them free is "to enjoy [nature] and to respect its laws, laws that are as wise as they are simple, that are written in everyone's heart, and it is only necessary to interrogate this heart to discern there its impulse" (498–99;303–04). Because humans are natural, the freedom from fable is as simple as reading or understanding oneself. The fable and the laws of its creatures are to be replaced with an enlightened, reasoned, education in human institutions, as human a lesson in human autonomy (self-legislation) and autolegibility. Laws do not need to be dictated from elsewhere, interpreted by others through their puppets, when they can be read freely and independently in each human (body and spirit).

Immediately, however, the status of these laws is put in question as well—which is the point at which we entered this structure some pages earlier. If gods have been first displaced by humans, it does not take very long—only another effort—to remove humans from any position of privilege: we need only quote again Mme. de Saint-Ange's first fable. "These absurd laws are the work of men, and we must not submit to them." Not only divine animation but also human law is "only a fable, whose existence is impossible." Where the first critique had seemed to suggest that it would suffice to "train [people] to cherish th[ose] virtues which, . . . without religious fables, make for individual happiness" (498;303), the second-order dismantling reveals those virtues to be just as aberrant as any religious belief. The rhetorical strategy that organizes this critique, and Saint-Ange's fable of freedom, becomes explicit later in "Français, encore un effort" when Sade theorizes the structure of similitude or resemblance (simile or metaphor) aimed at delegitimating the aberrant religious and human laws of prosopopeia and catachresis. Humans are born into, and hence like, nature. Nature levels.

The time has come for error to disappear; that blindfold must fall alongside the heads of kings. . . . Doubtless, we are going to humiliate man's pride by lowering him to the level of nature's other productions, but the philosopher hardly flatters small human vanities. . . .

What is man, and what difference is there between him and other plants, between him and all the other animals of nature? None, certainly. Fortuitously placed, like them [comme eux], on this globe, he is born like them [comme eux]; he propagates, increases and decreases, like them [comme eux]; he arrives like them [comme eux] at old age and falls like them [comme eux] into nothingness after the term nature assigns each species of animal. . . . [525–26;329–30]

Mutato nomine de te fabula narratur, as Horace expressed the law of fable. As when Mme. de Saint-Ange suggested that "the destiny of the woman is to be like the female dog or wolf [comme la chienne, comme la louve]"), here everything happens in the comme, the operator of the transition or the mutation between names. Like the real life fantasy of capital described by Marx in the first chapter of Capital, where the commodity form allows everything to be substituted for everything else, including people, nature treats all its creatures as the same: "to declare that all men are equal means that no creature is worth more than any other, all are interchangeable, "chacun n'a que la signification d'une unité dans un dénombrement in-fini" [each has only a signification of a unit in an infinite enumeration] (LS, 33;CJ, 54–55). Everything, to the extent that it can be treated and manipulated as a mere sign, can be compared with everything else: comme eux. Nature is this principle of similarity, the third term that provides the axis of resemblance around which humans and "other plants" can be compared. "What becomes of the tree when you transplant it from a soil full of vigor to a dry and sandy plain? All intellectual ideas are so greatly subordinate to the physicality of nature that the comparisons furnished by agriculture will never deceive us in morals" (529;333). Figurative language raises no obstacle to interpretation here; similarity slides easily into identity at the hermeneutic level, naturally. Fable is this structure of analogy, of metaphor, of comparison, the horizon of generality within which species can relate themselves as comme eux, like everything else (natural). Nature guarantees this resemblance or semblance; indeed, from the viewpoint of the "examining eye of the philosopher," the "rapprochements" between all the animals "are so exact that it becomes absolutely impossible . . . to perceive any dissemblance" (526;330). Thus fable is law, "law of nature" (525;329), "all individuals . . . being equal in the eyes of nature."[19] The appeal to nature made by this fable functions to remove the human from any position of privilege, in a gesture comparable to that of Nietzsche at the beginning of "Über Wahrheit and Lüge." Nature is not human—it comprehends, as the

19. Quoted without citation by Blanchot in "Quelques remarques sur Sade," Critique 3–4 (August–September 1946): 239–49, 243. Hereafter noted as QR.

whole to a part, the human without being reducible to it, the condition of possibility which cannot be comprehended by what it enables and which thus is entitled to give laws with authority and without prejudice. Compared to nature—and how could it not be?—humanity is itself but a prejudice.

> After the extinction of half the world, of its totality, if one wishes, . . . would [anything surviving] feel the slightest material alteration? No, alas! All of nature would not feel it either, and the stupid pride of man, who believes everything made for him, would be astonished, after the total destruction of the human species, were it to be seen that nothing in nature had changed. [529;332–33]

Nature is an example for us, as Saint-Ange told Eugénie, because it is so peculiarly inhuman, because it is a principle of likeness, of ineluctable comparison (*comme eux*), organizing the exchanges that articulate humanity with the plants and animals and enable their laws to address us as well. Nature displaces humanity by replacing it with anything, by inscribing it in a system of generalized exchange which denies it any privilege, by subsuming its specificity within the generality of everything. Nature exceeds humanity as (*comme*) the general rules the particular.

IV. THE LAW OF THE LAW

It appears that these first two critiques have left a certain unquestionable residue called nature as the genuine state of things, as the source and endpoint of our fables. This is perhaps Blanchot's strongest insight into Sade's writing:

> Nature is one of those words Sade . . . wrote most willingly. It is in the name of nature [*au nom de la nature*] that he waged his battle against God and against everything that God represents, especially morality. . . . For him, this nature is first of all universal life, and for hundreds of pages his whole philosophy consists in reiterating that immoral instincts are good, since they are facts of nature, and the first and last instance is nature. In other words, no morality: the fact reigns. [*LS*, 39–40; *CJ*, 62]

And yet. Although this attraction toward nature and the law, toward the principle of general resemblance and hence of generality itself, never ceases in Sade, it is interrupted or troubled at times by a very different impulse. Ultimately, there is no last instance, no final appeal, least of all to the law. For while the rhetoric of similarity can always perform its critical function, and does so with the ruthless indifference of generality, it too falls victim to the still more relentless force of something that resists the substitutive and symmetrical exchanges of the trope.

Finally, the strength of that "in the name of" and the force of that analogy (everything can be substituted for everything else, all individuals are equal, we are all natural) are what draws the most furious wrath of the Sadeian character. What must be questioned is the stability of the axis of comparison itself, the frame that organizes the exchanges and grounds the law.

> . . . always faced with this frame of reference [nature], Sade's man becomes gradually annoyed, his anger mounts, and before long his hatred for nature [becomes . . .] unbearable . . . : "yes, I loathe nature" [*LS*, 40; *CJ*, 62]

Sade's strangest moments turn on this extra effort of loathing, finding in the so-called laws of nature only another fable, another rhetorical confusion dangerously seeking to relate the unrelated. Blanchot quotes Juliette's apostrophe to nature, addressed as to a creature of fable: " 'perhaps you deceive me, as in the past I was deceived by the infamous deific chimera to which you are, we are told, submissive; we are no more dependent on you than you on him; perhaps the causes are useless to the effects' " (*LS*, 41; *CJ*, 64). To be free means to be free of comparison. The laws of nature, then, insofar as they attempt the metonymic substitution of cause for effect or indeed any substitution at all, are structured in the same confused and mistaken way as are the laws of gods or humans. The critical undoing of these errors in each case comes down to disengaging the pretended link between an abstract and a particular, between something general and something specific. This undoing is announced in the name of freedom, a freedom neither negative nor positive in that it depends on nothing (no obstacles to be overcome) and is ruled by nothing general (no law, not even one given by or read in the self). The *comme* that aimed to articulate everything within the synecdochal horizon of nature comes to be seen, with the eyes of a reader, as the enumeration of a stutter ("instead of analogy, we have enumeration, and an enumeration which never moves beyond the confines of a set of particulars" [de Man, "Anthropomorphism," 250]). Which is to say, there is nothing else to which to appeal, no frame or axis—nothing but the call "in the name of" . . . the name, in its singularity. One after the other, frames or names are tested—king, god, man, nature—and, as Blanchot argues, the test confers a certain value on them only in order that it may then in turn be resisted; "the experiment consists precisely in ruining them and nullifying them one after the other" (*LS*, 42/ *CJ*, 64). What is ruined in each case, in succession, is the claim to generalize, to exemplify, to draw (abstract) lessons from irreducibly singular events, . . . in a word, what is annihilated is the fable as the form of law.

"Français, encore un effort" turns of course to fable to make the case, offering the lesson of the general and its particulars as the fable of the general and his soldiers:

it will be agreed [that] to want to prescribe universal laws would be a palpable absurdity; this proceeding would be as ridiculous as that of the army general who would have all of his soldiers dressed in a uniform made to the same measure [of the same size]; it is a terrible injustice to demand that men of dissimilar [*inégaux*] characters all be ruled by the same [*egal*] law: "*ce qui va à l'un ne va point à l'autre*" [what goes for one does not go at all for another] [504–05;310]

What Sade, the philosopher or the text, revolts against, whether it assumes the figures of God, man, or even nature, is the law as such, the law of generality, universality, uniformity, measure.[20] "To the extent that he is particular, *any* individual is, as individual, alienated from a law that, on the other hand, exists only in relation to his particular being" (de Man, *AR*, 267). At stake is the structuring difficulty of the fable and the law: the terrible address of the law, open, to no one and only one in particular. In de Man's words, "no law can ever be written unless one suspends any consideration of applicability to a particular entity; . . . on the other hand, no law is a law unless it applies to particular individuals" (*AR*, 269). This means that the revolt does not seek to overthrow one law in the name of another, to replace a harsh law with a lenient one, to humanize divine law or naturalize human law. Sade aims at the very law of the law,[21] the possibility of articulating the general with the particular, the principle of relation or *rapport* itself that must be presumed by any law desiring to exceed the idiosyncratic or the private, which underlies as its condition of possibility any substitution (any example, any prosopopeia, any metonymy, any metaphor) with a common measure or trait.[22] Sade simply removes that commonality, that relation, and with it the foundation of the law, the law's law, in all of its disfiguring violence. If "Sade puts himself so completely outside generality, places himself so unconsciously far from the possibility of laws," then the only rule in the end (which is no rule and no end) must be: "Plus de lois, dit-il, presque pas de lois" (*QR*, 248). And if the emphasis in the example of the general and the soldiers was on a certain violence of uniformity, Sade understands it as a disfiguration superimposed on a 'prior' violence which begins by interpreting singularity as particularity in order to inscribe it as specificity within a system of generality. First, blinding, then a demand for visual distinctions: "Would the iniquity you would commit in this not be equal to that of which you would make yourself guilty if you wanted to force a blind man to distinguish between colors?" (505;310).

20. See William Connolly, *Political Theory and Modernity* (Oxford and New York: Basil Blackwell, 1988), 77–78.
21. A phrase which, as it turns out, I seem to have borrowed from Derrida's "Violence and Metaphysics," *ED*, 164; *WD*, 111. See also Hamacher's reading in "LECTIO," 179.
22. Jacques Derrida, "La Loi du genre," *Parages* (Paris: Galilée, 1986), 249–87; "The Law of Genre," trans. Avital Ronell, *Glyph* 7 (1980): 202–32.

The violence is the violence of relation, and thus we return to the declaration of independence Saint-Ange proposed for Eugénie. Act as the animals do, leave, with rights and without debts; you are obligated or connected to nothing but yourself, and even that "self-"relation is questionable since independence is self-exceeding and self-abandonment, the erasure of the *as*. No recognition, no debt, no relation. The fable erodes its own condition of possibility here, irreversibly. If the violence (what Derrida calls somewhere the nonethical opening of ethics, a violent opening)[23] can only be met with a certain violence, freedom requires that it occur

> without the destroyed object deriving the slightest value from this operation. This principle has another advantage: it assigns man a future without imposing on him the recognition [*reconnaissance*] of any ideal notion. [*LS*, 42; *CJ*, 65]

Blanchot reads this principle of future alterity as a kind of negation without position, and hence without negation in the strict sense: as an affirmative negation which attempts to disable the dialectical motion in which negation can be recuperated by the position it presupposes. It does so as the exercise of freedom. It is a "power which does not depend in any way on objects, which to destroy them does not even presuppose their anterior existence" (*LS*, 36; *CJ*, 58). Because of this freedom, this power without object is thus not the power of a subject, and certainly not of a subject which can enter into relations with other subjects, even to negate them—"*Mais quel peut être le rapport de l'exception avec l'exception?*," [what relation can there be between exceptions]? Blanchot asks (*LS*, 25; *CJ*, 46). And the structure of the *encore un effort* deploys this relation without relation (even or especially to our "self") over time: we have a future, but it has nothing to do with and thus owes no recognition to any past. If there is an other, it occurs only to the extent that we are incapable of recognizing it. This is what Sade calls *liberté*, freedom, this nonsubjective openness in textual space and time, a radical singularity that allows for no stable identity but only iteration without relation.[24] We are lacking only the freedom to consider this liberty (of absolute exceptionality without comparison, which is to say of the simple fact of difference), as anything but a matter of language.

Language, like reading, proves difficult, though, because it works by relying on and erasing the difference between singularity and generality— between the name as sign and as call, between *comme* as "comparative simile" and as "enumerative repetition" (de Man, "Anthropomorphism," 249–50), between the individual as singular and as example—by enforcing a law of exceptions. That the singular claims its freedom as a law, that free-

23. See also Jacques Derrida, "Violence and Metaphysics," *ED*, 188; *WD*, 128, on "the irreducible violence of the relation to the other" which opens that relation.
24. "Iteration alters," writes Derrida in "Limited Inc," 40.

dom is the "entanglement"[25] of no difference (equality) *and* no relation (exceptionality), that one fable undoes another (without opposing it from any other privileged ground)—this permanent predicament always demands another effort. Sade's strange rigor, his irony, is to entrust the task of teaching this lesson to fable: example of the singular, thus example of nothing, nothing but example.

V. FABLE SPEAKS

In other words, there is no evading the fable, the appeal to an elsewhere to which the last name given is that of nature. But that does not imply that this appeal could ever occur once and for all, that this last instance could last. The fable is the call that invents the place from which the imperative (the law) is uttered and robs it of any authority, submits it immediately to the law of its own undoing: yet another effort. Fable "itself has no ground and the ground that it is able to offer, by positing imperatives, for example, bears the mark of possible contingency, possible groundlessness, possible impossibility" (Hamacher, 188). The imperative, the law, finds its necessity in just this unreliability of ground: everything must be said, and again, because there is no guarantee that it can. Without justification, but not without fable.[26]

Which is why we never read just once: "Nous sortons de sa lecture, . . . nous reprenions la lecture" (Blanchot). Why must we leave off reading only to return to it? What is its difficulty such that it does not simply frustrate us but instead incites us, regardless of our desire for simplicity, for the simplicity we associate with our selves, necessarily to return to what is impossible for us? What would reading be if we could do it, if we could finally succeed, stop reading? This *sortie*, and its retraction, is no accident, but rather the very condition of reading, in its necessity and impossibility. "If it is still possible to read, then only in the aporia of undecidability articulated by literary texts themselves. In all writing and in all meaning is read the imperative: *Sors de la lecture. Sors*" (Hamacher, 179).

25. Blanchot: "The world of Sade is constituted by the entanglement of two systems: in one, beings are equal, each counts equally. But in the other . . . not only are individuals not equal, but the inequality is such that there are no relations [rapports], no reciprocity, possible among them" (*QR*, 244).

26. Oddly, this coincides with Luce Irigaray's call to "'Françaises,' ne faites plus un effort" (in *Ce Sexe qui n'en est pas un* (Paris: Minuit, 1977), 195–202; "'Frenchwomen,' Stop Trying," *This Sex Which Is Not One*, trans. Catherine Porter (Ithaca: Cornell University Press, 1985), 198–204). No more effort means no more nature. "Don't even go looking for that alibi. Do what comes to you, what pleases you: without 'reason,' without 'valid motives,' without 'justification'" (202; 203). This doing without, without ground, is just what we mean by another effort (of reading, politics). We translate: *plus d'effort*.

The call to fable, then, is structured like the excessive call of naming Blanchot found so internally violent. In the name begins our responsibility. What calls for reading in these affirmations, these compulsive namings, that by their very movement make it so difficult? What allows it?

(1) Nothing—it has no ground, no foundation or basis, no law other than what Hamacher calls "the law of the impossibility of identifying any epistemological instance that could secure the meaning of language and even its very capacity to mean" (179). Naming makes reading possible only by withdrawing it, by paying the price of the imperative.

(2) Everything—"*N'avons-nous pas acquis le droit de tout dire?*" [Have we not acquired the right to say everything?] asks "Français, encore un effort' (525;329). Foucault evades the rigor of Sade's formulation when he translates "the exact object of 'sadism' " as "everything that could have been said [tout ce qui a pu être dit]," because *possibility* does not restrict the scope of this everything—possible or not (not a question to be answered epistemologically), an imperative is in force here. Blanchot: "Everything must be said [Il faut tout dire]" (*IM*, 20;*MI*, 50). Indeed, an imperative or a right is required, acquired, *because* the possibility of saying (everything) is just what cannot be taken for granted. If it were simply possible, rights would be unnecessary. Whether or not it can be, everything demands to be said, and it demands its rights and its freedoms.

If Blanchot is correct—

> . . . The "everything" at stake in this freedom to say everything is no longer only the universality of encyclopedic knowledge . . . or even the totality of an experience in which meaning is achieved by the movement of a negation carried to term—a circular discourse which is thus the closed and completed affirmation of a mastery of everything. Sade's *tout dire* . . . goes even farther. It is no longer everything possible that is given and expressed. Nor is it . . . the whole set of values that a religion, a society, and a morality interdicts us from saying. [*IM*, 20; *MI*, 50–51][27]

—then to whom does this freedom and right belong, or to whom is the demand addressed? The right has nothing voluntary about it. A subject cannot choose to exercise this right, to say everything—nothing separates the right from a responsibility, an ineluctable or irrevocable call. Blanchot insists that this everything is nothing possible (not knowledge, not the experience of mastery, not even what is prohibited) but something else that he associates in Sade with the political:

> Everything must be said. The first freedom is the freedom to say everything. That is how he [Sade] translated the fundamental demand [*exi-*

---

27. Compare Foucault on the "prétention de tout dire," 49; 61.

gence]—in the form of a claim [*revendication*] that for him was henceforth inseparable from a true republic. [*IM, 19–20;MI, 50*]

The right and freedom to say everything is a political one *because* it is not necessarily possible; its possible impossibility makes it breach the limits of any subjectivity, opens the one that claims the right onto the impossibility of making the other, the others, and thus language, its own. To be free is to be responsible here, but this fundamental equation of all ethico-political metaphysics encounters the disruption of its subjectivist (whether liberal or communitarian) prejudice in the terrible double bind that constitutes the predicament of this responsibility: it may not be possible, separated as it is from any ground in knowledge or meaning, but that makes it necessary.

Sade's effort, in its recurrence, to say everything and his claim that this is not merely a possibility or an essence but a *right*, and more exactly an "acquired" right (hence something ethico-political, the exercise of which constitutes an affirmation or an intervention), leaves his text and any reading of it open to a constant encounter with the condition of its possibility—language. This is a lesson in language as the open extent of saying, the freedom of all that must be said. Without knowing, without pathos.

Which is not to say, without politics. For reading, like politics, if it is still possible, must be unavoidable, allowing no opting out nor requiring any commitment (in the sense of cognitive decidability and intention). Its irresistibility or necessity means that its freedom cannot simply be a matter of choice or decision, a willed relation of a subject to an exterior object, but an *effort*, and always another effort. "Français, encore un effort" teaches this effort of reading in its inevitable recurrence as politics.

Politics and reading have their necessity in the withdrawal of security. These fields, because they expose us to events that cannot be calculated, programmed, "settled by experts or machines,"[28] demand responses (in another vocabulary, decisions) that cannot be referred to anywhere else, to something we know or mean. Our freedom is defined by this responsibility, nor by that of a subject that knows what it does, which is why politics is not finally a matter of interpretation. We read, ethically and politically, when something (others, for example) demands a response we cannot give, at least not on the basis of anything we know or have under our control, but that we cannot avoid giving. If what we did could be authorized by something we knew (nature, truth), doing it would have nothing of the political or of reading about it. Unreadability only frustrates politics to the extent that politics is understood as something a subject does when it knows. Otherwise, it

28. Berlin, "Two Concepts," 118, distinguishing between the technical and the political.

offers a chance to think about a politics open to the future, to others, others "within" and without us. Indeed, the possible impossibility of reading makes politics—freedom and responsibility—ineluctable.

In politics speaks the imperative of this exposure to all language: "Everything must be said [*il faut tout dire*]. The first of all freedoms is the freedom to say everything" (*IM*, 20).[29] What Sade calls the "revolution" is built on this linguistic structure, which is why another effort is needed if we are to be republicans. The irony, as Blanchot insists, is that this revolution comes from nowhere else, has no privilege or guarantee of its own, but is just as fabulous as the state it would threaten.

> It is not enough to live in a republic to be a republican; . . . nor is having laws enough for that constituting act, that creative power, to persevere and maintain us in a state of permanent constitution. An effort must be made, and *always* another effort—there is the invisible irony. . . . Sade calls it *insurrection, the permanent state of a republic* [510;315]. In other words, the republic knows no state, but only a movement. [*IM*, 25–26;*MI*, 53]

No state, no state of security, no standpoint or present in which knowledge and action might be coordinated. Rather, a permanent state of emergency. Thus the invisible irony of the title—invisible, which is to say, unrecognizable to those who read only what is readable—the irony of the unending exigency of another effort, the law of another fable. Just as fable undoes fable in a structure that cannot finally be reduced to opposition or demystification (a cognitive, recognitive critique), so revolution and the law lock themselves in a double bind whose temporal deployment is what we call history.[30] Politics aspires to this condition of revolution, and when it happens—everyday and everynight?—"freedom aspires to be realized in the *immediate* form of *everything* is possible, everything can be done."

> A fabulous moment—and no one who has known it can completely recover from it, since he has known history as his own history and his own freedom as universal freedom. Fabulous moments, in fact: in them, fable speaks; in them, the speech of fable makes itself action. [*LDM*, 309;*LRD*, 39]

Only a fable could teach this, if it could be taught.

---

29. Elsewhere Sade himself makes it imperative, and gives the task to philosophy: "A quelque point qu'en frémissent les hommes, la philosophie doit tout dire" (quoted *IM*, 51; MI 63).

30. See de Man: "revolution and legality by no means cancel each other out, since the text of the law is, per definition, in a condition of unpredictable change" (*AR*, 266–77).

V.

YVES BONNEFOY

Poetry and Liberty

What does the word "liberty" mean to us?

First, a certain situation. We are permitted certain acts, which will cost us no more risks than those slumbering, hidden or unhidden, in the heart of uncontrollable forces. But the ant, too, can do as it pleases, on the threshold stone, or the hawk when it hunts over some forlorn place, yet one would hesitate to say that in this the hawk or the ant are free beings. For in the very idea of liberty which we have fashioned, there is also our respect for it, the feeling of its creative value; there is sometimes, if not often, the conviction that liberty is a constitutive part of our humanity, one of those few means at our disposal, apart from language, to distinguish ourselves, precisely, from the ant, and from all those other animal lives which are, we surmise, only prey, sexuality, and sleep.

Understanding liberty in this way—as part of our self-definition and, consequently, as one of our absolute rights—is obviously what Georges Cottier and Jean Starobinski had in mind in their opening remarks to this gathering, when they asked us to reflect on what can help to protect it in our society, which, although more or less democratic, remains nevertheless incapable of foreseeing or instituting the means which would guarantee its exercise.

And here is an a priori—somewhat metaphysical, it will be said, if not outright theological: in a word, an act of faith, as is the case in Christianity, but one which I am entirely willing to make my own due to a conception of language, and of speech, which I have come to take. A questionable conception, to be sure, and one which you will perhaps shortly question; but one which I still think I can expose, in our reflections on liberty, since it has at

YFS 79, *Literature and the Ethical Question,* ed. Claire Nouvet, © 1991 by Yale University.

least one virtue. This thought, it seems to me, accompanies, upholds, more or less consciously, the kind of activity we call poetry: and therefore it will be able to shed light on, if not explain, the necessity which some of us have for poetry, precisely—a longing so badly explained by contemporary criticism, which, in the poem, distinguishes the text, and knows how to analyze a number of forms and effects of this text, but which hardly bothers to ask itself why Hölderlin or Rimbaud or Mallarmé sacrificed so much of ordinary existence simply for the adventure of a few remaining pages.

II

Let us begin, then, by this idea of language which I should like to propose: an idea or even, say, an impression immediately experienced, almost physical, but of the kind one experiences in some unusual situations, as when walking in the mountains, with the mist closing in and just a bit of sun to reflect the murmur of a source. You know the feeling one experiences at such moments: words are no longer anything for us, the reality which we glimpse seems not yet permeated by our speech, and is felt, therefore, as a oneness, since division is no more thinkable when words disappear—a oneness wholly present at each of those points where it offers itself to our senses. And you know as well that at such moments one senses that one is present to this presence in a way unapproachable by intelligence alone, but nevertheless felt to be all the more real, as if the words we left behind had until now only given us a surface representation of ourselves, illusorily differentiated and multiple.

This impression of partaking of a reality suddenly more immediate, and yet more whole, and more intimate to our own being, this is what I have come to designate with the words *presence,* sense of presence. And the fact that such partaking, at times so spontaneous, is ordinarily denied us, this, I will today call *linguistic estrangement.* Language has deprived us of a good which we still sense, but which we are no longer able to make our own. Speaking, fashioning sentences, thought, action: this breaks up the wholeness of the world, drawing, at this or that point, spectral figures of what is, weaving a set of relations from one figure to another,—which leaves us to dwell in what is, hereafter, the irreality of one vast image. This image, which is language,—an image in place of the world—can be quite beautiful, surely, and more easily habitable than those precarious dwellings of the animal condition, but it is no less pernicious. If, in fact, it answers to our needs, it does so not without erasing from our consciousness a virtuality which is, nonetheless, the most important one, one which I would even call redeeming: for only it could satisfy what is still a need in us, perhaps the deepest need of all.

Let us go back, indeed, to what can be glimpsed in those moments of mist, of slight sounds, of silence. Time, our experience of duration, appears there to us in a light that dissolves the idea we held of it. For, on the one hand, it exposes itself in all its evidence, as it never does at any other moment of our lives. That leaf falls from the tree with all the time it takes: as if unfurling, before our eyes, an almost infinite lapse between the beginning and the end of its brief fall; and yet, at that same instant, one no longer knows that here is time since, in the whole, in the palpably appearing unity, beginning and end—whether that of a falling leaf or of a galaxy senselessly shining in space—are but the same spuming foam, the same surface tracings, the same endless absence of beginnings and ends. Time's form has displayed itself, but our notion of time no longer holds for us. And a similar kind of transformation appears potentially to take place in our relation to what we are. We now perceive ourselves to be mortal, it is true, and in a way never before so immediate; but it is also as if there were no more death, since we no longer have any separate reality in that oneness where our own lapse of a leaf's fall from the tree reinscribes us. Thus, a disburdenment of all our being. One has the premonition of what a divine gaiety might be like.

But we have only to return among words, in situations of speech, and this good is lost, fatally. It is not that our discourse ignores the existence of time, for it can explicitly render time's most fearsome aspects as well as its seductions, but it does so with notions and with figures; and these, like everything which partakes of the sign, are intemporal: so that, suddenly, even if we know ourselves to be mortal, even if we measure the ambiguities of finitude, we do so by imagining another mode of being, timeless, as the background to such incipient knowledge, making an enigma of our lives, a lack, inciting us to dream we might escape, if only in spirit, the natural condition. Where dying was originally just another form of life, death has now left its stain, ink-blot of nothingness in every word. Language brought death into the world, as it brought the dream. After which we strain to protect this dream—ideology or belief—from the lies that other dreams give it. Hence the rivalries, the combats, the wars, with that blind and murderous something that characterizes the human species, all the more savagely as the rift between its natural origins and its historical belonging widens across the centuries. Language renders mad, spawning worlds whose inner lack condemns us to go beyond all measure, and to search for that very death we seek precisely to deny. So that here we can say: words have been the fall, the fall from the midst of the real, except that we must refrain from giving to this figure a historical dimension, which would be but another way of dreaming. To say that language fragments oneness, that it deprives us of that which still heaves in our breath, beats in our veins, makes us hunger and desire, is not to claim a "before," a time when some human or prehuman consciousness would have enjoyed the immediacy we now lack; for there is no consciousness without a system of signs and, before language, there is no relation of parts to a whole that is not akin to dumb stone. Indeed, the speaking being creates the very universe from which his words exclude him.

And he knows this dialectic so well that his search for oneness has, throughout history, either led to a mystical experience, which tends to free itself from chronological notions of "before" or "after," as from other linguistic categories; or has imagined prelapsarian consciousness as yet another language, lived simply in an enigmatically more open and more intuitive way, thus turning this other usage into a possibility one hopes to renew, in some future, as well as into a remembrance of an origin. This is the case in Genesis, for example, where it is said that it was through knowledge of good and evil that humanity lost the garden of Eden, which should instantly discredit language; but, no, the biblical text also says that Adam and God decided on the words together, which saves the chances for an encounter between divine word and human speech. . . . Unless these be, perhaps, nostalgias of a golden age, of saturnian times, felt, as for them, only in times of profound social change, when hope—for a truer order, for happiness of being—is rekindled. *Jam redit et Virgo. . . .* It is as if the very evidence of linguistic estrangement were for many of us the occasion to denounce not language, but the misuses of language: with the consequence that one might therefore oppose, to the anguish in the face of death, and to the disordered projects of conceptual thought, a new ground, venturing into powers of speech still unknown to us.

And, indeed, such a venture has already taken place: it is the thinking of religion, which, as the etymology of the word *religion* suggests, seeks to bind together that which is scattered, showing that the world, fractured in the many faces of the mirror of language, has been thought, and consequently spoken, in a more onelike way by a God beyond. In thus lining the figure of each thing with the transcendence of a Word, one gives to things and beings an intensity which the relations of word to word in language no longer teach us to see: this is the function of myth. But to achieve this, one needs an account of those relations between the visible and invisibility, a story with signifiers in which, after Freud, it is easy to detect the unconscious wishes of a society, thereby rendering it less credible. So that this possibility is now closing up.

In short, the relation of the speaking being to oneness remains there, before us, in us, as a lack always, and as an open question, a problem.

III

But it will at least permit me now to return to this idea of liberty—of liberty and its uses—which is the theme of our present encounter.

What is liberty? Although there is no more agreement over this question as over many others, the conflicting theses are few. There may only be three major ones. Common sense holds that to be free is to be capable of obtaining what one wants, and it thinks, consequently, in terms of possession, in the category of *having*. Philosophical thought responds to this simple intuition by interiorizing the problem, claiming that to be free is to be in a position of electing oneself, of fashioning oneself into whom one desires to be, despite social or natural constraints. This second interpretation constitutes the thinking of *being*, even if it remains posed as a demand, thereby risking becoming a trap, since the mode of being to which one attains can itself also be lived and administered as a mode of having. But there remains still the point of view of the Stoics, who define the free being as he who knows how to fully accept what is, what comes to pass, even if his consent comes at the expense of his desires. An absolute deconditioning where all expectation of having, if there was one, disappears.

This, then, is the state of the problem, appearing, it seems, in a most contradictory form, since it is either a question of having or one of being; either of altering a present state in order to attain what one desires, or of unconditionally consenting to a given state. But there is a ground, it seems to me, on which these conflicting theses are reconciled, where obtaining one's desires means also being whom one desires to be; and this, thanks to what is certainly an action, a revolt against many constraints, but which remains, nonetheless, a profound acceptance of what one already holds and already is. This ground is our most original relation to language.

Let us return to this loss of reality induced by language, to this experience to which the speaking being must submit: to be exiled in relation to a possible life in the midst of oneness, to be, literally, a prisoner of the outside. To experience such estrangement, which constitutes the specificity of the human condition, is this not also to want to end its constraints, to seek an escape from this prison: a desire for liberation and, suddenly, a need for liberty? At this level, liberty can still appear as the pursuit of a good, which is reality itself, that oneness missing in the site of signs. But this sort of liberty is just as much a desire for a way of being, since it bears the condemnation of an existence according to words; it is a refusal of those thousand models proposed by and through words. So that we must conceive the necessity of an act, of the most difficult kind even; but in this act we will have to open ourselves to a passive acceptance of a reality beyond words, that always self-same mass of oneness billowing beneath. To whomever grasps and refuses linguistic estrangement, being free is being prepared to desire, to truly desire a state which is indeed the pure act of being: this self-coincidence which characterizes, if unconsciously, the leaf's falling from the tree, between its beginning and its end.

In brief, at this level, all the possible interpretations of what liberty might be, merge; and it seems to me therefore legitimate to draw these diverse definitions back to that moment of inception where they are equivalent, that is to say, to that need for oneness we so constantly suppress—or, rather, neglect, the greater evil being that which we do not feel. This need, this desire, I will call the higher desire, to distinguish it from those others—*eros*, for example—which are but the diffractions of the body's demands in all the registers of language. And I will here venture to say that the hypothesis of this word-surpassing desire recovers, even confirms and illuminates, our intuitive idea of liberty, this liberty whose notion vanishes where life is purely animal.

First, in effect, the "higher" desire has, as its object, a transcendence. It seeks to perceive, as a whole, suddenly "one and indivisible," that splintered world, now experienced as if from the outside: the mind here does not move horizontally from one representation to another, as one turns the pages of a book, but rises sharply, by a sudden illumination to a place higher than our ordinary consciousness. Now that there is transcendence in the aim of all act meant to be free is something suggested by the philosophies of liberty. It has always been thought that the human condition, by its very nature, seeks to reach outward, beyond itself.

Moreover, we have here confirmed that the right to liberty is one of the constitutive aspects of the speaking being's relation to himself, and that, as has often been remarked, it constitutes as much an obligation as it does a mere right. Whoever has the right to be free, and claims the right to demand from society those conditions of life that will permit him, if he chooses, to devote himself to a project of inward freedom, has also the duty to exercise this liberty; for if our mind does not mobilize against the inertness that lies at the heart of its very words, it risks,—I will come back to this later—seeing its most profound intuitions taken over by verbal stereotypes, its motivations ursurped, its decisions ignored, becoming a thing, and thus ending our adventure on this earth.

And, finally, it seems to me, one could show that the various practical liberties which moral reflection has reclaimed throughout its long history, are the means, or the symbolic representations, of that right, and of that duty which are the specificity of the human, if not until now its success. What, for example, do those "commandments" say, that are the laws that liberty gives itself in every religious or civil tradition? "Thou shalt not kill thy neighbor": the first, or almost first, commandment. What brings us to recognize the place of oneness beneath the brushlike undergrowth of signs if not our bestowal of something transcendent, something sacred, to that other, close to us, whom ordinary discourse so quickly reduces to the mere idea it holds of him, that is, to a disposable abstraction? Bearing witness to oneness cannot but be, in us, and from the beginning, the recognition of the Other, since he is the very site of its emergence.

IV

Liberty is definable from the moment one opens enough silence in oneself to look, to really look, and to see: from the beginning to the end of its sense and reasonless course, the leaf slowly falling—but what does "slowly" mean?—from the branch. We even know why liberty has been so forcefully demanded throughout history.

But also we can here begin to understand the thorough fragility of this need for liberty, the precariousness of such a demand: they rest on the apprehension of something absolute in the very fleetingness of a falling leaf; that is on an object of thought specifically abolished by the very words we use to utter it. Our most fundamental need or, if you will, our highest possibility can, at any moment, not simply renounce but dissipate themselves, self-forgetful, unremembering of their previous existence—and this because of a break in the already fleeting contact with the absoluteness of the world. Our possible is grounded in impossibility. And it follows that what was yesterday an intermittence might today altogether cease, given certain facts of our time.

This time our modernity is that which has witnessed a profound and extensive transformation in the very web of conceptual relations. These are no longer tied, ever since Galileo and Descartes, to sensory qualities; they seek their explanatory principles under the surface of appearances; and there is no danger here, in this tricking with the surfaces of the phenomenal, since the mind will encounter beyond them other, as yet unmanifested, phenomena, whether in the immense or in the infinitesimal, in the starry skies or closer to the atom, in life or in matter: something to keep alive,—increasing, why not,—the feeling that reality transcends what remains of it in notions—the feeling of mystery. But scientific investigation has secondary effects which can be catastrophic. The knowledge it produces, for example, is not verifiable through immediately perceptible proofs; its truth is given bit by bit, with difficulty, even to the best intellects; and in this way it favors a new kind of revery, that of the reader of theories, who no longers tries to think, really, to the end, or to verify, choosing to believe that he enjoys the benefits of an absolute and definitive teaching, which someday, when he truly begins to study, will grant him the key to knowledge. An obscure discourse is no inconvenience to such reveries, it does not arouse suspicions—well on the contrary. But what a victory, in each case, of the word's abstractness over its demonstrative, referential capacities! For language is thickened not in the truthwork of science but in near-likenesses and in counterfeits.

But it also happens that the exact formulation, the discovered law, increase the autonomy of language in our apparently simplest behaviors. To give only one example, among many possible others: the psychologist detects a reflex, some predictable effect with which a metaphor or a metonymy conditions desire; no sooner does he state that such reactions can be elicited from a large number of individuals, than commerce will avail itself of this chain of stimulations and effects: they will be linked to products which it will seek to sell in greater quantities. But to do so it will also have to dismantle, to de-actualize, other uses of these metaphors. And to achieve that, it will endlessly shout the most striking slogans, reducing a person, through these repeated blows, from within reducing him to phrases that no longer know anything of what is. One suspects today that the human being might soon become nothing more than a thoroughly semantic field, where commodities appear and disappear, not without leaving their imprint; archetypes of sham universes where the forest, the oceans, the mountains themselves appear here and there as those objects of consumption that dot the commercial street, where the leaf that falls from branch to branch would quite soon become just another advertisement.

There is, in short, the great risk that oneness might disinhabit consciousness, leaving the spirit of liberty to dry up at its very source: a confirmation of this, sadly, being what happens in our rich and, as they say, technologically advanced societies. The history of liberty is tributary to events of language. One has seen it at the time of the American Constitution, and of the Declaration of the Rights of Man, a period coinciding with the decline of the authority of the Churches, which retained the desire for liberation outside the social space, in the realm of inner experience.

But there is today, nevertheless, a practice where the memory of this oneness that the words cancel subsists, in a precise use of language. This use is poetry.

V

Let us listen to a poem, if only, indeed, to one of its lines, letting the vibrations of a string of words echo in us, words at once confounding and evident, oracular words, light-traversed in their still-water simplicity as if they were at times captured by a storm, their surface breaking, as if a substance from beneath all sensorial perception were here raised and dispersed. What is this? Words, certainly, but at work in the phrase in a way I have not yet mentioned, having up to now only considered those ties linking notion to notion in the space of signifieds. Yes, words, and with them meaning, but this time sounds as well, and rhythms, forming in this other kind of speech, from one vocable to another, a new ground of associations, of searching, even, one could say, waiting ahead of all thinking. From these diffractions, the economy of concepts, if it is not altogether destroyed, if it is at times even intensified, carried beyond its ordinary logic, is nonetheless troubled, very profoundly, disjointed: a reading of the world which language peacefully pursued, a work of building which it carried out around us and in us are, for an instant, as if suspended. And there appear, of course, new forms of consciousness, in this unpiecing of the image which language had set in place: but there are,—it is the fact that we must perceive, now—two ways of understanding this phenomenon, one interpretation being more current today than the other.

As you know, there are many who consider that in this disarticulation of the code which regulates the usage of words, what appears is simply more language: the movement of notions which have been freed from certain constraints but which remain, therefore, all the more willing to lend themselves to new constructions and, sketching these, all the more ready to abandon them, to go on to others, adding up dreams, shamelessly contradicting themselves in this unmoored place, one freed from all moral, social, or even logical responsibility; the proper place, they tell us, and the right, of artistic creation. Is not the unconscious, according to psychoanalysis, a relation between words, established as much by sound, in the signifier, as by the force of tropes? And this life of words in the depths of a poem, is it not, therefore, simply the effect of desire at work, building stages where it can dream and claim its pleasure, thereby ruining the credibility of discourse, but multiplying, in what is called the "text," those possibilities of articulation which only vegetate in ordinary speech? The poem would explode sense through sound only to free the virtualities of meaning still chained in language. It would deny the authority of a figure of the world but just to acknowledge the fact that it is unconscious desire which, in a mobile society can best take up the work of invention, a task that classical rhetoric ranged under the sign of the intellect. And if there be invention of this new kind, and consequently poetry, it would be because the picture of the world which our society has given itself, with its objects as with its values, is not sufficiently in accord with the true needs of the natural being we are; this natural being well known, on the other hand, to the unconscious desire, and reclaimed and announced by it. It follows from this that poetry would be— still in the field of language, still among concepts—an act of mutual readjustment between culture and the body, an act that might well cease some day, its mission duly accomplished.

I am not, for my part, of those who would care to minimize, in poems, the importance of those verbal clusters which desire intertwines, collapses, restarts, all to the greatest benefit of that plasticity so essential to speech. There is no doubt that the principles and values that ground a society are but an ensemble of representations, in part arbitrary, which must be opened to the criticisms that the body, with its great demands, poses by means of the imaginary. Those poets who have been the most willing to defend the specificity of poetry have also been the first—well before, that is, the analysts of textual matter—to sense the work that takes place in their writing at the level of words, a work which tends, in its way, to "change life." But I must also stress that the poem is not just that self-centered transgression, in some measure unconscious, of structures of ideality judged to be repressive. Whoever writes in a serious manner pays attention to all the givens of his being-in-the-world; he knows the affections that guide him, he seeks to give meaning to his existence, he cannot answer the promptings of his desire without also remembering his responsibilities toward society, and to those near to him. From all this emerges a figure of the world whose value lies, it is true, in its being more demanding, less conformist, one closer, that is, to the unconscious than are all collective propositions, yet one whose coherence will nonetheless predominate over the flow of the imaginary. In the poem, desire has no doubt been regained closer to its source; it has been permitted, freely enough, to invest itself in imaginary and symbolic situations which overturn moral interdictions and common necessity—a fate that lived experience cannot permit itself. But it has still been retained, at the threshold of dispersion, and for the greater satisfaction in its very dream; held back by all sorts of natural and cultural considerations: so that the work that expresses it is a stable scene, a richly abundant yet relatively ordered setting, an ensemble of values and perceptions: in short, the equivalent in private existence of a civilization. Because it is not a *"divertissement"* [diversion] that fails to capture the reader, who mostly is interested in models for life, in some teaching for his own, a poem has the traits of a language somewhat fixed and precise, one that creates and speaks a world. And foremost among these traits is a coherence, the primacy of lasting, if not constant, forms over the flux of more fleeting, wayward imaginings.

Now one must not miss recognizing this coherence in a poem that is, this world-structure under its guise of free-play, for the sake of its transgressive aspects, its revolts, because the most far-reaching comprehension of poetry proceeds from it. One of its consequences is, first of all, the charm exercised by certain poems, in that almost magic way suggested by Valéry's famous title. Poems please, not because they jostle codes, but because they offer universes in other keys, beautiful for being freed from necessity by dreams *vastes portiques*, says Baudelaire, season-dyed in a thousand hues of fire.* It is in such worlds, according to this or that wish of ours, that our longing is stilled, our impatience diffused. Here we touch catharsis, as Aristotle this time tells us.

But remember, too, that such spells are not free of reservations even for

---

*The reference is to Baudelaire's poem "La Vie antérieure": "J'ai longtemps habité sous de vastes portiques / Que les soleils marins teignaient de mille feux."

those who experience them. If Aristotle values poetic creation, Plato only sees in it the lie, loving poetry but excluding poets from the decisions of society. And in that same poem, "La Vie antérieure," where he speaks explicitly of the world, resembling Claude Lorrain's, that his poetry open up to him, Baudelaire says, too, that he who elects to live there only "languishes," for some unknown—or unavowed—yet painful reason.

VI

Why this ambivalence? The reason is simple: a world-image, a text which structures itself according to the law of a language that is in itself a world, is, once again, language—language in its specific act and place; and, therefore, once again, this imprisonment within words, this loss of reality that I have already defined. The worlds of poetry may be more beautiful, they may be free of those cruel and painful aspects we stumble across in life, its prison may be vaster—it is no less a prison which, being forever there, forever locked, remains all the more mysterious. Thus the pain claimed by Baudelaire, and that melancholy so often associated with poetic creation. Happiness is annulled for the reader of the poem by the linguistic estrangement he finds there still whole; and it is this discovery, we now see, that brings *"ces malédictions, ces blasphèmes, ces plaintes"*; at times, even, those cries of horror and those tragic *hauntings* which are as frequent and as violent in poetry as they are in the Rembrandts, the Pugets, or the Goyas we see in the mirror of "Phares" in the *Flowers of Evil*.

To sum up, in distinguishing the world-image in the poem, I am not forgetful of the anguish and the rage which it can bring because of the closure that are words, *autant qu'il aura donné le bonheur du rêve* [as much as it will have given the happiness of the dream]. I do not forget that poetry is as much in Antonin Artaud or, in Baudelaire, "Une Charogne," as it is the pleasures and pastimes of "L'Après-midi d'un faune." But this is not, however, the true problem of the poetic. For beneath this dream, under this rage, there remains a layer which I have not yet touched, even though it is the most important one of all.

And it is this: the poem, the poem as that text from which has taken form, with its phrases, its figures, its imaginations, its values—the poem is words dislodged from a simple conceptual economy but ransomed—we have seen—by desire, by *eros*, and therefore still enfolded in a movement of language. This recapturing leads many minds to see in poetry only an intensification, a multiplication, of the possibilities of language. And it is also this recapturing—but lived otherwise, as proof that the dreamt-of world is still a prison—it is this which builds poetry as a theatre of pain as much as of hope.

And yet why should there be a feeling of cell-like enclosure, of a fall from reality, at precisely the very moment when the imaginary world unfolds itself? Is it not because the memory of a reality outside language, a memory of oneness, has succeeded in maintaining itself in poetic activity despite the spell of the universes it conjures? And should one not, therefore, infer that there is somewhere in poetry a point where this memory is marked?

This point exists. It is, simply, it is once again, the word; the word whose materiality of sounds has not protected the discourse of the text; but which can now be heard, at a level which is, indeed, imperceptible for those who are not inhabited by the "higher" desire of which I have already spoken. The concept is neutralized in the poem, knowledge and ordinary law are there effaced, and in their place the dream outspreads: restarting a language, reaffirming language? Yes, but at the very beginning, in the very first second, when no thought has come to join it to anything in that vacant space between an undone knowledge and a dream to come; when, as if virgin, original, on the whiteness of the page, the *word is there,* all the same; and what does it then evoke if not a thing itself disengaged from that which ordinarily veils it, a thing in this way solidary, solidary still, with that fund of reality, of unity, always vanishing in discourse. It is the *"absente de tout bouquet"* which appears, fleetingly. A face, suddenly, instead of its many features. I sketch a verse, from a rhythm within, by concurring sounds, colors glimpsed across words, and as long as the verse does not take form, the word *"fleur,"* the word *"arbre,"* the words *"soleil"* and *"mer",* or even the word *"portique"* will not close into some idea of these things; they will instead allow me to perceive even here in my daily life: the tree, a shore, the light from the sky and from the land, as when these are sometimes given to us in moments of silence, those moments when we no longer hear in us the suggestions of language. One says "une fleur"—just that—and this of course is language, since a flower exists only because language decrees it so; but to say, "a flower," like that, in that dawn of speech where the word, I would say, is conceptually vacant, its referent with as yet no care of a signified, this is also to let the flower emerge from oneness, barely surfacing, onelike, keeping speech in the experience of immediacy our mind that seeks, how true, to become once more language.

A trace of oneness has remained, an instant's drops imbued to the window-pane, this side of our speech. Let the word be only emptiness, suspended meaning, and drawing from silent intuitions, it will be able to fill the half-conceived line with our experience of the whiff that is all, of the beyond to our projects and our dreams, our anguish and passions, which is the cause of a joy, that purifies and redeems all others. In thinking poetry, is this not an event which must count as much as the shattering of codes, the subversion of idealisms—subversion which moreover risks creating new dogmatisms?

So that, from the moment one perceives this spring of poetic intuition, one can recognize, in its light, at least among the greatest poets, a labor which cannot at all be confused with their creation of world-images since, in fact, it critiques and battles such dreams; and, losing the battle in each poem, quickly wages it anew; winning, sometimes, in the end. How is this work carried out? How can one fissure the world-image? Through *images*, precisely, taken this time in the sense given to them by surrealist poetics, in Breton's "soleil cette nuit," or in the "lions en barre" and the "aigles d'eau pure" of Paul Eluard; that is to say, not in the sense of figures—not in those tropes which know only how to place signifieds in relation to each other, to the greatest profit of language—but in the sense of word associations that transcend all figures, discourage explications and are therefore disruptive of any emerging verbal structure. It is through images of this sort that language is short-circuited, its current no longer passes through words, those lights are extinguished which marked our few paths; or, if you will, it's like those grainy knots in the glass of old windows: through them we see things fragmented and disfeatured but their edges are luminous, iridiscent. And another way of moving, through words, toward oneness, another negative way, but one which tends toward positivity, would be, in these lines that are sound, the birth of music. The little time left will not permit me to consider this question.

Little time is left, but I have arrived at the point I had intended to reach. What is poetry? It is not the subversion of the discourse of law by a discourse of desire; it is not the invention of imaginary worlds, but their destruction, their renewal, and again their vanishing: and this, because they preserve in them, like a coming of impatience, this thought of oneness, whose flashes in the word when it is withdrawn from sentences. Poetry is thus a testimony, a reminder. Even if nothing immediate—nothing real—is retained at the end of such labors, the reader can at least perceive, in whatever fashioned form offered for partaking, that sight has been distended, beyond disunions, beyond exiles, toward a great outward object *dont ainsi lui est rendue la mémoire* [whose memory is thus given back to him].

VII

Poetry is the memory of oneness. This definition will now enable me, I hope, to answer the question I asked earlier concerning the risk of losing, at this end of the twentieth century, precisely this memory of oneness; and of no longer feeling, therefore, this "higher" desire which awakens, in situations of estrangement, the need for liberty and the consciousness of liberty's own obligations. It is true that the discourses of knowledge are becoming ever more dense, that the need to understand things—or to dream that one will understand them, or to believe that one has already understood—increasingly takes over our intelligence; it's true, as well, that commerce assails us with its slogans, which refer only to fictitious realities, deathlike and abstract. But to preserve the great, redeeming intuition, there is still poetry. Poetry and, of course, certain works of the cinema or of painting, since the arts also form part of those sign-systems which can be short-circuited, blasted, by the perception, in a painting for example of a brushstroke of pure color, nonmediated, absolute. Indeed, painters and poets share the demand for presence as a common possibility, and those theories of *ut pictura poesis* cited them to hold the same discourse only to keep them better together in the prison-house of language.

There is still poetry. And when one has taken measure of this fact, two questions pose themselves, two questions which I can here only sketch, for lack of time, but to which we might return in the discussion to follow.

To begin with, can one expect more from the activity of poets than this essentially negative work of which I spoke? Could one think, for example, that an awareness of the symbols that seem to come forth in the natural world might allow the poem to open up a space where men and women might act, speak—speak to each other—without ceasing, thereby, to be *in presence?* This would justify the dream of a right and good usage of words which we have seen in religious traditions.

And then, if poetry is a resource, should we not be concerned about the very resource itself? I do not believe that poetic experience today is any poorer than at other times, despite the habitual counterfeits. I believe even less that those who truly assume the task of poetry are fewer than before. But we all know that the place granted to poetry in the realm of culture is increasingly limited and marginal since it disturbs too-powerful interests: those of ideology, for example, and especially those of commerce, which instills in us the desire for *having* and not that of *being*. So that it would be useful, then, to ask how one might grant poetry the more central place which would answer to the need of all. It would certainly not be an initiative of the public powers, who are blind to the matter; it would be, rather, the initiative of poetry itself, poetry becoming critical thought—as Baudelaire had wanted—, a thinking that would inform the critics and the researchers, who are involved today in textual analysis and more or less control the teaching of literature, that is to say, the transmission, as well, of serious information. These critics dispose of means and methods—psychoanalysis, for example—which all bear on meanings, or on stylistic form, and which therefore lead them to account for the work on the level where it is language. But in so doing, they risk not understanding poetry, becoming blind to it, forgetting it; or, rather, reclaiming its great works in order to take them apart according to other laws. Let us lead them to admit what takes place in poetry—an admission no more difficult than is, for the phenomenologist of religions, the idea that transcendence can determine human conducts—and those very methods that now veil the poetic will come to unveil it, revealing that what they consider the positivity of the poem, and its happiness, is only the tunic of Nessus which the poet seeks to cast off.

Who knows, these methods might even help the spirit of poetry to strengthen itself, allowing it, perhaps, to better understand the illusoriness of the making of those world-images, to whose pleasures it abandons itself, forgetful of the very intuition it bears. How many kingdoms of our dreams which, in the end, clothe only a very ordinary Oedipus, one who now limps more than ever. The critic might help the poet to demystify his words, to free things earthly from their vain adornments, to recover the language of simple things, the one through which oneness, the infinitely near, might most easily come toward the window, knocking.

Translated by Alfredo Monferré with the collaboration of the author.

Contributors

MAURICE BLANCHOT, whose work examines and transforms relationships between literature, philosophy, and literary criticism, is a writer. Among his books most recently appearing in English translation are *Thomas the Obscure, The Unbearable Community,* and *The Writing of the Disaster.*

YVES BONNEFOY, France's great lyric poet, holds a chair at the Collège de France. He has been a visiting professor at Yale many times. He also writes, among other things, on painting and is the translator of, among others, Shakespeare and Yeats into French.

CATHY CARUTH is Assistant Professor of English at Yale University. She is author of *Empirical Truths and Critical Fictions: Locke, Wordsworth, Kant, Freud* (Johns Hopkins University Press, 1990), and has edited a special issue of *American Imago* entitled *Psychoanalysis, Culture and Trauma* (Winter 1991).

SHOSHANA FELMAN is Professor of French and Comparative Literature at Yale University. She is the author of many books, including *The Literary Speech Act: Don Juan with J. L. Austin, or Seduction in Two Languages* (Cornell University Press, 1983) and *Writing and Madness* (Cornell University Press, 1985); the latest to appear is *Jacques Lacan and the Adventure of Insight: Psychoanalysis in Contemporary Culture.* (Harvard University Press, 1987). She is currently working on Testimony. The article in this issue belongs to a larger work forthcoming from Routledge (see p. 39). It is also appearing in French.

THOMAS KEENAN teaches in the English Department at Princeton University and is working on a book called *Responsibilities.* He is coeditor, with Werner Hamacher and Neil Hertz, of Paul de Man's *Wartime Journalism* (Nebraska, 1988) and *Responses* (Nebraska, 1989), and with Deborah Esch of two forthcoming volumes of Jacques Derrida's writings on politics and institutions, *Institutions of Philosophy* and *Negotiations.*

270

CLAUDE LANZMANN is the editor of *Les Temps Modernes*. He is the producer of the films *Shoah* and *Pourquoi l'Israël?*

NATHANIEL LAOR, M.D., Ph.D., is Associate Clinical Professor at the Yale Child Study Center and Director of the Tel Aviv Mental Health Center. He has written a number of articles which have appeared in psychoanalytic journals, many of them on Lacan.

RUTH LARSON is a graduate student in the department of French at Yale University.

RICHARD LIVINGSTON is a student in the Department of Comparative Literature at Yale University.

ALFREDO MONFERRÉ is a graduate student in the French Department at Yale University.

JEAN-LUC NANCY is a Professor at the Université de Strasbourg. His book on Bataille, *La Communauté désoeuvrée*, in translation is forthcoming from the University of Minnesota Press.

KEVIN NEWMARK teaches at Yale University and is author of *Beyond Symbolism*, forthcoming from Cornell University Press. He is currently working on Schlegel, Baudelaire, and Nietzsche.

CLAIRE NOUVET teaches French Medieval Literature at Emory University. She has worked on fourteenth-century literature and completed a book entitled *An Open Dream: The Romance of the Rose*. She is presently working on a new book: *Abélard and Héloise: The Evil of Letters*.

VINCENT P. PECORA is a member of the Department of English at UCLA. His book *Self and Form in Modern Narrative* was published in 1989 by the Johns Hopkins University Press. He has written on modern literature, contemporary criticism, and most recently on architecture.

JILL ROBBINS is Assistant Professor of English and Comparative Literature at the State University of New York at Buffalo. She is the author of *Prodigal Son/Elder Brother: Interpretation and Alterity in Augustine, Petrarch, Kafka, Levinas*, forthcoming from the University of Chicago Press.

D. N. RODOWICK is Associate Professor of American Studies and Comparative Literature and Director of Film Studies at Yale. He is author of *The Crisis of Political Modernism: Criticism and Ideology in Contemporary Film Theory* (University of Illinois Press, 1988) and of a forthcoming book on sexual difference and film theory. He has published widely on French, German, and American film and issues in current criticism.

ELIZABETH ROTTENBERG is a student at Yale University majoring in French Literature; she is compiling translations of Bataille's texts for her senior project.

PAUL WEIDMANN is a free-lance translator and reader of Blanchot, Artaud, and Genet.

The Duel
Its Rise and Fall in Early Modern France

François Billacois
edited and translated by Trista Selous

This engrossing book traces the evolution of the duel in early modern France and discusses its implications for French politics, morality, and religion during that time. Published in France in 1986, it is now available in English for the first time.

"Mr. Billacois's study...**takes a rarely viewed part of the French tapestry and shows it in all of its brilliance and color.**"—Richard Bernstein, *The New York Times* $30.00

Vilna on the Seine
Jewish Intellectuals in France since 1968

Judith Friedlander

This intriguing book tells the story of two generations of French Jewish intellectuals—one from the turn of the century, the other from the 1968 student uprisings—who have defined their identity as modern Jews through the example of Lithuanian Jewish life in old Vilna.

"A **compelling** account of how Jewish intellectuals in Paris have grappled with the right to be different in a state that has long insisted on a unitary national culture."—Barbara Kirshenblatt-Gimblett 16 illus. $27.50

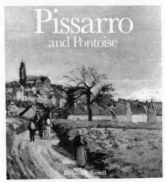

Pissarro and Pontoise
The Painter in a Landscape

Richard Brettell

In this **lavishly illustrated** study, Richard Brettell offers a new interpretation of the works of the patriarch of Impressionism, Camille Pissarro, arguing that Pissarro was a vanguard artist whose own alienation from modern society was clearly expressed in his numerous landscape paintings of the small provincial French town in which he lived from 1866 to 1883. 54 b/w + 120 color illus. $45.00

Now available in paperback

Cardinal Richelieu
Power and the Pursuit of Wealth

Joseph Bergin

"Here is a vivid and fascinating guide to the financial basis of high society in Louis XIII's France, and a precise account of how Richelieu gained and maintained his position in government. ...**Meticulous and scholarly.**"
—Roger Mettam, *History Today*

"A **brilliant, fascinating, and elegantly written** book."—*American Historical Review* $16.95

Yale University Press

Dept. 561, 92A Yale Sta.
New Haven, CT 06520

The following issues are available through **Yale University Press,** Customer Service Department, 92A Yale Station, New Haven, CT 06520.

63 The Pedagogical Imperative:
   Teaching as a Literary Genre
   (1982) $15.95
64 Montaigne: Essays in Reading
   (1983) $15.95
65 The Language of Difference:
   Writing in QUEBEC(ois)
   (1983) $15.95
66 The Anxiety of Anticipation
   (1984) $15.95
67 Concepts of Closure
   (1984) $15.95
68 Sartre after Sartre
   (1985) $15.95

69 The Lesson of Paul de Man
   (1985) $15.95
70 Images of Power:
   Medieval History/Discourse/
   Literature
   (1986) $15.95
71 Men/Women of Letters:
   Correspondence
   (1986) $15.95
72 Simone de Beauvoir:
   Witness to a Century
   (1987) $15.95
73 Everyday Life
   (1987) $15.95

74 Phantom Proxies
   (1988) $15.95
75 The Politics of Tradition:
   Placing Women in French
   Literature
   (1988) $15.95
   Special Issue: After the
   Age of Suspicion: The
   French Novel Today
   (1989) $15.95
76 Autour de Racine:
   Studies in Intertextuality
   (1989) $15.95
77 Reading the Archive: On
   Texts and Institutions
   (1990) $15.95
78 On Bataille
   (1990) $15.95

Special subscription rates are available on a calendar year basis (2 issues per year):

Individual subscriptions $24.00   Institutional subscriptions $28.00

- -

ORDER FORM   **Yale University Press,** 92A Yale Station, New Haven, CT 06520

Please enter my subscription for the calendar year
☐ **Special Issue (1991)**   ☐ **1991 (Nos. 79 and 80)**   ☐ **1992 (Nos. 81 and 82)**

I would like to purchase the following individual issues:

_____

_____

For individual issues, please add postage and handling:
Single issue, United States $2.75   Single issue, foreign countries $5.00
Each additional issue $.50   Each additional issue $1.00
Connecticut residents please add sales tax of 8%.

Payment of $ _____ is enclosed (including sales tax if applicable).

Mastercard no. _____

4-digit bank no. _____ Expiration date _____

VISA no. _____ Expiration date _____

Signature _____

SHIP TO: _____

_____

_____

- -

See the next page for ordering issues 1–59 and 61–62. **Yale French Studies** is also available through Xerox University Microfilms, 300 North Zeeb Road, Ann Arbor, MI 48106.

The following issues are still available through the **Yale French Studies** Office, 2504A Yale Station, New Haven, CT 06520.

Add for postage & handling

Single issue, United States $1.50
Each additional issue $.50

Single issue, foreign countries $2.00
Each additional issue $.75

- -

YALE FRENCH STUDIES, 2504A Yale Station, New Haven, Connecticut 06520

A check made payable to YFS is enclosed. Please send me the following issue(s):

Issue no.	Title	Price
_____	_____	_____
_____	_____	_____
_____	_____	_____
	Postage & handling	_____
	Total	_____

Name _____

Number/Street _____

City _____ State _____ Zip _____

The following issues are now available through Kraus Reprint Company, Route 100, Millwood, N.Y. 10546.

36/37 Structuralism has been reprinted by Doubleday as an Anchor Book.
55/56 Literature and Psychoanalysis has been reprinted by Johns Hopkins University Press, and can be ordered through Customer Service, Johns Hopkins University Press, Baltimore, MD 21218.